WHO WAS EDGAR CAYCE?

Edgar Cayce was born in 1877 in Hopkinsville, Kentucky, and lived sixty-seven years that were sometimes painfully eventful, but tremendously enlightening. He had developed a gift in former lifetimes which gave him the capacity in this life to enter a state of altered consciousness. He was able to be in touch with the akashic records and the information in what he called the Universal Consciousness.

In his state of altered consciousness, Cayce would respond to questions and often would give special dissertations on a variety of subjects. Two thirds of his nearly 15,000 readings had to do with healing of the human body. He is well-known, too, for his predictions on earth changes and with readings on reincarnation, dreams, soul development, Christ consciousness, astrology, Atlantis, ancient Egypt, and emotional development. Cayce's readings evidenced a very close relationship with Jesus and his teachings, and it is not surprising that he advised hundreds who sought his counsel to take Jesus as their pattern for living in these troublesome times.

Cayce could also contact the unconscious mind of individuals far distant from where he was giving a reading, and could describe not only their past lives, but also the state of the inquirer's physiological functioning and what needed to be done to return that individual to full health.

Cayce's legacy for the world can be found not only in the hearts and minds of millions of individuals whose lives he has changed, but also at the Association for Research and Enlightenment (A.R.E.) Library in Virginia Beach, VA, which houses the Cayce Readings.

Edgar Cayce called his work the work of the Christ, and anyone who studies these readings to any depth will most likely agree.

William A. McGarey, M.D.

BOOKS IN THE EDGAR CAYCE SERIES
FROM ST. MARTIN'S PAPERBACKS

EDGAR CAYCE'S ASTROLOGICAL REVELATIONS

JOHN WILLNER

St. Martin's Paperbacks

EDGAR CAYCE'S ASTROLOGICAL REVELATIONS

Copyright © 1996 by John Willner.
"Who Was Edgar Cayce?" Copyright © 1995 by William A. McGarey, M.D.

ISBN: 0-312-96551-6

Printed in the United States of America

St. Martin's Paperbacks edition/March 1998

10 9 8 7 6 5 4 3 2 1

This book is dedicated to Priscilla, my wife, who knows she has received benefits from Edgar Cayce's readings. It is also dedicated to Barbara, Paul, Ross, Lance, and Claude; and to spouses of the first and last two children, Carlos, Cathy, and Deborah, who have been most attentive and supportive.

CONTENTS

In order to reproduce and preserve Edgar Cayce's readings as close to the original as possible they were transferred electronically from a CD-ROM recorded by the Association for Research and Enlightenment. Gladys Davis had originally taken down the readings in shorthand and typed them afterward on a mechanical typewriter of that period. Capital letters for emphasis, punctuation as would be entered on a typewriter (rather than word processor), use of the words *Akashic* and *Akashian* to mean the same source, and other artifacts doubtless approved by Edgar Cayce have been retained. Only a few obvious duplications of words and typos have been corrected.

There are astrological urges latent that become manifested through the application of the will of the entity.

Well that those influences, that are so easily misunderstood and misconstrued by man in his seeking for knowledge and wisdom, be understood. Knowledge without wisdom often is dangerous, even in man's material—and more in his spiritual and mental—life.

                                                    1081-001

PREFACE

BY NOW MOST adults should have heard or read about Edgar Cayce, who was clairvoyant. For those who haven't, an excellent description of his life may be found in *There is a River* by Thomas Sugrue, A.R.E. Press, Virginia Beach, Virginia.[1] Reading about his life that was dedicated almost exclusively to helping other people would provide excellent background information for the thoughts expressed in this book. In summary, he was a deeply religious man born in Hopkinsville, Kentucky, on March 18, 1877. His formal education did not extend beyond grade-school level. As a young man he learned how to induce self-hypnosis. While in trance, questions could be put to him and omnipotent answers would be forthcoming. They were often couched in archaic language but provided deep insights into the mysteries of life. These queries and responses became known as readings. Virtually all of his early readings were for ascertaining the nature of illnesses, and they were accompanied by recommendations for cures. When his fame began to spread, the orthodox medical profession raised a storm of protest. After all, he had no formal training in medicine, nor did he have the obligatory degrees. Therefore, they claimed he was practicing without

---

[1] Early editions were published by Holt, Rinehart and Winston, Inc., and by Dell Publishing Company.

a license. Investigations and legal proceedings were instigated. Most of them ended in uncertain conclusions and stalemates.

In his waking state, Edgar Cayce had no knowledge of many terms he was expressing while in trance. The cures were often as strange to him as to others. Once discovered and publicized by the press, however, investigations began. Self-appointed experts, including university professors, were bent on exposing the assumed hoax. Yet none of these learned men could figure out how he—or his source of knowledge—was so uncanny at deducing the exact causes of illnesses.

The remedies he prescribed in trance were holistic in nature. They ranged from spinal manipulations and colonics to preparations commonly available from pharmacies, grocers, or other accessible sources. Drugs prescribed by doctors of this period were not among his recommendations, although some patent medicines were. When his advice was followed by patients, most of them were successfully cured. Yet he did not remember what he had said when coming to a waking state.

Although briefly jailed once, he continued to give readings when he realized that he was helping people get well. This was the humanistic and religious thing to do. Edgar Cayce was a very religious man. He responded to all who asked for help, giving up to three readings a day. This regimen was exhaustive and caused strains on his health that eventually led to his death. The people he had helped, however, became his supporters.

The normal procedure was for Edgar Cayce to loosen his tie and lie down on a convenient sofa or pallet. He would then put himself into trance after which questions were asked of him. Often these questions were asked by his wife, by a guest, or later by his sons. He would then proceed to give responses in a clear voice. When a topic had been concluded, he would end the session. Suggestions were then given for him to wake up.

Fortunately, a decision was reached fairly early to record these readings. A young secretary named Gladys Davis became almost a member of the family. Throughout the years until his death on January 3, 1945, more than 14,000 of these hypnotic sessions were recorded out of about 18,000 that he gave. Not all of them were transcribed by Gladys Davis, but she was involved with the majority. They now reside at the Association for Research and Enlightenment in Virginia Beach, Virginia. The legacy of his readings and the hopes they inspired have spread worldwide. His words have elevated spirits and convinced thousands of people to lead better lives.

Eventually, the readings expanded beyond purely medical problems and covered a large variety of questions and answers on primordial and esoteric topics. The start of this expansion in subject matter occurred one day in 1923. A printer from Dayton, Ohio, named Arthur H. Lammers arrived in Selma, Alabama, where the Cayces were living at the time. He wanted questions to be answered that were nonphysical in nature. Lammers was a student of occult philosophies, and he wanted information on those subjects. In fact, he was so wrapped up in the possibility that Edgar Cayce could provide beneficial answers, that he offered to pay Cayce's way to Dayton, Ohio, where he lived. This was when the first questions about astrology were asked. The clairvoyance of Edgar Cayce was just as insightful as it had been for illnesses. Responses were profound and intermingled with a radical view of life on this earth and during periods between births. Reincarnation was implicitly embedded in these responses without qualification. This whole series of readings became known as life readings to distinguish them from the physical readings he had been giving up to this time. Among life readings that followed were those devoted to horoscopes.

Upon awakening from the first reading on astrology, Edgar Cayce was initially surprised and a bit fearful of the answers he had given. In fact, up until that time in 1923, he thought horoscopes were fakes. Mr. Cayce, as he was referred to by his wife Gertrude, had no more training in astrology than in medicine. Neither he nor his family knew what to make of the strange information that was imparted. Being very religious and God-fearing, Edgar Cayce was concerned that this might be the work of the devil. References were given while in trance to planets and their characteristics, to planetary sojourns, and to physical or mental conditions influenced by the stars. It took a number of serious reviews and considerable persuasion by Lammers to assuage those fears. The readings themselves said the information came from Akashic records or the Universal Mind. This information was not clearly understood at the time but was transcribed for future reviews and analyses. Edgar Cayce eventually came to accept further inquiries along these lines, because he realized his own questions about his mission in life were being expressed in Lammers' words. Then he began to understand that his responses were continuing to benefit mankind.

In 1967 the A.R.E. Press booklet *Astrology and the Edgar Cayce Readings* by Margaret H. Gammon was written and first published. It surveyed readings containing astrological infor-

mation, citing many examples. A good overview of the subject
was given, and differences with traditional astrology were indicated but not deeply explored. Those differences were eventually recognized as having implications of great importance.
According to Edgar Cayce, modern astrologers were making serious mistakes that needed to be understood and rectified. One
failing was a lack of consistency, and that caused opposition
from scientists and methodical thinkers. That situation still exists
over seventy years later.

I personally heard about Edgar Cayce for the first time when
quite young—in the 1930s. He was mentioned in a sort of awe-
struck manner by my mother. She said he had a gift from God
and was healing sick people. This was a cause for reverence. His
life readings were not discussed at that time, probably because
they had not yet been extensively publicized.

In fact, books about Edgar Cayce were not printed until much
later. I did not read any of them until the 1950s. Another decade
passed before Edgar Cayce's life readings were studied at some
length. Bits and pieces of astrology were found in a large quantity of his responses. By then a perception arose that contemporary astrologers who tried to interpret a few of his astrological
readings somehow were not understanding exactly what his
words meant. They appeared to be missing the main points and
trying to relate Edgar Cayce's clairvoyant statements to sayings
they had learned when studying astrology. That seemed to be a
mistake, because some of those sayings were apparently on the
wrong track. Additionally, these writers were making guesses
about meanings that were questionable and offering no proofs.
Important concepts were omitted.

My credentials for these conclusions are based upon over half
a century of study and experience. I first read astrological
books—some very old ones indeed—at the tender age of twelve.
Many books were bought and absorbed during formative years
and intermittently thereafter. In 1942, an elderly benefactor introduced me to certain hidden astrological mysteries that he had
received in a like manner when he was a young man. It consisted
of both a philosophy and formulas. I was aware that his decision
to pass on this information was an act of kindness, yet he
charged me a stiff price for the elemental methodology. While
the retelling of this incident might arouse suspicions of chicanery, I never regretted the transaction. His philosophy was that
nothing in life worthwhile is free, and nothing worthwhile should
be given away without payment, work, or effort—because then

it would not be highly regarded. If I were to value the knowledge being transferred to me, sacrifice was important. I also had to agree never to give the exact particulars away. As he predicted, these mysteries have proved to be extremely valuable, because they establish a solid foundation for the study and practice of natal astrology. It is most intriguing that later, when Edgar Cayce's readings on astrology were discovered, the imbedded precepts and the wisdom previously transferred to me were in complete agreement. Indeed, Edgar Cayce's revelations provided confirmations of conclusions that had been independently derived over years of application.

My learning about astrology occurred well before studying science and engineering, earning several degrees, becoming a director of advanced technology, gaining experience in new frontiers of exploratory scientific investigations, and managing numerous research and development projects. Without this head start in astrology, I might have viewed the subject differently and issued self-righteous condemnations as some of my less-informed peers have done periodically. On the other hand, my natal Uranus established the interest.

What is so fascinating and ironic about this state of affairs is that astrology properly interpreted fits well with science as we think we know it. In many ways the missing humanistic links are to be found therein. But one would not draw that conclusion from occasional rhetoric snubbing this great ancient body of learning. The well-known reason, of course, has been that impostors, mountebanks, and quacks claimed astrology for themselves as well. Hence, Greek critics were writing about improper practices as early as the time of Plato, and new critics have appeared in every generation thereafter.[2]

Unfortunately, the belittlers of astrologers (not necessarily of astrology) place a veil between the beholder and the kernel of wisdom underneath. Modern cynics have usually not investigated.[3] Therefore, they do not fully realize and comprehend the reasons why revered wise men of old were both astrologers and scientists. These older scientists mastered all phases of ancient knowledge. As late as the Reformation period, great minds, such as Johannes Kepler, Tycho Brahe, and Sir Isaac Newton,

---

[2]For example, Carneades, a pupil of Clitomachus, who taught in Plato's academy and was one of his successors.

[3]The ranks of astrology are filled today with those few who did investigate and crossed over.

practiced astrology. That fact runs counter to the beliefs held by many twentieth-century astronomers, as well as physicists, chemists, mathematicians, and other highly trained professionals. However, the stark reality is that scientific pioneers practiced astrology up until only a few hundred years ago. A few hundred years is a very short period in the history of the world and the history of astrology. These records cannot be taken lightly or made to disappear.

Meanwhile, the revelations of Edgar Cayce on astrology have not been adequately explained to the general public, to those scholars who might be privately interested, or to astrologers themselves. Ideally, the most learned men and women should do the explaining, but many of them have already voiced their disdain. Therefore, it is fairly obvious that their biases would prevent objective reviews of Edgar Cayce's life readings. Similar biases interfere with scholarly reviews of historical records that deal with astrology and cause them to be less than objective. But there is another reason. Unquestionably, most scientists are outstanding in their chosen fields of endeavor. However, these super-rational human beings can be, and often have been found to be, distressingly uninformed when they venture beyond their chosen fields of investigation. It seems as though all of their careful scrutiny of evidence and meticulous procedures are thrown out the window when in unfamiliar territory. The unknown creates fears.

At an opposite extreme another ironic conclusion was reached long ago. Conventional astrologers do not appear to be qualified to interpret Edgar Cayce's words either. This is in their own field of endeavor. Reviews read long ago kept trying to relate his readings to catechism-like phrases learned by rote, like "seventh house is for open enemies" or "prisons and hospitals are shown by the twelfth." The information Edgar Cayce was offering ran much deeper than those sayings. Quite a few astrologers, while perhaps more willing than scientists to open their minds to unorthodox subjects, behave as though they are wearing blinders. That type of reviewer could not be wholly objective either.

Somehow much time has elapsed, and the connections with Edgar Cayce's messages are still unexplained. Yet, if scholarship has any bearing on the subject, far more astrologers today have advanced degrees than most outsiders would realize. Here and there learned investigations are taking place without being cluttered with prejudices. That is a very encouraging sign.

Meanwhile, armed with privileged information, my perceptions of Edgar Cayce's astrological revelations have been growing for decades. As readings were interpreted, they were mentally filed. When a test could be devised to provide proofs that did not exist before, such tests were conducted. Correlations with Edgar Cayce's prophetic words were observed repeatedly. I continued to identify elements of ancient wisdom first comprehended in my teens that conformed with ideas expressed by this man. During all of this time, no one else has stepped up to the plate to decipher the mysterious passages and dispense this knowledge in a way that could be understood by a broad segment of readers. A goal was therefore formed, spurred by the blockbuster nature of the information, that sooner or later an attempt must be made to set matters straight.

However, I encountered many mental difficulties in how to handle the material. The complexities of Edgar Cayce's wording caused much concern about how best to present it. Edgar Cayce often made statements that did not conform with prevailing ideas. Startling concepts that run counter to popular opinions are always difficult to handle. One runs the danger under these circumstances of being branded an impostor. Moreover, conjecture attends some of the interpretations, and there is no easy way to validate some of the conclusions. When detailed probes of ideas could be tested, it had to be acknowledged that they would probably not be easy to explain to a less-informed public. Appealing to scientific mentalities would be extremely difficult in the face of published objections. Many learned people associate astrology with fortune-telling, and they would oppose anything smacking of the occult. Notwithstanding, it would be necessary to show that the images conveyed by those positions are actually improper. Convincing arguments would not be easy to present. To make matters even more difficult for astrologers who could benefit the most, they will most likely have to unlearn some of their lore, and that is always a difficult task. If they do not accept identified errors, these jewels of knowledge could be reduced to matters of unending debates. Thus, many hours were devoted to these assumed problems. It would be most fortunate if none of them actually materialized. Also, many more hours were applied to optimization of possible approaches for disseminating the truths Edgar Cayce had volunteered. To be perfectly honest, none of them seemed to be adequate.

However, knowledge gained was sitting there waiting to be conveyed, and it grew. Apparent proofs were added from time to time. After many years a goal emerged. It was to find some way to make this controversial material more palatable. Then it became a galvanizing obsession. The approach had to be simple. A clear-cut purpose had to be defined and adhered to. Thus, before proceeding, the objectives of this book had to be established in terms most people could readily understand. With the unwitting help of others, the main thrusts began to gel. The objectives of this book are now established. They are to fill an enormous gap in interpreting Edgar Cayce's readings on the controversial subject of astrology, and to provide readers with information about how such disclosures can benefit them in their daily lives. This means all readers.

A third goal is to approach each subject with intelligence and a minimum of fantasy. It was recognized that in order to be comprehensive, Edgar Cayce's astrology requires knowledge drawn from many sources—modern physics, medicine, mathematics, astronomy, esoteric principles unknown to the vast majority, statistics, history, religion, psychiatry, acceptable verification techniques, physical or spiritual associations of underlying forces, etc. Such a broad scope, of course, presents more challenges. First, no single human being may rightfully claim encyclopedic knowledge of all these subjects, let alone myself, even though I may have enjoyed a wider array of experiences in life than most. Second, any presenter with less than total understanding faces the problem of how to learn, interpret, and write this material in a way that can be readily understood by laymen and laywomen without erring. Third, an element of conjecture still remains that cannot be readily confirmed using stringently controlled tests. Fourth, philosophical controversies surround many of the positions taken. Hence, this enormous breadth of information is acknowledged as being extremely difficult to cope with. Yet it must. A timely need exists as astrology slowly cycles back into popularity during the later part of this twentieth century, and it deserves attention. I have now volunteered to fulfill this mission. Astrologers know the timing is correct. The Aquarian Age has arrived.

The writing of this book took a number of months. While reviewing the completed manuscript, it occurs to me that several comments are in order about the tone. The choice of words has been affected by intended readers who fit into at least three diverse categories: technologists and well-intentioned critics, astrologers themselves, and the general public. The choice of words and the way one would speak to a scientist differ from the way one would talk to an astrologer or communicate with the general public. Therefore, the style is not the same as for other New Age books, and that is the category this book belongs to. If the words sound more like they should appear in a professional journal and appeal to my colleagues among technologists, then I apologize and hope the rest of you will understand. If the words sound more like they are directed toward advanced compatriots in astrologers, then I hope you will understand again. Moreover, since a considerable portion of the material interprets flaws in current practices pointed out by Edgar Cayce, it is hoped that none will be offended and all will learn by the process. If the words appear to be oriented more toward the general public and other people merely curious about astrology, I really have no defense because that was intended also. A huge number of acquaintances and friends fall into this last group, and my desires are for them to gain as well. Having a Taurus sun sign, my leaning is toward practicality and usefulness. I am convinced that rightly used, these revelations can help everyone. My wishes will be fulfilled if you, the reader, acquire a greater understanding of the true meaning of life with its astrological rudiments from Edgar Cayce's incredibly potent messages.

                                                    John Willner

1
FIRST ASTROLOGICAL READING

THE INFORMATION IMPARTED to those present when the first astrological questions were asked was startling and revolutionary, because it combined a concept of reincarnation with influences of the planets and the destiny of man.

In October 1923, not long after Edgar Cayce arrived in Dayton, Ohio, at the invitation of Arthur H. Lammers, a profound reading was given on the subject of astrology and its mandatory role in life. Virtually all of Edgar Cayce's readings prior to the summer of 1923 had been for the purpose of determining the causes of illnesses and offering remedial actions. Gladys Davis, who did most of the recording, discovered that once back in 1911 he had alluded to reincarnation in an offhand manner. These comments were passed over, however, and no one apparently questioned them. It was not until Edgar Cayce had arrived in Dayton that a series of questions that Lammers had been preparing were asked. The first series were on the subconscious mind, philosophy, metaphysics, and psychic phenomena. These were subjects that Lammers had been studying and for which he wanted answers. The fourth session in the series was devoted to astrology. Preparations had been comparatively thorough. Initial responses to ten questions on the subject of astrology and their answers were so important that they are given in their entirety: numbers were assigned to individuals in these readings to shield their identities.

An individual assigned the number 3744 asked the questions. The answers were unexpected. They described unimagined concepts about astrology's substantial role in furthering the destiny of man. Reincarnation and astrology were discussed in an integrated manner, and eventually a determination was made that neither could be properly understood if separated. Essential functions of the planets in life on earth and in life outside the earth plane were disclosed. Each question received an esoteric and sometimes jolting answer. Some of the questions went off on tangents that were based upon concepts held by the requesters. The answers, however, usually provided further insights on these related subjects. Because the information given in this first reading is so profound, a review and discussion will follow each question-answer pair:

TEXT OF READING 3744-4

This psychic reading given by Edgar Cayce at the Phillips Hotel, this 24th day of November, 1923, in accordance with request made by [5717], [953], [294], and others.

PRESENT

Edgar Cayce; Linden Shroyer, Conductor, Gladys Davis, Steno.

READING

Time of Reading   Phillips Hotel,
3:30 P.M.   Dayton, Ohio.

Q-29. Please give a definition of the word astrology.
A-29. That position in space about our own earth that is under the control of the forces that are within the sphere of that control, and all other spheres without that control. That is astrology, the study of those conditions.

In the beginning, our own plane, the earth, was set in motion. The planning of other planets began the ruling of the destiny of all matters as created, just as the division of waters was ruled and is ruled by the Moon in its path about the earth; just so as the higher creation as it begun is ruled by its action in conjunction with the planets about the earth. The strongest-force used in the destiny of man is the Sun first, then the closer planets to the earth, or those that are coming to ascension at the time of the birth of the individual, BUT LET IT BE UNDERSTOOD HERE, NO ACTION OF ANY PLANET OR THE PHASES OF THE SUN, THE MOON, OR ANY OF THE HEAVENLY BODIES SURPASS THE RULE OF MAN'S WILL POWER, the power given by the Creator of man, in the beginning, when he became a living soul, with the power of choosing for himself.

The inclinations of man are ruled by the planets under which he is born, for the destiny of man lies within the sphere or scope of the planets.

In unmistakable terms Edgar Cayce stated, "The inclinations of man are ruled by the planets underwhich he is born." Astrology is the study of forces exerted by planets in our solar system and forces exerted by the "so-called" fixed stars outside our solar system. Its application is only to a region in space where these forces impress their effects upon man. The Moon as it was set in motion about the earth came to rule all divisions of liquids. This is important, because both the physical bodies of human beings and our planet earth are more liquid than solid. As the planets were planned for the higher creation of man, each one assumed a distinctive influence. Hence, planets rule the destinies of all matters created in this region of space. One may interpret the word "matters" to mean entities as well as flesh-and-blood people. Companies, countries, states, cities, and agreements are examples of entities.

Because the Sun is the center of our solar system, it has the strongest influence over man's destiny. Next to the Sun in ability to mold the individual are those planets closer to the earth or coming to the Eastern horizon at birth (and the Eastern horizon itself, i.e., the Ascendant of a horoscope). Whereas the Sun establishes the skeleton or framework of the body and its character or individuality, the Ascendant and planets near the Ascendant establish the physical shape of the body and its personality within racial boundaries. The influences of all planets are intermingled, and the variety of their natal and progressed aspects number in the tens of thousands. For all intents and purposes, they are present constantly for every human being throughout life, ebbing and flowing at many different frequencies. No day passes without some planetary aspects forming. Every one of these aspects has an influence.

Yet the Creator gave man control when he became a living

soul. The will of man can supersede any single or combination
of planetary influences. Most planetary influences occur in
groups so that more than one planet is producing urges at any
one time. These combinations add spice to life and interesting
complexities. Individuals may choose independent courses of action. However, those choices are made in concert with, and usually in response to, planetary inclinations. They vary widely in
power and tenor. The strongest progressed aspects of planets
and nodes correspond with major milestones. The weakest relate to less important everyday affairs. A huge assortment of
decisions are prompted along the way.

All inclinations of man are ruled by the planets under which
each individual is born! These inclinations define the framework
or vistas leading to destiny. Exercised willpower uniquely defines the paths taken in arriving at personal destiny. Thus, destiny is shaped by a series of freewill choices when reacting to
complex urges emanating from planets. Freewill choices can
overcome the cast or makeup of any planetary force or forces.
Therefore, for every instigation of an urge, the will can acqui-
esce, oppose, or ignore. It can choose to cooperate with the
nature of the urge, or stand against it, or become preoccupied
with something else. In any case, the variety of human experiences fits the traits of the planets and the domains in which they
are found.

Q-30. Do the planets have an effect on the life of every individual born?

A-30. They have. Just as this earth's forces were set in motion, and about it, those forces that govern the elements, ele-
mentary so, of the earth's sphere or plane, and as each comes
under the influence of those conditions, the influence is to the
individual without regards to the will, which is the developing
factor of man, in which such is expressed through the breath
of the Creator, and as one's plane of existence is lived out from
one sphere to another they come under the influence of those
to which it passes from time to time.

In the sphere of many of the planets within the same solar
system, we find they are banished to certain conditions in developing about the spheres from which they pass, and again
and again and again return from one to another until they are
prepared to meet the everlasting Creator of our entire Universe,
of which our system is only a very small part. [See 900–25,
Par. 3-A.]

Be not dismayed [deceived]; God is not mocked; "Whatsoever a man soweth that shall he also reap." [Gal. 6:7]

In the various spheres, then, through which he must pass to attain that which will fit him for the conditions to enter in, and become a part of that Creator, just as an individual is a part of the creation now. In this manner we see there is the influence of the planets upon an individual, for all must come under that influence, though one may pass from one plane to another without going through all stages of the condition, for only upon the earth plane at present do we find man is flesh and blood, but upon others do we find those of his own making in the preparation of his own development.

As given, "The heavens declare the glory of God, and the firmament sheweth His handyworks. Day unto day uttereth speech, night unto night sheweth knowledge." This from the beginning and unto the end. [Ps. 19:1, 2]

Just in that manner is the way shown how man may escape from all of the fiery darts of the wicked one, for it is self, and selfishness, that would damn the individual soul unto one or the other of those forces that bring about the change that must be in those that willfully wrong his Maker. It is not that which man does or leaves undone, but rather that indifference toward the creation that makes or loses for the individual entity. Then, let's be up and doing—doing—"be ye doers [of the word], and not hearers only". [Jas. 1:22]

No one escapes astrology, whether believed in or not. The planets affect everyone and every matter on this earth, including every element in the earth's plane or sphere. These influences are present irrespective of will. In fact, they are essential to prod the will into action along prescribed paths. The exercise of will represents the developing factor of man. Thus, anyone disclaiming astrology is railing against what the Creator gave to us and denying the modus operandi of their own destinies. To shape the destiny of a person, no matter how lofty in social rank, while chastising others for acknowledging the way such destinies are formed must surely represent an offensive error that will be paid for in another life.

Make no mistake about this reading. It goes far and states in unequivocal terms that astrology is intimately bound together with reincarnation! One's existence is lived out from one sphere to another. Planetary influences affect each sphere through which a soul passes. Other lives will be lived by every one of us who has not reached a state of perfection. Other lives include those on earth and those on other planets to which we are from time to time banished. So pity the intellectual who believes in neither astrology nor reincarnation. Such individuals, perhaps without realizing what they are doing, have relegated themselves to a class occupied by atheists and agnostics who deny the existence of a Creator or express nonbelief. They face being "banished to certain conditions in developing about the spheres through which they must pass." Their banishments may be more severe than for other mortals, because "God is not mocked. Whatsoever a man soweth that shall he also reap." [Gal. 6:7]

Yet the critics probably will not be alone in reincarnation. All of us must return again and again until prepared to meet the everlasting Creator of our entire universe. So those of us who are believers have no room for being smug. All must come under the influence of planets again and again, although some may not have to go through all of the stages.

Then another curious statement was made, ". . . only upon the earth plane at present do we find man is flesh and blood, but upon others do we find those of his own making in the preparation of his own development." We can infer that flesh-and-blood man lives only on earth (in this solar system), but other spheres are conditioned by the individual's own making. While self and selfishness are cause enough for the repeated needs of further development, the worst offense is *indifference toward the creation.*

Were these the only readings on astrology and reincarnation, the authority of this single question-and-answer session might possibly be contested. But the general idea of repeated incarnations with inclinations from planets spurring each individual to make decisions that affect their destiny was repeated hundreds of times. Hence, astrology by itself should no longer be approached as an isolated study and practice. It must be considered in the context of an accompaniment to every incarnation upon earth.

Horoscope patterns ought to be interpreted in terms of composite inclinations that prod the individual in making proper decisions to gain redress with the Creator. Planetary aspects should be interpreted in terms of their individual contributions to decision-making and soul-development. Progressed aspects must be regarded as calendarized energy surges that embody the characteristics of every opportunity to gain advancement toward a higher destiny. Hence, one of the greatest astrological benefits to mankind is not the revealing of good and bad fortunes but understanding the what, why, how, and when of every challenge in the path leading to destiny. To a person who can interpret horoscopes, advanced notifications are conveyed that describe the nuances of every inclination. How a person responds is up to that individual, but these spiritual maps of routes and timetables provide focus, and they can facilitate decision-making.

This topic deserves much more discussion, and it will be revisited many times in a number of different ways. However, all of the remaining questions and answers of this reading will be addressed first:

Q-31. Give the names of the principal planets, and the influence on the lives of people.

A-31. Mercury, Mars, Jupiter, Venus, Saturn, Neptune, Uranus, Septimus. Influence as is given by many of those in and about the earth plane is defective. Many of the forces of each is felt more through the experience, by the entity's sojourn upon those planets than by the life that is lead other than by will, for will is the factor in the mind of man that must be exercised. The influence from any is from what planet that soul and spirit returns to bring the force to the earth individual, as it is breathed into the body, from whence did it come? that being the influence. Not the revolution of the ideas as given from those who study of those forces, but study those that come, as the Star of Bethlehem came to the earth as the individual pointing out the way to Truth, the Light, and others can only be such as prepare their way through that light and influence.

Edgar Cayce gave this reading in 1923. Pluto, regarded today as a principal planet, was not discovered by modern astronomers until 1930. Therefore, it could not have been identified readily until it was named seven years later. Septimus is Latin for *seventh*. The old way of counting was to start with the initial position, not the next one down the line. Counting from the earth as one, Mars as two, etc., Pluto becomes the seventh planet out in our solar system.

After Pluto was discovered, Edgar Cayce associated the name Pluto with Vulcan. Septimus had been a numbered placeholder. Refer to Greek and Roman mythology for allegorical information about Pluto and Vulcan. But that is a digression.

This answer to question 31 is one of the first, if not the first, to state that a soul and spirit may have planetary sojourns. It clarifies the part of answer 30 that talks about existences lived out from one sphere to another. An influence from a planet that has been a stopping place for the soul and spirit is stronger than when that planet has not been visited. Furthermore, the experiences may have differed to some extent or been far more intricate than the natural influences attributed by most astrologers to the same planet. Therefore, interpretations may be defective when the total powers of such experiences are not taken into account. That could present difficulties to those unable to see these nuances through psychic impressions or other means. A Mercury, Mars, or Venus in one horoscope, for example, will have some characteristics in common but will not carry the same implications for one person as they do for another! Most astrologers already knew that the subject they studied was complex. What this message portends is a complexity beyond what most of them might have imagined. Moreover, computer interpretations of planetary influences popular today can only be of marginal value at best. Any recipient of an astrological computer analysis should henceforth be aware of this inherent weakness. If any individual has sojourned on other planets, the computer will not know about them. The programmer was not privy to that knowledge, and no known software expert can sense the unique experiences gained by every individual during such planetary sojourns.

Edgar Cayce said that in order to understand these influences they had to be studied with an attitude pointing the way to Truth and Light. This is a different approach than for customary delineations of horoscopes wherein the recipient is typically looking for a jackpot. It may be compared with understanding the vast implications held by the Star of Bethlehem in contrast with any other visible star or planet. To be effective, interpretations of planetary inclinations must be given in a way that show each individual how they might prepare their way. Explanations in terms of good or bad fortunes are therefore inappropriate and might be detrimental. Edgar Cayce used the word defective to describe customary delineations, the way they are typically given now. Astrologers will gain if they apply all of their resources to correcting such defects in the information they convey.

Q-32. Are any of the planets, other than the earth, inhabited by human beings or animal life of any kind?
A-32. No.

This answer is acknowledged by scientists as being correct for our solar system. It might be the height of human egotism, however, to believe no other planetary system contains life. We are such a small speck in the total universe.

Q-33. Give the description of the planet nearest the earth at the present time, and its effect upon the people.

A-33. That planet now fast approaching the earth, under whose influence the earth's minds trend, will be for the next few years, as time is known here, is Mars, who will be only thirty-five million miles away from the earth in 1924. The influence will be felt as this recedes from the earth, and those of that nature; that is, given through sojourn there, express in their lives upon the earth the troublesome times that will arise, only being tempered with that of those who may be, and will be, coming from those of Jupiter, Venus and Uranus, those strong ennobling forces tempered by those of love and strength.

The fact that this question was asked at all implies that the author believed a planet close to the earth would affect the populace more than one farther away. There is more to a planet's effect upon the populace than closeness. However, this idea is known to be very old. When Mars approached earth, it was especially feared by ancient peoples.

As a matter of fact, the earth's orbit lies between the orbits of Venus and Mars. The likelihood of any other planet being as close as one of these two would have a comparatively low probability. On November 24, 1923, when this reading was given, Mars was closer than Venus. It came closest in August of 1924, when in the same sign and degree as earth. Edgar Cayce simply answered the question directly without further elaboration. Mars on that date was closer to earth than any other heavenly body except the Moon. But he also said that when receding from earth, Mars would be more troublesome to those who were susceptible, i.e., after August 1924. Individuals who had previous sojourns on Mars would be affected the most. During that fall period, Jupiter, Venus, and Uranus were forming strong aspect angles with each other. The combined effects were forecast as being ennobling, tempered by love and strength. Those words fit Jupiter, Venus, and Uranus.

What is known about the Cayce family in 1924 was that money was scarce. Lammers became involved in lawsuits, and this source of money dried up. Mars can usually be associated

with strife. The family survived mainly on readings given to individuals. During this trying period, however, ideas of building
a bigger base for the work did not cease. Edgar wanted to form
an association and erect a hospital where patients could be
treated in accordance with their physical readings. But life readings said that Virginia Beach was where they should be located,
not Dayton. Funding would require love and strength. That
caused the breakup of an initial attempt to form a society in
Dayton. But preparations for the move to Virginia Beach did
occur, and it had to have been an ennobling transition. The
combative and inflaming forces of Mars were evident.

Q-34. What effect will the planet, Uranus, have on the people during the next two years?
A-34. We find in this planet those of the exceptional forces,
those of the ultra forces, those that carry the extremes in every
walk of physical life and forces, and these are those that will,
in the next two years, especially, give of their strength to the
greater force, as has been given. Those, tempered with the
forces as received there, find in the tumultuous times that are
to arise, the setting ready for their again forces. Well may the
earth tremble under that influence in 1925 and 1927.

Edgar Cayce described the general nature of influences from
Uranus. Exceptional and ultra forces can occur in any arena
when Uranus is providing impulses. Webster's dictionary defines
"ultra" as going beyond others, or beyond due limit—extreme.
During this two-year period, Germany suffered its economic depression, and Adoph Hitler increased his power through writing
and speaking about his revolutionary ideas. There was much
poverty throughout the world. On the other hand, the first air-
plane was flown between continents by Charles Lindbergh. Uranus also pertains to the electrical and electromagnetic revolution
taking place during this period. Television was invented. Extreme changes in everyday living took place, and they were tumultuous changes. Individuals who had been tempered by
sojourning on Uranus found a setting ready for them to apply
their talents. Many scientists and engineers were in that category.
Uranus was in the second half of Pisces during most of this
two-year period from 1925 through 1927, touching Aries only
briefly before returning by retrograde motion. Retrograde is a
term applied to an apparent backward motion of a planet when

viewed from the earth. Pisces is the perspicacious sign, giving awareness about a multitude of factors. Uranus is inventive and radical in disposition. Modern is better than the passé. Many contacts with other planets occurred during this period, especially the outer planets that produce dynamic changes. The year 1925 was the year that Edgar Cayce and his family moved lock, stock, and barrel to Virginia Beach, Virginia. The Association for Research and Enlightenment was formed in 1927. Doubtless, Uranus had a hand in both, and the earth has trembled. It trembled for other Uranian reasons as well, including earthquakes.

Q-35. Is it proper for us to study the effects of the planets on our lives in order to better understand our tendencies and inclinations, as influenced by the planets?

A-35. When studied aright, very, very, very much so. How aright then? In that influence as is seen in the influence of the knowledge already obtained by mortal man. Give more of that into the lives, giving the understanding THAT THE WILL MUST BE THE EVER GUIDING FACTOR TO LEAD MAN ON, EVER UPWARD.

This was one of the all-time important messages about astrology that Edgar Cayce gave in his readings. No question about its validity can be sustained. The worth to man is exceedingly great. He emphasized that it was proper when studied aright, meaning that in many cases astrology was not being studied aright. However, influences from the planets were known by mortal man. These influences have been known for aeons by many different people in many different lands. While some may have studiously avoided knowing about these influences, or harassed those who did, such actions do not make the influences go away. What is important is to give more of this knowledge into lives while emphasizing that will is the ever-guiding factor to lead man on toward his destiny. That complete understanding of the dichotomy between the prodding of the planets and the necessity of applying willpower for development of the soul is absolutely necessary. It is one of the missing links in astrology as it is being practiced today. The complete picture must be given for interpretations to be aright.

Q-36. In what way should astrology be used to help man live better in the present physical plane?

A-36. In that which the position of the planets give the tendencies in a given life, without reference to the will.

Then let man, the individual, understand how WILL may overcome, for we all must overcome, if we would, in any wise, enter in. Not that the position gives man the transport, but that that force as manifested in the creation of man wherein choice between the good and evil, exercising highest will force, may be manifested the greater in man. DO THAT.

The main way that astrology can be used to help our fellow man is to identify tendencies given by the positions of the planets in their horoscopes, leaving decisions to be made up to the individual. The recipients of astrological information need to know that their own will can overcome the problems that present themselves in life. The exercise of willpower in meeting challenges is consequential to their development. Making choices between good and evil manifests the highest use of a person's faculties. Such choices in themselves do not provide transport back to the Creator, but they are necessary steps in getting there. Astrology is the study that can provide the signals of when to act and comprehension of the complexities that need to be considered to act more efficiently.

In translating the astrological information for another person, leaving self out of the picture is important. Imposing one's own will on another, or even directing specific, detailed, and mindless courses of action for others to follow, can interfere with that person's progress. It is better to offer guidelines for mutual benefit than narrow procedures that stifle individual expression. Hence, these ideas should be understood by every manager of people. Their employees should be directed in a manner that allows them freedom to think and act. Given this leeway, they will perform better for any organization and for themselves than when every move is dictated.

Q-37. Who were the first people in the world to use astrology, and what time in history was it first used?

A-37. Many, many thousands, thousands of years ago. The first record as is given is as that recorded in Job, who lived before Moses was.

Most historians, archaeologists, and astrologers would answer this question by citing the Chaldeans as the people and about 5,000 years ago as the time. This incorrect response would be based upon the earliest surviving artifacts of an astrological nature uncovered by archaeologists. Ancient manuscripts allude to this same era. However, Edgar Cayce said that astrology is much, much older than that. One needs to read Job in the Holy Bible to find this record that is tens of thousands of years older. Job lived before the time of Moses in the land of Uz. The Uzbek were known to be a Turkish tribe located in what is now Russia.

The thirty-eighth chapter of Job makes specific astrological references, and they had to be familiar to the people of Uz during this ancient period:

31. Canst thou bind the sweet influences of Pleiades or loose the bands of Orion?

32. Canst thou bring forth Mazzaroth in his season? or canst thou guide Arcturus with his sons?

33. Knowest thou the ordinances of heaven? canst thou set the dominion thereof in the earth?

Pleiades and Orion are constellations known for their astrological influences. The Pleiades are characterized as being established by young females in mythology. It would be natural to think of them as sweet. Orion has the bands of a hunter. Mazzaroth refers to the obscure or hidden part of the zodiac at any season. The hidden part is on the other side of earth that cannot be seen when looking into the sky. Arcturus is a first-magnitude star having significance to souls in their journeys, according to other Cayce readings. The ordinances of heaven have known rulerships over compartments of life. "Dominions thereof in the earth" can be translated into what astrologers call houses. Perhaps domains would be a more appropriate term for compartmentalizing influences in the human experience. However, all of these references are unmistakably astrological in nature, and the period was very long ago—thousands of years before the Chaldean involvement.

Q-38. Are the tendencies of an individual influenced most by the planets nearer the earth at the time of the individual's birth?

A-38. At, or from that one whom is at the zenith when the individual is in its place or sphere, or as is seen from that sphere or plane the soul and spirit took its flight in coming to the earth plane. For each planet, in its relation to the other, is just outside, just outside, relativity of force, as we gather them together.

This is another profound answer to a simple question. The initial part of the answer is straightforward. It states that planets near the zenith (Midheaven) in a sphere (horoscope) influence the individual more than any planet close to the earth. This answer needs to be contrasted with Answer 29 that referred to the Ascendant. Question 38 pertains to the planet that will sway the individual the most or provide the strongest urges. The Ascendant and planets close to the Ascendant set the personality and appearance. Their effects were manifested at birth. In essence, their influences have already been established in the body and mind of the individual. Therefore, the answer is correct. Planets near the Midheaven or zenith have strong continuing influences upon any individual. They mold that person's reputation.

Nearness to the earth of planets has been recorded in ancient astrological texts, because there was a great fear of Mars when it approached. But the levels of influence upon man from proximity are not as strong as planets at the zenith. This issue appears to be a continuation of the same one expressed in Question 33. While a force acting between two bodies in physics varies as the square root of the distance between them, that is not the only physical phenomenon existent. Otherwise, for example, the influences of Pluto could never be as strong or stronger than those of the Moon. Yet those who have attempted to gauge the strengths of astrological aspects have found that apparent constancy of position in relation to the location of an individual being rotated diurnally on the surface of the earth is a greater measure of influence. This means that the more distant outer planets have the strongest influences on average, especially when they near the zenith of the horoscope. Since the outer planets move even more slowly in declination than in celestial longitude, those aspects when appearing at the zenith are stronger still. On the other hand, nearness of Mars or Venus to the earth is a consideration not often spoken of today.

Edgar Cayce went further in his explanations. He told of the place from which the soul and spirit took flight. The position of this area of departure is on a sphere or plane and directly over the spot where the baby will be born—at the zenith. Moreover, that sphere or plane is just outside relativity of force, as souls and spirits gather together. They are apparently beyond the effects of strong gravitational forces, but close to earth in terms of relative distances between celestial bodies in space. Thus, the flight paths are comparatively short (and the transitions fast as we would understand speed). That might be necessary to fix the horoscope within a fraction of a second of the time chosen so that influences do not change perceptibly in the interim between takeoff and arrival. Souls and spirits gather together at these launching pads. Reincarnations take place from locations directly above human bodies as they are born. Planets in line with such paths, or close to them, have the greatest impact in horoscopes as the individual matures.

This is an intensely esoteric side of astrology that will be explored at greater length later on. Modern sophisticates may have difficulty accepting this line of reasoning at face value. It is probably a matter that the majority of people have never considered. However, God should not be mocked, nor should Edgar Cayce! The arrangement for horoscopes to be injected almost instantaneously makes a lot of sense. Moreover, undeviating correlations with other statements fortify this idea.

In these ten questions and answers may be found a number of missing links that wise modern men and women must learn if they would consider themselves to be educated in the ways of life and this world we live in. If you, the readers, are startled with their content, then think about Edgar Cayce when he came back to a waking state and read these words for the first time. No wonder the information was a matter of deep concern to him personally and to his family. They had many discussions before acquiring a degree of comfort in the subjects explored. Further readings along these lines hinged upon much convincing on the part of Lammers and a realization that mankind might be benefited by such revelations. Edgar Cayce made the decision to continue his participation, and many hundreds of nonphysical readings given thereafter contained more astrological wisdom.

2

REINCARNATION

THE INITIAL TEN questions answered by Edgar Cayce opened several complicated topics, starting with the role played by astrology in reincarnation. Not only was the information controversial, but it spoke of a grand plan that will be incredible to many.

Before proceeding, perhaps it would be best to clearly identify four assumptions that may be inferred from the initial astrological reading and those that immediately followed. First is the subject of reincarnation having an integral and dependent relationship with astrology. Second is the ability of a soul and spirit to enter a baby's physical body when in the process of being born and the astrological options available at that time. Third is the mystery of where the soul and spirit reside within human bodies and/or where horoscopic influences are stored and triggered. They would have to reside somewhere within or about the human body in order to establish a framework for living. Fourth is the scientific and medical compatibility of these new astrological ideas that must somehow be integrated, whether acknowledged by the respective professional communities or not.

Each one of these subjects has enormous implications. The readings approached them from many different angles. Remarkably, a number of readings were given years apart, but they remained consistent. Confidence in the authenticity of this information has accumulated through undeviating repetitions of the same themes. Explanations have connected a multitude of complex threads between related subjects with no discernible flaws. Subsequent affirmations by other people have added to the case for validity. Analogous experimental data, where it could be obtained, have in every case provided support and further agreement. Therefore, short of finding tangible justifications that could be exhibited to everybody, the position will be taken that if Edgar Cayce gave pertinent information on a topic, that topic is worthy of honest intellectual review. Acceptance is a personal matter, but that may only be a question of familiarity. People tend to fear those things they do not understand. Those same people usually drop their fears when the subject is understood.

To review and collect thoughts, Edgar Cayce has already spoken as though reincarnation was a universally accepted fact. That is not quite true, although the idea in our modern Western world is growing. He also stated that visits (or banishments) to planets between lives on earth provide experiences that are brought with the soul to the next incarnation. That is a comparatively new embellishment of an old belief to most people.

Then Edgar Cayce went on to say that souls gather outside the earth as the time nears for entering the bodies of newborn babies. A choice has to be made by a specific soul to become injected into a particular body. Such choices are alleged to have astrological significance because they are based largely on astrological factors. These choices affect the intensity and character of urges, depending upon where the planets are at that instant of flight back to earth into the newborn baby's body.

The information contained in a horoscope has to be stored somewhere. Perhaps this issue arises from frail human logic. Storage within the child's body would be the expectation, whether at, prior to, or after birth. An interesting conjecture has been promulgated in esoteric circles that such storage takes place in one or more endocrine glands. This latter idea could be controversial to scientists or those in the medical profession, even though cogent. Storage has to take place somewhere if it is to activate influences and trigger responses in the human body. So what better places are there than the endocrine glands when corresponding planetary and bodily functions are considered together? The heart alone or the brain alone do not appear to be wholly commensurate. Correspondences with the ductless glands need to be analyzed for better understanding. Secretions from these ductless glands have been identified by medical experts, and many of their functions are known.

Underlying the information given by Edgar Cayce is the thought that none of it would be revealed if untrue. Truth in a modern world means that all of the implications must fit intellectual, physical, and behavioral guidelines of society as known today. This definition includes medical and scientific guidelines. It would be best if all of the phenomena were observable and measurable. Those properties are not available in some cases, or important relationships have not been clearly identified. Without real data, beliefs might be stretched thin. However, certain associations and compatibilities can be identified. They might aid mental harmonization with those elements that at this moment could be labeled imaginary. Repetitive, complex associations that were given in the readings have to be construed as more than coincidences. Associations are key factors in discovery.

Returning to the question of reincarnation, several observations come to mind that might be worth mentioning. Reincarnation is a belief held by the cultures of many races. It was known to the pharaohs of Egypt as depicted in their funerary artifacts. It was described in Sanskrit, the old Indic language spoken from the third century B.C. onward. From this source it became an integral part of the Hindu and Moslem religions. Aborigines on every continent have some belief in afterlife. Thus, reincarnation is not just a religious philosophy confined to selected groups. It is to be found among the beliefs of many independent races who had no known communications with each other. Furthermore, despite contemporary inattention in the West, reincarnation is entrenched in Christianity. Supporting statements appear frequently in the Holy Bible, although concerted efforts were devoted to weeding them out after the time of Christ. Certain chapters were dropped as a part of this project.

Clerics may speak out against reincarnation, as they sometimes do against astrology, but that is a sign those particular individuals do not fully comprehend their own specialty. The Bible is filled with references to both subjects, and Edgar Cayce often cited the passages. Even though some outspoken professionals are known to hold reincarnation at arm's length, Edgar Cayce was not combative in his responses to their expressions of doubt. He simply stated these truths as observed through his clairvoyant vision.

Q-25. I have heretofore disliked the idea of reincarnation but I want truth. Is there any evidence that I have been here before.

A-25. The urges that have been indicated for the entity here should answer this. For, there must ever be the answer within. For, "My spirit beareth witness with thy spirit sayeth the Lord."

3228-001

Q-29. About how much time have I spent in reincarnation up to the present time?

A-29. Almost in all the cycles that have had the incoming from period to period hast thou dwelt. Thine first incoming in the earth was during those periods of the Atlanteans that made for the divisions. Hence, counting in time, some twenty thousand years.

707-001

These readings leave the skeptic with his own inner thoughts and several more shockers. The controversial race of Atlanteans is brought up in a matter-of-fact manner. According to Edgar Cayce, reincarnations haven't happened one or two times. Most people have been reincarnating over and over again for tens of thousands of years. The necessity for so many returns to earth indicates that man must be making progress toward a final destiny very slowly, or in many cases taking backward steps. Humans probably make forward progress until they slip back into patterns that are detrimental and from which they must recover. Those regressions must be what requires so many additional reincarnations.

In reading after reading that followed the initial one prompted by Lammers, all kinds of related questions were asked. When Edgar Cayce was queried about biblical references in support of reincarnation, this is typical of his responses. They were given unhesitatingly, and they were precise. He always seemed to have the answers at the tip of his tongue:

Q-24. What part of the New Testament definitely teaches reincarnation?
A-24. John, six to eight; third to fifth. Then the rest as a whole.

452-006

Still other questions were more inane:

Q-53. Does the soul's entity change in reincarnation?
A-53. The ENTITY? The soul is the ENTITY! The entity is the soul and the mind and the body of same, see? These only enter matter, or a new house, in incarnations.

1494-001

A recent poll shows that about 50 percent of the population of the United States has some form of belief in reincarnation. Thus, the concept of rebirth of the soul in another body may be only half controversial in America. European beliefs are not known to differ by any sizable margin from those in the United States. In the Middle East, Far East, and many other areas of the world, a far greater percentage of the population does not find this subject to be controversial at all. Thus, it might be expected that a majority of the people of the world already accepts the idea of reincarnation. A majority on any subject does not constitute proofs or even a better judgment. Yet an inquiring mind might question why, if incarnation is a truth, any portion of the population would be nonbelievers. The answers heard so far are not altogether rational or convincing. They appear to be a result of noninvolvement more than cogent thinking.

Most members of the Association for Research and Enlightenment, the organization left to spread Edgar Cayce's words, are familiar with this subject. Most of them have read books and circulating files of his readings. They know that Edgar Cayce frequently discussed reincarnation as a step for continuing progress in spiritual development. A reincarnation is considered to be one example of an earthly sojourn. Hundreds of examples were given, but the right to another stay on earth is implicit in all of them:

For each soul-entity enters a material experience not by chance but as a purposefulness—fulfilling that whereunto it has been promised that He hath not willed that any soul should perish, but that each should know and become aware of its relationships to Creative Forces.

Then, as to whether there is the developing or retarding of a soul through any particular sojourn depends upon how the entity applies self—or as to whether or not it is being true to that it sets or chooses as its ideal.

1767-002

These words reaffirm that a soul-entity is not a chance encounter, but a mission that has purposefulness. A soul does not perish with death, but lives on in another form. An entity develops or retards, depending upon how the applications to life are made. Applications to life are spurred on by astrological urges.

Many additional details are given in the complete reading that follows. It is quite religious in its tone. The essence and purpose of reincarnation are given. Edgar Cayce did not differentiate between reincarnation and religion, but treated them as a single item. Additionally, arguments for and against reincarnation are supplied as though anyone on earth would beg the question. Did Edgar Cayce anticipate the doubters? If so, he gave appropriate answers. Do the doubters lump reincarnation and astrology together as they should? Probably not, but if so, that would be fine. Astrological ties to reincarnation are given mainly in the questions and answers that came at the end of this dissertation:

TEXT OF READING 5753-1

This psychic reading was given by Edgar Cayce at his home, on the 16th day of June, 1933, before the Second Annual Congress of the Association for Research and Enlightenment, Inc., in accordance with request by those present.

PRESENT

Edgar Cayce; Gertrude Cayce, Conductor; Gladys Davis, Steno. And approximately thirty-five other people attending the Congress.

READING

Time of Reading
5:00 to 6:00 P.M.

1. GC: You will give at this time a comprehensive discourse on reincarnation. If the soul returns to the earth through a succession of appearances, you will explain why this is necessary or desirable and will clarify through explanation the laws governing such returns. You will answer the questions which will be asked on this subject.

2. EC: Yes. In giving even an approach to the subject sought here, it is well that there be given some things that may be accepted as standards from which conclusions—or where parallels—may be drawn, that there may be gathered in the minds of those who would approach some understanding, some concrete examples, that may be applied in their own individual experience.

3. Each soul that enters, then, must have had an impetus from some beginning that is of the Creative Energy, or of a first cause.

4. What, then, was—or is—the first cause; for if there be law pertaining to the first cause it must be an unchangeable law, and is—IS—as "I AM that I am!" For this is the basis from which one would reason:

5. The first cause was, that the created would be the companion for the Creator; that it, the creature, would—through its manifestations in the activity of that given unto the creature—show itself to be not only worthy of, but companionable to, the Creator.

6. Hence, every form of life that man sees in a material world is an essence or manifestation of the Creator; not the Creator, but a manifestation of a first cause—and in its own sphere, its own consciousness of its activity in that plane or sphere.

7. Hence, as man in this material world passes through, here are the manifestations of the attributes that the conscious-

ness attributes to, or finds coinciding with, that activity which is manifested; hence becomes then as the very principle of the law that would govern an entrance into a manifestation.

8. Then a soul, the offspring of a Creator, entering into a consciousness that became a manifestation in any plane or sphere of activity, given that free-will for its use of those abilities, qualities, conditions in its experience, demonstrates, manifests, shows forth, that it reflects in its activity towards that first cause.

9. Hence in the various spheres that man sees (that are demonstrated, manifested, in and before self) even in a material world, all forces, all activities, are a manifestation. Then, that ability to be one with, becomes necessary for the demonstration or manifestation of those attributes in and through all force, all demonstration, in a sphere.

10. Because an atom, a matter, a form, is changed does not mean that the essence, the source or the spirit of it has changed; only in its form of manifestation, and NOT in its relation with the first cause. That man reaches that consciousness in the material plane of being aware of what he does about or with the consciousness of the knowledge, the intelligence, the first cause, makes or produces that which is known as the entering into the first cause, principles, basis, or the essences, that there may be demonstrated in that manifested that which gains for the soul, for the entity, that which would make the soul an acceptable companion to the Creative Force, Creative Influence. See?

11. As to how, where, when, and what produces the entrance into a material manifestation of an entity, a soul:

12. In the beginning was that which set in motion that which is seen in manifested form with the laws governing same. The inability of destroying matter, the ability of each force, each source of power or contact—as it meets in its various forms, produces that which is a manifestation in a particular sphere. This may be seen in those elements used in the various manifested ways of preparing for man, in many ways, those things that be speak of the laws that govern man's relationship to the first cause, or God.

13. Then, this is the principle:

14. Like begets like. Those things that are positive and negative forces combine to form in a different source, or different
manifestation, the combinations of which each element, each
first principle manifested, has gained from its associations—in
its activities—that which has been brought to bear by self or
that about it, to produce that manifestation.

15. Hence man, the crowning of all manifestations in a
material world—a causation world, finds self as the cause
and the product of that he (man), with those abilities given,
has been able to produce, or demonstrate, or manifest from
that he (the soul) has gained, does gain, in the transition,
the change, the going toward that (and being of that) from
which he came.

16. Periods, times, places: That which is builded, each in
its place, each in its time.

17. This is shown to man in the elemental world about him.
Man's consciousness of that about him is gained through that
he, man, does about the knowledge of that he is, as in relation
to that from which he came and towards which he is going.

18. Hence, in man's analysis and understanding of himself,
it is as well to know from whence he came as to know whither
he is going.

19. Ready for questions.

Q-20. What is meant by inequality of experience? Is it a
strong argument for reincarnation?
A-20. Considering that which has just been presented, isn't
it the same argument?

Q-21. Is experience limited to this earth plane?
A-21. As each entity, each soul, in the various conscious-
nesses, passes from one to another, it—the soul—becomes
conscious of that about self in that sphere—to which it, the entity, the soul attains in a materially manifested way or manner.
Hence the entity develops THROUGH the varied spheres of
the earth and its solar system, and the companions of varied

experiences in that solar system, or spheres of development or activity; as in some ways accredited correctly to the planetary influences in an experience. The entity develops THROUGH those varied spheres.

Hence the sun, the moon, the stars, the position in the heavens or in all of the hosts of the solar systems that the earth occupies—all have their influence in the same manner (this is a very crude illustration, but very demonstrative) that the effect of a large amount of any element would attract a compass.

Drawn to! Why? Because of the influence of which the mind A soul, an entity, is as real as a physical entity, and is as subject to laws as the physical body as subject to the laws in a material world and the elements thereof! Does fire burn the soul or the physical body? Yet, self may cast self into a fire element by doing that the soul knows to be wrong!

What would make a wrong and a right? A comparison of what the soul knows its consciousness to be in accord or contrary-wise with, in relation to that which gave it existence.

Q-22. Are not transferred memories misappropriated by individuals and considered to be personal experiences?

A-22. Personal experiences have their influence upon the inner soul, while disincarnate entities (or that may be heavenbound) may influence the thought of an entity or a mind.

But, who gives the law to have an element to influence, whether from self or from others? That same as from the beginning. The WILL of the soul that it may be one with the first cause. In the material, the mental, and the spiritual experience of many souls, many entities, it has been found that there BE those influences that DO have their effect upon the thought of those that would do this or that. Who gives it? Self! Just as it is when an entity, a body, fills its mind (mentally, materially) with those experiences that bespeak of those things that add to the carnal forces of an experience. Just so does the mind become the builder throughout. And the mental mind, or physical mind, becomes CARNALLY directed!

The mind is the builder ever, whether in the spirit or in the flesh. If one's mind is filled with those things that bespeak of the spirit, that one becomes spiritual-minded. As we may find in a material world: Envy, strife, selfishness, greediness, avarice, are the children of MAN! Longsuffering, kindness, brotherly love, good deeds, are the children of the spirit of light.

Choose ye (as it has ever been given) whom ye will serve. This is not beggaring the question! As individuals become abased, or possessed, are their thoughts guided by those in the borderland? Certainly! If allowed to be!

But he that looks within is higher, for the spirit knoweth the Spirit of its Maker—and the children of same are as given. And, "My Spirit beareth witness with thy spirit," saith He that giveth life!

What IS Life? A manifestation of the first cause—God!

Q-23. Explain, in the light of reincarnation, the cycle of development towards maturity in individuals.

A-23. As an individual in any experience, in any period, uses that of which it (the soul or entity) is conscious in relation to the laws of the Creative Forces, so does that soul, that entity, develop towards—what? A companionship with the Creative influence!

Hence karma to those disobeying—by making for self that which would be as the towers of Babel, or as the city of Gomorrah, or as the fleshpots of Egypt, or as the caring for those influences in the experience that satisfy or gratify self without thought of the effect upon that which it has in its own relation to the first cause! Hence to many this becomes as the stumblingblock.

It is as was given by Him, "I am the way. No man approaches the Father but by me." But, does a soul crucify the flesh even as He, when it finds within itself that it must work out its own salvation in a material world, by entering and re-entering that there may be made manifest that consciousness in the soul that would make it a companion with the Creator?

Rather is the law of forgiveness made of effect in thine experience, through Him that would stand in thy stead; for He is the way, that light ever ready to aid when there is the call upon—and the trust of the soul in—that first cause!

Has it not been given that there IS an influence in the mind, the thought of man, from the outside? Then, would those that have lost their way become the guides and both fall in the ditch? or would the soul trust in the Way, and the Light, and seek in that way that there may be shown the light?

What caused the first influences in the earth that brought selfishness? The desire to be as gods, in that rebellion became the order of the mental forces in the soul; and sin entered.

Q-24. What is the strongest argument against reincarnation?
A-24. That there is the law of cause and effect in MATERIAL things. But the strongest argument also, turned over, the strongest argument for it; as in ANY principle, when reduced to its essence. For the LAW is set—and it happens! though a soul may will itself NEVER to reincarnate, but must burn and burn and burn—or suffer and suffer and suffer! For, the heaven and hell is built by the soul! The companionship in God is being one with Him; and the gift of God is being yet apart from Him—or one with, yet apart from, the Whole.

Q-25. What is the strongest argument for reincarnation?
A-25. Just as given. Just turn it over; or, as we have outlined.

26. We are through for the present.

"That the created would be the companion for the Creator" is the first cause. Thus, becoming worthy to be a companion of the Creator is the guiding principle behind reincarnation. This is an unchangeable law and standard. Our souls become entities as a manifestation of the Creator. All things on earth are likewise manifestations of the Creator for use by mankind and to aid in becoming companionable. Attributes from the planets are a part of this grand plan and in total harmony with its precepts. Man was given free will to make choices. We either direct our own actions toward good or toward evil with appropriate consequences. "For, the heaven and hell is built by the soul!" Is Edgar Cayce saying that heaven and hell fall into these cycles of reincarnations and planetary sojourns?

A number of signs are given to us of the law. For example, matter can neither be destroyed nor created by man. Matter can only be transformed. Physicists and chemists, who know this law well, should take note of the underlying significance. Matter and souls are akin. This state of affairs was ordained by the Creator, and no mortal can change His law. Yet the positive and the negative can be readily combined to form chemical combinations, or compounds, with different characteristics. Positive and negative souls can also be combined to form families. A family's traits are different from either soul alone. The atoms that make up a chemical combination remain unchanged, but the resulting compound is another material. Souls that combine to form a family remain unchanged, but the family unit is unlike either person alone. Both kinds of mixes or blends represent new characteristics and new gains. Chemists and married couples understand these principles readily. But do they really understand the makings of the law that governs?

Other signs are that effects have causes. Like begets like. Powers from spheres set in motion cannot be escaped, nor should there be any desire to do so, because they have a beneficial purpose. All of the planets rotate on their axes and in orbits about the Sun. These forces exist and manifest themselves because of their rotary and curvilinear motions and the desires of the Creator.

The issue of karma was raised. Karma is a term common to Hindus and Muslims describing the totality of one's actions carried forward into a succeeding incarnation. These actions include conditions of uncompensated guilt. Self-gratification, evil conduct, and oppressive acts must be atoned for, and that is where justice often comes about—not in this life always, but in the next or next. Man, trying to behave as gods, has let sin enter. Hell on earth or in one sphere or the other may be the result. Karma has a cause-and-effect relationship that is better understood when the justification against reincarnation is turned over. A negative response to any of the planetary influences can require karmic revisiting of that experience and another chance for making better decisions. A positive response can result in heavenly advancement. Goodness will prevail, even if realization does not come until the soul has entered another sphere, or another . . .

Q-9. Must each soul continue to be reincarnated in the earth until it reaches perfection, or are some souls lost?

A-9. Can God lose itself, if God be God—or is it submerged, or is it as has been given, carried into the universal soul or consciousness? The SOUL is not lost; the INDIVIDUALITY of the soul that separates itself is lost. The reincarnation or the opportunities are continuous until the soul has of itself become an ENTITY in its whole or has submerged itself.

Q-10. If a soul fails to improve itself, what becomes of it?

A-10. That's why the reincarnation, why it reincarnates; that it MAY have the opportunity. Can the will of man continue to defy its Maker?

826-008

Individuality is the Sun, and the Sun of an individual can be lost. But the soul cannot be lost. Of that we have received assurances. The opportunities are continuous until the soul becomes an entity.

3

A Soul's Choices

ONLY A FEW people in this world who accept reincarnation may know about a soul being able to make far-reaching, astrologically dependent choices before returning.

> For, there is ever the choice by the soul-entity as to the environs, as to the path to be taken in its application of opportunities EXPRESSED in material consciousness.
>
> 2650-001

During reincarnation the soul, according to Edgar Cayce, can pick a country, state, town, home, and family in which to be born. He also stated that the soul can choose a path of life. A path of life is portrayed in a horoscope and its progressions. In this context Edgar Cayce did not use the astrologer's word horoscope. Rather, he spoke of cosmic forces. The next reading cites cosmic or God-force choices in a material world. In addition, he refers to familiarization of the soul with those forces in preparation for celestial influences that direct activities and cause associations of ideas and conditions. This passage equates astrological forces with God-forces, and that is an extremely important connection.

> For, as has oft been given, the soul is that which is to be made one with the Creator, through experience and through

the application of that knowledge and understanding respecting the laws of the cosmic or God-Force in a material world. And what the soul, the individual, does respecting such laws, such activities, makes for that preparedness within the inner self for the companionship with those celestial influences that make for the directing and the associations of ideas and of conditions in the realm of whatever activity in which the entity finds itself.

In the present, then, the associations make for those conditions wherein and whereunto the soul must make its choice; as to whether things are to be viewed from the material angle or from the soul's development—that must live on and on. And the choice also makes for the realm of activity in which are those things and conditions upon which every soul's development must depend. For, will and choice is the gift of the soul—that it may make of itself that which may be in the closer relationships with the spirit of truth, of life, of understanding.

556-001

The soul has options to either pursue a material angle, to further its own development, or to try to do both. It must first pick an environ, a family, and then seek expression. In doing so knowledge and understanding respecting the laws of the cosmic or God-force in a material world are applied. "Companionship with those celestial influences that make for the directing of things upon which the soul must depend" is an integral part of the decision. Again and again references were made to choices available to the soul as though every option had already been identified in considerable detail and those options were limited. Thus, the complete depiction of each potential new life as embedded in specific horoscopes would have to be known to the soul so that a single best choice could be made. Each individual horoscope would have to be for a precise time.

In every entity's activity there are urges latent and manifested. The astrological influences, as termed in physical consciousness indicate choices that have been or were made by the entity. Thus these indicate to the entity, or to others, those periods when such influences are retroactive in the experience of an individual entity.

Thus has grown that comprehension or interpretation of astrological aspects.

2629-001

The background of latent and manifested urges to be integrated during the decision-making process would be experiences resulting from all prior choices made during previous incarnations. These influences are reflected in astrological aspects to the physical consciousness, and they are retroactive. Choices by the entity indicate periods when such influences are active. Comprehension and interpretation of astrological aspects grow from observations of these experiences.

> No entity enters a material sojourn by chance, but from those realms of consciousness in which it has dwelt during the interims between earthly sojourns, the entity chooses that environ through which it may make manifest those corrections—or those choices it has made and does make in its real or in its inner self.
>
>   3027-002

Realms of consciousness between earthly sojourns affect the selection of a new environment. Every potential choice of a new body and horoscope would, of necessity, portray a different path or a different set of opportunities for beneficial corrections and improvements. A choice without understanding every potential horoscope and its progressions is unthinkable, because this type of choice is a serious matter whose effects last for eternity. Attunement to the infinite would be a vital necessity.

As the next reading states, the soul must find a body-mind adapted to a myriad of requirements, among which is compatibility of the physical experience in the material world as shown by the astrological signatures.

> For as is the hope, the expectancy of the entity, it will be a conscious entity through eternity. Then it has been a conscious entity from the beginning, but not aware of those experiences save as the entity may attune its spiritual abilities and spiritual activities to the infinite. For the entity finds itself a body, a mind and a soul, or a body-mind adapted to the environs of a physical experience in the material earth with urges latent and manifested, and these urges magnified or minimized according to the activities of the entity in relationships to such urges.
>
>   4082-001

Urges latent and manifested are exactly what astrology is all about. Lest anyone think that choices are made by the soul without considering the astrological significance of each option, quite a few other readings refer specifically to the astrological. To be more precise, the astrological influences were the main choices. They funnel the heterogeneous mass of urges being carried forward into specific patterns. Influences retroactive in the experience of an individual entity would have to be considered, as well as all of the upcoming influences that will accord activities of a lifetime. Those activities will be preordained, and the decisions based upon them will be eternal.

Unless all reviews of horoscopes forward and retroactive could be completed in a flash, and that is most unlikely, it is extremely doubtful that an infinite number of horoscopes could be reviewed to cover such a vast panoply of information. Much more likely would be the expectation that a finite number of horoscopes would have to be reviewed, and even then with comparative speed. This thought recurs at almost every reading on the subject of a soul attempting to optimize its choice, and especially when the situation calls for urgency. The idea of a finite number of potential horoscopes is not new to astrology, but the exact method of arriving at the times is unknown to most contemporary astrologers.

A centuries-old astrological concept holds that births cannot occur at any moment on an analog scale. They can only occur at discrete moments consonant with pulses of energy. These pulses of energy have an affinity with modern quantum mechanics. The smallest packet (unit) of energy is called a quantum, and it cannot be observed or directly measured. Each packet (unit) occurs in an instant of time. Likewise, if Edgar Cayce's information is correctly interpreted, spiritual births are instantaneous, coming from just outside the earth's sphere and from locations directly overhead. They occur in the midst of the rather lengthy physical birth process that starts with the first labor pains and could end after the umbilical cord is cut.

> For, each soul, each entity, enters not merely by chance but through the grace, the mercy of a loving Father; that the soul may in and through its own choice work out of those faults, those fancies, as would prevent its communion wholly with—and an atonement with—the Creative Forces.

> Hence, from the life experiences in the earth, the material and mental circumstance, and those latent forces from astrological aspects, we find these as a composite or as a hetero-

geneous mass of urges, latent and manifested, in the present
experiences of the entity.

                                                    459-012

The amount of time needed by a soul for a complete review
of personalities and all other factors to make a well-considered
choice is an open question. Perhaps time outside the earth plane
is not the same as time the way we humans understand it here
on the earth plane. Yet to review such a large amount of information would probably not occur in a short instant of time.
Moreover, a separate review would be required for each choice.
Then, the times for all of these individual reviews must be added
together. Birth could occur only after a decision had been
reached following a complete review.

Heterogeneous masses of astrological urges can change swiftly
during the gestation period if the mother journeys or is moving
about a large area. Thus, if a prospective mother is traveling
when birth is due, a soul's decision might have to be accelerated.
Such relocations near the term of birth would impose different
birth times and cause the entire set of horoscopes and their progressions to be different as well. Potential body shapes, personalities, and timetables of milestones would be altered if new
birth locations are imposed upon the soul for any reason.
Therefore, if a mother remains in one location near her term,
the soul might have an easier task. Or perhaps the review of
available horoscopes might be more thorough.

3. As we find, while time is fast approaching when the body
should be delivered of the body within the body, all of the
activities are very good. It should be near to full time, unless
some unusual incident or accident should occur to body. And
while it will not be, as might be said, entirely free from over-
anxiety, there should be a very normal, nominal deliverance.

4. Ready for questions.

Q-5. Is there anything which may or should be done to facilitate the timing of the birth of the child to coordinate with
the purpose and spiritual development of the soul which will
enter this body?

A-5. As just indicated, this will be near normal. Unless there
are undue excitements or happenings of some kind, it should
be a normal, nominal delivery, and full time.

                                                    1505-006

Every horoscope is dependent upon the exact location of birth and the exact time. Even without travel the need for a fast response on the part of the soul might be heightened by events applying to the pregnant mother. An accident could be such an event requiring swift action. A presumption is that the soul might have to choose a time other than the one tentatively selected. Yet no flippant or hasty decision can be imagined. The choice is simply too important not to use care. Moreover, horoscopes of both the father and the mother must be taken into account. The child's horoscope has to conform with the parents' horoscopes. Many other factors must fit that add complexity. The soul does not have an easy assignment even when a long period for decision-making is available. When only seconds are available, one might question whether or not a sudden decision was forced. However, we continue to be reassured, because the soul appears to be reviewing every choice continuously, whether the potential birth times are shifting or not.

Know that it is not by chance that one enters a material experience; rather the combination of minds as would create the channel to be offered for the expression of a soul, and the soul seeks same because of those desires of the two making one, thus bringing the opportunity.

Thus, those environs may change; and those activities of individuals may be changed by those influences that appear to be without the scope or cope of man's activity. All of these are oft visioned by the soul before it enters, and all of these are at times met in tempering the soul.

For, remember, He hath not willed that any soul should perish, but hath with each temptation, with each experience offered a channel, a choice whereby the soul is enlarged, is shown that the choice brings it nearer, near yet, to that purpose for which expression is given of same in the material world; even as He, the way, the life, the truth, came into life in materiality that we, through Him might have the advocate with the Father, and thus in Him find the answer to every problem in material experience.

1981-001

Edgar Cayce said, "All of these [changes] are oft visioned by the soul before it enters, and all of these are times met in tempering the soul," possibly meaning that in some instances they are not met until a different sojourn can be secured. That might happen if the conditions for birth are unstable or subject to drastic changes. However, babies are born in spite of untoward events, and every baby must receive a soul. We are also told that souls do not perish and no entrance is by chance. That entrance must conform with desires of a combination of minds, starting with the parents. The requirement to meet conditions tempers the soul. But how much tempering does a soul need? Cooperative actions, if known, might give the soul a better chance to refine its decision-making. Would it not be better for an expectant mother to be aware of the soul's problems and to somehow aid its decision-making as the blessed moment nears, or does it matter? Is noninterference the best policy, or would a particular mood or frame of mind help? Would focusing on goals for the new life be beneficial? It is recognized that a mother suffering labor pains is not in the best condition to do more, and the important decisions have probably already been made. At any rate, the soul's choices are modulated by all related happenings.

When emergencies occur, one has to believe that the soul has a right to change selections and defer the original first choice until another incarnation. If the array of birth times remaining are untenable, is it possible that a body might be abandoned by one soul, presumably to be a candidate for another? Such questions continue to surface, whether they contribute to understanding or not. The concern is whether the soul might be helped in some way. Every parent should want the best for their offspring, and they might ponder their actions when a baby is due.

As has been indicated through these channels respecting that which takes place at the moment of conception, as to ideals and purposes of those who through physical and mental emotions bring into being a channel through which there may be the expression of a soul-entity, —each soul choosing such a body at the time of its birth into material activity as its physical being controlled much by the environs of the individuals responsible for the physical entrance. Yet, the soul choosing such a body for a manifestation becomes responsible for that temple of the living God, when it has developed in body, in mind, so as to be controlled with intents, purposes and desires of the individual entity or soul.

263-013

A soul intent upon rebirth in the earth plane must be very persistent about ideals and purposes, because the environs control the actual expression of a soul-entity. Yet the soul remains responsible. Whatever the circumstances, rebirth must happen with controlled intents, purposes, and desires of the individual entity. Additionally, it would seem logical that a sufficient number of souls must have decided in favor of rebirth to match all of the babies due to be born.

The quantity of souls has been a question puzzling some of the people who lean toward reincarnation. Another issue is whether or not lower levels of life can move upward and become human souls should more be needed. In general, Edgar Cayce squashed such thoughts. They may not be valid considerations, let alone comprehensible. However, whether we understand or not, at least one soul must be present to attend every birth. There is no evidence to the contrary, and that assuages many fears. One soul at least seems to know about the prospective parents, about the many different periods, environs, or sojourns of the past and prospects for the future. That particular soul brings submerged memories and expectations with it into physical being.

In entering an experience in the material plane, the entity or soul sees through what environs it may pass. That man has divided into time and in different periods of an entity's experience in the earth (being divided into expressions of one environ and another) is viewed as a whole or as a unit, from the soul's sojourn in entering. And the soul's manifestation depends upon what the soul-mind may do with the opportunities that may be presented to that body or soul through an experience. As to what, is asked? That which may be to the soul the more worthy expression of that which is creative, or that which is the activity of what has rightly been termed to man as the fruits of the spirit, or truth and light, and the expression of man's relationship to the Creative Forces in the activity. That man in the realm of man's sojourn may only express or manifest same upon or to the associates or those whom the soul or the entity may contact is as an expression that is viewed by all.

Then, in entering, each soul comes to manifest that it has NOT so well learned in the lessons of hope, patience, tolerance, brotherly love, kindness, gentleness, meekness, and such. These are the fruits of the spirit. And the manifestation of these attributes in the experience of each soul brings, as the

Master of Masters has given, that awareness of self of the soul that is the gift of the Creator, that is the birthright of every individual that may be wasted in attempting to gratify those things that are of the earth, or of the carnal forces, and thus become weakened and less aware of its experience or existence in the affairs of man. Yet the soul finds its experience, no matter in what environ; and the ENVIRON is that created by what the soul—the inner self—has done, does do, about the manifestations of Creative Influences in the relationships to its fellow man.

505-004

So, in the final analysis, each of our souls knew about potential existences and opportunities as units before entering. Units apply to discrete cosmic patterns or horoscopes. The environ of birth is a choice based upon what we have done before. Our souls must be very perceptive entities, very brilliant mentalities, to know all of those things and to take decisive action.

But no matter how accomplished the last decision was, challenges in the pathway to destiny continue. Therefore, souls will benefit by continuing their education about such matters once maturing to an age of understanding.

9. Study also astrological subjects, not as termed by some, but rather in the light of that which may be gained through a study of His word. For, as it was given from the beginning, those planets, the stars, are given for signs, for seasons, for years, that man may indeed (in his contemplation of the universe) find his closer relationships.

10. For man is made a co-creator with the Godhead. Not that man is good or bad according to the position of the stars, but the position of the stars brings what an individual entity has done about God's plan into the earth activities during those individual periods when man has the opportunity to enter or come into material manifestations.

5124-001

Studying astrology helps man find his closer relationships. A unitary position of the stars brings prior accomplishments into earth activities. An opportunity to select a singular configuration of the stars comes once as each new life is entered. Preparations are like lessons, one lesson per lifetime. Preparations in terms of learning astrology are key to further understanding. However, learning astrology must be approached from the standpoint of studying His word, and that is not necessarily the way it is taught today. We should know by now that the future rests upon what we do about the manifestations of Creative Influences in relationships with our fellow man. Our challenges are before us. Let us ever try to make the right decisions.

4

HOROSCOPE TIMES

ONE SIGNIFICANT CONCLUSION from the readings is that the most egregious fault in the practice of astrology today is the use of incorrect horoscope times! It follows that this error has been the root cause of most objections to astrology.

> Q-36. Are the zodiacal divisions of the body proper and do they have any relation to this?
> A-36. Only relatively. For this is as we have given again and again in reference to same; for as they have been set as the zodiacal signs, correct. As they have moved in their orb or their sphere about the earth, these have just recently passed and have become—as has been indicated—a very different nature to them.

281-029

Edgar Cayce made the point about timing errors again and again. Astrologers are constantly choosing the correct planetary settings in their zodiacal signs. Astrologers are then choosing incorrect times for the movement of these planets and signs in their sphere about the earth. That sphere in motion moves twelve signs past a birthplace horizon during one twenty-four-hour period. Thus, the coordinates are rapidly changing, due to the rotation of the earth, and small errors in time can amount to large errors in angular nodes of the sphere.

Correct timing of horoscopes for review by souls before birth and strong evidence of errors being committed by astrologers after birth are considered so important that this chapter, devoted to exposing these problems, has been interspersed between the one on soul choices and the one that is now going to follow about where horoscope data might be stored. When Edgar Cayce revealed that a soul must review all potential horoscopes and many other factors in order to make a choice for entry, a question of practicality came to mind. Only so many thorough reviews could be conducted during a short period established for birth. He did not say, by the way, that the choice of a horoscope induced birth. Rather, the inferences were that an assortment of such planetary configurations, as well as their progressions, were reviewed for selection. Once a selection was made, then birth would follow in a natural sequence. Rapid, if not instantaneous, execution of the birth of the spirit would be a requirement. The gathering of souls just outside the earth's sphere would facilitate this swift flight. The one horoscope time from several available must be an accurate manifestation.

Yet, as contemplated earlier, while a soul is reviewing conditions for birth, the earth continues to spin on its axis. The apparent rotation of planets and zodiacal signs stops for no one. The personalities shown by the Ascendant sign and degree are constantly changing. They change at the rate of approximately one-fourth degree for every minute of time. In four minutes another degree has passed by. If the soul's milestones as indicated by day-for-a-year progressions are to be pinned down to an exact day, much greater accuracy is needed than is the current norm for astrologers. Their birth times to approximate hour and minute are unacceptable for timing! And some births occur without much warning down here!

The old astrological doctrine mentioned earlier permits calculation of potential birth times with as great an accuracy as deemed appropriate. An accuracy to seconds or tenths of a second can be obtained. Accuracies to that level correspond with the concept that only one of the available times would be acceptable to a soul. Only one extremely accurate time produces a horoscope correct for all uses, and it must enter instantaneously. Then Edgar Cayce came along and essentially confirmed that point.

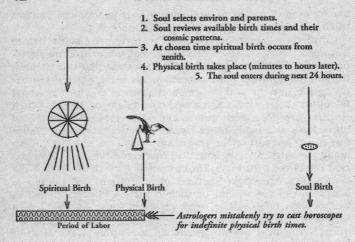

1. Soul selects environ and parents.
2. Soul reviews available birth times and their cosmic patterns.
3. At chosen time spiritual birth occurs from zenith.
4. Physical birth takes place (minutes to hours later).
5. The soul enters during next 24 hours.

Spiritual Birth   Physical Birth   Soul Birth

Period of Labor   ← *Astrologers mistakenly try to cast horoscopes for indefinite physical birth times.*

Figure 1. Normal sequence of births. According to Edgar Cayce, spiritual and physical births are monitored by the soul, although it is possible for them to be reversed. The soul enters last. Cosmic patterns enter during spiritual birth.

Old astrology books that might have alluded to this theorem of limited horoscope options are long out of print. And so today's astrologers, who are constantly looking for a new panacea, either time horoscopes for the first breath, or they rectify for some one event, or they use a time quoted by a member of the family, or they try to go by some prenatal epoch, or they subtract fixed times from the physical birth time as given, or they subtract fixed arcs from the calculated Ascendant, etc. These disparate approaches are real, by the way. They were obtained by questioning astrologers directly and by recalculating horoscopes. As might be expected, almost none of them arrives at exactly the same time for a horoscope, nor do they arrive at a time selected by the soul. Those who rectify might come the closest, but success in picking correct horoscope times is not shown by published charts. Those who publish may or may not be among the best astrologers, but they are at least representative. Of those horoscopes checked, only a very few have been found to be the same as one of those the soul might have reviewed. Such horoscopes are not wholly functional. Day-for-a-year progressions do not coincide with significant events in these erroneous maps of the planets, and that is a most important check.

In earlier times much of the best information about astrology was passed down verbally from master to pupil, and no records of this oral tradition exist. Only the pupils who survive know what they learned that is not published. Thus, references cannot be given of books, articles, or scrolls that speak about a limited number of finite birth times. However, from earlier teachings the Sun, Moon, and Uranus have a hand in determining the times reviewed by a soul. That contribution to astrological lore in itself has many far-reaching implications. However, the mathematics are complex, and not easily disseminated. No further details will be given at this time, because this book is about Edgar Cayce's revelations.

Edgar Cayce did not refer to any methodology for calculating horoscope times. Perhaps that is just as well, because techniques are quite complicated and could not be explained in the time of a typical reading. Rather, he simply answered questions about birth times and occasionally spoke of philosophies relating to the soul's choice of a horoscope. He also continued to confirm in many readings that astrologers were making errors.

Q-12. Give exact minute of physical birth, Feb. 11, 1911, to enable entity to ask for explanation of astrological laws governing entity.

A-12. This, as we find, as the record has been made of same, is near right—to the second; and while at the entrance of the entity into the earth's plane and the spiritual and physical birth varied little, there was the PHYSICAL under one sign and SPIRITUAL under another! Hence the doubts that often arise, from an astrological view.

Q-13. Give time of soul Birth.
A-13. As indicated

488-006

An astrologer would have cast a horoscope for the physical birth. The soul would have reviewed and picked a horoscope cast for the spiritual birth!

Of the various approaches to timing physical horoscopes already mentioned, a large percentage of astrologers are fixated to the first breath theory. They believe that horoscopes are fixed when a baby, as an independent being in this world, takes its first breath. In many ways that seems to be a logical assumption. It is a noteworthy event that can be timed, although one might question how precisely such events are observed and recorded on average—certainly no better than to the closest minute and more frequently to the closest hour or half hour. But a fascinating idea of this type spreads. Some fathers acquainted with astrology try to time the first cry they hear as accurately as possible, thinking it will yield a better horoscope. But that kind of accuracy might prove irrelevant, because none of them have been found to agree with calculated times for spiritual births, one of which is believed to match the soul's choice without fail.

Of course, the real question to ask along the same lines is "Does the horoscope cast by an astrologer for any physical birth time agree with the one chosen by the soul?" Since none have been observed that do, the probability is exceedingly low. Therefore, the broad answer to that question is no, or not likely. This truth has created enormous problems. Astrologers' horoscopes on average agree only partially with the people for whom they are intended, and any two astrologers generally produce a different horoscope for the same person. The planets might be in more or less correct positions, but the wheel itself with its house cusps differ. Edgar Cayce constantly spoke of these differences between recorded times of physical birth and the times of spiritual entry. Thus, astrologers, whatever their personalized methods, are mostly missing the mark.

In reality, there are two points of contention. The first one questions the idea that horoscopes can be set for any time on an analog scale, because that is what most astrologers are doing. The converse thought contends that a limited number of precisely timed horoscopes can be studied and reviewed by a soul for the selection of one of them. The horoscope selected is injected into the body in a flash. The second point rejects physical birth times that astrologers predominantly believe they must use. No physical birth time has been found to agree with a soul-chosen time or to produce a horoscope that can be verified. No first-breath horoscope was found to be entirely relevant. None have been found to be totally functional!

The first issue contesting discrete versus analog times is supported both by the logic of Edgar Cayce's statements about soul choices and by confirming results from the old astrological theorem that cannot be easily referenced. The second point about physical birth times was addressed many times by Edgar

Cayce. The following reading was the first discovered to show significant differences between physical and spiritual birth times. This was the reading that was in substantial agreement with documented experiences over more than half a century that used the theorem of the first part. It was the only agreement from external sources encountered in all of those years, but a resounding one. The experience was potent and deeply gratifying, because it just had to be correct. It marked the beginning of a period filled with new realizations about the mysteries of life and the profound intelligence constantly being unveiled by Edgar Cayce:

> In giving the interpretations of the records as we find them here, these we choose from the records upon time and space, as recorded in the mental and physical activities of the entity through those periods of sojourn in the earth as well as those realms of consciousness outside the physical body, which are termed astrological but have little to do with the common term of the astrological aspects. Though oft they are correct, more of ye find them in variance. For most astrologers are nearly thirty degrees off in their reckoning in the present.

> 3376-002

Thirty degrees off! Thirty degrees is another sign on the Ascendant! Thirty degrees represents about a two-hour mean difference in time at the equator, more or less at Northern or Southern latitudes, depending upon the season. Thirty degrees is close to the average of the differences that had been computed and recorded over many years. Sometimes the Ascendant was in the same sign as the horoscope for the quoted physical birth, but mostly at an earlier degree. Sometimes the Ascendant was in the sign preceding. Sometimes the Ascendant was two signs back. On rare occasions it was three signs back. When this subject was pointed out to other astrologers, most of them were skeptical of the findings. But perhaps the subject had not been broached properly. Of great importance was the emphatic statement by Edgar Cayce that in the reckoning of his source of information, most astrologers were at variance. They are very much at variance! No truer statement could have been made. And, incidentally, the records of time and space cannot be found in a published book either.

This was only the first of the Edgar Cayce readings that was spotted and ascertained to be in essential agreement with evidence separately compiled. Many more readings contributed additional evidence. Of course, there were all of those horoscopes that had fit their subjects perfectly. There were all of those progressed aspects that timed the presence of forces to the day and, when needed, to the hour. Other astrologers were honest in admitting they had not been able to obtain those kinds of predictions, or they were obtained infrequently. There were the repeated sensations of perfection in matching horoscopes to individuals and the magnificent comprehension of uncovered truths. There was what is now believed to be recognition of soul's choices. Such recognitions are not derived from ordinary, unverified horoscopes. Each one is much more akin to the realization of a precise chosen horoscope for an exact time that is verifiable. Each one comes with an accurate timetable for proffering inclinations, and that is the most important check of all:

> As there was in the entering of the entity's inner forces into this physical body, the first will come at the age of seven, at fourteen, at twenty-two—these will be decided changes, or one will so lap over the other—but may be said to be periods when changes will come to this entity; for there was some lapse of time (as time is counted from the material) between the physical and the spiritual birth.
>
> In giving, then, the astrological influences, these would vary considerably from that as would be seen from the spiritual—or the entity or soul experience in the earth's plane. Were this entity's experiences given from the purely astrological science, as accepted in many quarters, these would vary entirely from this which may be given here, or that is viewed from here—for these are the Akashian records of the entity's or soul's development.
>
> 566-001

It follows that the type of horoscope Edgar Cayce mentions as having astrological influences applies to a spiritual birth. This horoscope differs radically from one for physical birth that so many astrologers try to use. Physical birth horoscopes accepted in many quarters represent the majority. Almost invariably the horoscopes for spiritual births do not compare with those for physical birth, so much so that one might question the value of any horoscope for a physical birth time at all. Horoscopes timed in this manner do not appear to serve a useful purpose. But on the other hand, that might be a bit rash. The physical birth time is useful in an unexpected way. It marks a beginning point for performing essential calculations to obtain the spiritual birth time. It is a point of departure that should never be used directly, but without which there would not be much to go on. Furthermore, conventional astrologers with well-developed psychic abilities do glean much from these physical horoscopes.

Alliance of the spiritual horoscope with Akashian records of the entity's or soul's development is a tremulous thought. Being able to duplicate and interpret a spiritual horoscope could be like reading a very small portion of an Akashian record. Might it be that horoscopes produced by the old doctrine cast aside by modern astrologers are in such accord? One of the times generated by that doctrine for each entity has always proved to be totally functional and verifiable. One and only one. That is the kind of evidence that could mean correspondence with the Akashian records.

Having strong evidence of the validity of spiritual horoscopes versus physical horoscopes, a fundamental issue still remains. Is there a relationship in time between the soul's arrival at the site of a chosen body and the ensconcement of categorized and scheduled energy portrayed by a spiritual horoscope? This question omits physical birth from consideration. Many times Edgar Cayce said they were not the same, and differences up to many hours could occur. Many times the requesters of such information confused their terminology. The ultimate conclusion is that the soul oversees the fixing of the horoscope and the physical birth. The soul is usually born fairly close to the physical birth time, but later. This idea agrees with more of the readings that follow:

Q-45. What was the time of my physical birth?
A-45. In the afternoon, three to four.

Q-46. What was the exact time of my soul birth?
A-46. Almost at the same period. For the union of the activities in the bodily forces was purposeful. We would give as an hour's difference, if we would measure time by such, between the physical and the soul or spiritual birth.

1336-001

This reading might be construed in several ways. Edgar Cayce seems to have spoken of the soul or spiritual birth as occurring at the same time, although that is not a certainty. Nor is it likely, because at other times they were separated. The physical birth was always different. In the above case the soul birth and physical birth were separated by an hour. The spiritual birth was probably separated from the physical birth by an hour as well. From what is known now the soul's time difference was probably positive, or later. The spiritual time difference was probably negative, or earlier.

The next reading is going to be discussed at greater length, because it is on this same subject and has been frequently misinterpreted. While a blandly simple question was asked, it was not asked correctly. Edgar Cayce often admonished the querist when a question was not properly framed. This time he did not, and the result is that this one reading out of many has become controversial among astrologers who have read the material. They claim it supports their opinions. Edgar Cayce did refer to "oft confusing experiences." That should have been a warning. However, the controversy about it needs to be gotten out of the way. At the same time a very important confirmation is included in the wording that needs to be understood and seems to have been missed by others in their zeal to claim a proof for their first breath theory:

Q-5. Should an astrological horoscope be based on the time of the physical birth or the time of soul birth?

A-5. On the time of physical birth; for these are merely IN-CLINATIONS and because of inclinations are not the influence of will. WILL is that factor of the spiritual forces or the gift, as it were, to man . . . as he came into material form, with which choice is made, see? Hence if astrological aspects are to be assumed, then physical. But these make for oft confusing experiences to those casting such charts and reading from that which has been the version [interpretation] of same.

For as we have indicated, there are two, yea, three phases or schools through which such information, such charts, such characters have been carried—the Egyptian, the Persian, the Indian.

The Persian is a combination and the OLDER of all of these, and these are as logos [?], or as charts that have been set. That they have become as experiences in the activities of individuals, to be sure, is not disputed; but the world does not governs MAN, MAN governs the world! And the

inclinations astrologically show whether man has or has not
applied will!

Then the inclinations are good, but they may be stumbling
stones if one submerges will to listen at inclinations!

826-008

In this reading Edgar Cayce again stated that physical birth
and soul birth occur, or can occur, at different times. As a
matter of fact, on several occasions he confirmed that soul
birth could occur as much as a day later. However, in other
readings births were also said to be tripartite in nature. The
three parts are spiritual birth, physical birth, and soul birth as
indicated in Figure 1. The above reading only referred to two
of these three. He made an appropriate allusion to this third
(spiritual) birth by saying, "WILL is that factor of the spiritual
forces . . . as he came into material form, with which choice is
made, see?"

In first reviewing Edgar Cayce's response, an open question
arose: "What is the instant of birth upon which a horoscope
should be based?" That specific question was not asked nor was
it answered. The actual question asked was far more general,
and it received a generic answer. Given the simple either-or
choice, the central logos of the answer was that the idea of a
horoscope for soul birth is wrong. It can be deduced from what
was said that souls themselves do not have astrological horoscopes. Thus, a soul would not directly respond to inclinations
in the spiritual plane. Inclinations acting upon the soul as dif-
ferentiated from the human body would be inappropriate.
Therefore, a horoscope for soul entry does not make sense. By
default it has to coincide with the second of the two choices
offered in the question. A horoscope has to be based upon what
is going on during physical birth, as opposed to soul birth. But
it is a factor of spiritual forces.

A number of astrologers cite this question-and-answer passage as being proof that physical birth occurs at first breath. So
that is the time according to them for which the horoscope
should be cast. It is this unfortunate interpretation that is the
cause of so much controversy. As a matter of fact, Edgar Cayce
did not use the words "first breath" in this reading nor convey
any such idea. Therefore, the precise time of the horoscope remains an unasked question in this isolated passage taken alone.

References to Egyptian, Persian, and Indian schools of astrology appear to be afterthoughts that point out differences

between the many versions of Tropical and Sidereal astrology that can add confusion to interpretations. Interpreting a horoscope is a complicated matter. There are plenty of complications because of the divisions among Egyptian, Persian, and Indian schools of astrology. Edgar Cayce said that the Persian school is favored. It leads to the Tropical system of astrology as we know it today.

However, in this explanation he seemed to be confirming an earlier point that has already been made. He said, ". . . and these are as logos [?], or as charts that have been set." Yes. Very much so are they logos and are they charts that have been *set*. The idea of set horoscopes for review by the soul has been stated in no uncertain terms.

While in trance, Edgar Cayce gave many other answers to questions concerning details of time differences observed at physical birth. By contrast with the prior reading, the next one indicates a two-sign discrepancy in an astrologer's reckoning. Two signs is typical of variations between correct horoscopes and those cast for reported physical birth times. Some writers have tried to explain this two-sign difference by citing precession of the equinoxes. Other possible reasons have been offered. But those are misplaced thoughts, and they indicate a lack of understanding about spiritual and physical births. The difference between the Tropical and Sidereal zodiacs due to precession of the equinoxes as late as 1995 when this book is being written is less than one sign. Therefore, such a theory cannot apply when the discrepancy is two signs, and it must be set aside:

> Hence the entity was born into the earth in what signs? Pisces, ye say. Yet astrologically from the records, these are some two signs off in thy reckoning.
>
> 5755-001

Close inspection of this reading shows that the words *signs* and *these* were used, and both are plural in form. The principle two signs of a horoscope are the Sun sign and the Ascendant sign. The Sun sign is rarely, if ever, mistaken, because it is carefully calculated and one of the most closely followed of all. It appears in every ephemeris and almanac, as well as many calendars, magazines, and newspapers. The Ascendant sign, on the other hand, is another matter. Degrees on the Ascendant move rapidly, and all twelve signs cross that point during one day.

More often than not, the Ascendant is two signs off. That would be impossible for a first breath horoscope. A two- to four-hour difference in time equates to a two-sign difference. A two-sign difference, by the way, means with virtual certainty that Capricorn was the sign on the Ascendant of 5755.

The next reading not only emphatically states that soul choices are made, it also shows consideration of who the mother, brother, sister, and father will be. Moreover, soul vision is utilized to review the choices available. To reiterate, a time-consuming additional requirement is imposed. Potential choices include consideration of the variations of character among relatives.

Q-59. Why was I separated from my parents at such an early age?

A-59. These are experiences that may best be known by the paralleling of some of the associations. For, there are conditions—especially in the soul experience, not from the physical. For, remember it is the soul choice, the soul vision in which there are choices made for entrance into material experience,— so that little of the channels, save as a channel, enters into the developing or retarding. For, as to soul—"Who is my mother, my brother, my sister: He that doeth the will of the Father!"

2301-001

"Paralleling of some of the associations" means finding common or interrelated traits in the respective horoscopes of the entity and the parents, brothers, and sisters. Soul vision can apparently make such comparisons prior to entrance into material experience. Soul vision evidently confines horoscope selection to the one showing family members in a manner that "doeth the will of the Father." Signatures of family members and associates are sufficiently important that a later chapter will be devoted to what the soul must look for in selecting the correct horoscope.

As to the experience of the entity from the astrological and from the earthly sojourn, the entity's entrance into the material plane as for the physical birth was in the evening, while the spiritual birth was close to what is called the witching hour.

1391-001

The degrees on the Ascendant are swiftly changing this very moment. Thus, the Ascendant of a spiritual horoscope could easily be in a different sign than the physical horoscope with only a few minutes separating the two. The witching hour and evening were hours apart.

The unremitting conclusion is that astrologers are providing disservices unless they comprehend these truths and determine how to change their ways. The common practice of simply casting a horoscope for any time received from any source is a sloppy procedure. It may be psychically read in part by one who is practiced in the art, but the records show much is also being omitted. Current astrological delineations are imperfect on average and riddled with errors. Yet enough truth is present to carry the subject onward. And so astrology survives in spite of these limitations.

The next reading not only shows time differences between physical birth and spiritual birth, it speaks of destiny—another word for fate. It indicates that the soul's free will becomes destiny, and that is another important piece of evidence. Note the change between "soul birth" in the question to "birth spiritual" in the answer. This time Edgar Cayce left no doubts:

Q-3. Give exact time of physical and soul birth on Jan. 17, 1913, in the present incarnation?

A-3. Yes. There was, as counted as time, thirty to thirty-five minutes difference in birth physical and birth spiritual. The variations as occur, as has been given, are as the elements that make for those forces as termed hereditary influences, with environmentals as builded for; as with this entity in this particular experience, through the environments of that, or the present sojourn, would meet those of the cosmic forces, or meet the karmic forces in cosmic AND physical influence in the present. Hence some call it, or such relations, destiny. Some call it meeting such, when the conditions have been prepared by the activities of self.

275-005

The spiritual horoscope is where cosmic forces are met. It has already been ascertained that a horoscope for the soul would be meaningless. More and more of the readings repeated the truth of these time differences and the coincidence between the choice of times and destinies established on earth. Destinies include meeting karmic forces, cosmic forces, and physical influences.

No further readings were uncovered that left the slightest doubt about such timing differences.

> As to the time, we find this was at 10:58 A.M. and the completion of the entity, soul, spirit and the physical completed near noon.
>
> 234-001

> Q-11. How long a period between the physical and spiritual birth?
> A-11. Some four and a half hours.
>
> 566-001

The two previous readings gave in no uncertain terms the magnitudes of timing differences that took place. The first time differed by about one hour and two minutes. Coincidentally, four-and-a-half hours matches the most negative difference between a calculated spiritual birth and the reported physical birth time that has been experienced to date. But what of positive differences? What about their magnitudes?

> Q-6. Does soul enter child at conception or birth or in between?
> A-6. It may at the first moment of breath; it may some hours before birth; it may many hours after birth. This depends upon that condition, that environ surrounding the circumstance.
>
> 457-010

This question was about soul entry, not spiritual birth. We have already realized that the soul and spirit do not typically enter an infant's body at the same time, although they may be fairly close together. Our evidence on spiritual birth times is mainly from confirmed horoscopes substantiating what Edgar Cayce provided. No way to determine a soul's entry has been discovered.

The most important task of the soul is to oversee spiritual birth. The onset of a physical birth period is initiated earlier by the soul in time for the spiritual birth to capture the selected time and cosmic influences. Remaining behind for the conclusion of physical birth does not appear to be extremely important to the soul when things are going well.

The closest verified horoscope time to an alleged first moment of breath horoscope over a fifty-year period was about three minutes. In this particular reading Edgar Cayce made no specific mention of the tendency for a vast majority of correct horoscopes and spiritual entries to occur before completion of physical birth. Physical birth is actually a lengthy process lasting sometimes for hours, and the astrologer's practice has been to rely on the end time. Thus, the average spiritual horoscope time has been found to be negative in relation to the physically recorded birth time, but occurring between the moment when labor pains were initially felt and the moment when the baby made physical entrance into the world. The average negative separation between spiritual birth and physical end times has been found to be about one-and-a-half hours. Other informed investigators claim an average of about two hours. No questions were asked that would cause Edgar Cayce to confirm these averages. But, in retrospect, it is easily possible for a spiritual birth to take place more than two hours before physical birth and for the soul to enter before as well.

The largest positive time discrepancy that has been encountered to date was about twenty-one minutes. The reference point may have been an iffy reported time. Yet in the preceding passage Edgar Cayce spoke as though a spiritual birth or a soul birth could occur quite a while after physical birth. The clause ". . . it may many hours after birth" is a distinct possibility that has never been observed for a horoscope, and one must ask why? There would be no great surprise if larger positive deviations did exist. However, if such a deviation were found possibly "that environ surrounding the circumstance" would have to be most unusual. It would most likely be related to a shocking event that triggered the onset of labor, such as an accident. A shocking event of this type might force the soul to delay making a choice, or it might want to wait for an upcoming preselected time. The soul might have tentatively settled upon a considerably later birth time, and the sudden change in circumstances would require a complete review of horoscopes immediately at hand. The nearest time might not be acceptable. It should not be necessary for a soul or a human to respond instantly to such an unexpected major aberration. There would be so many things to consider—a different personality, a different timetable of events, a radically different appearance, a completely different orientation toward life, the proper placement of parents, future offspring, relatives, uncles, aunts, friends, etc. In fact, several hours later would be very swift decision-making indeed. Thinking on earth can only occur at a rate consistent with the speed of memory recall and processing of information. For a soul, the time required for thinking might be faster, or it might not be much different. We simply do not know. An unexpected situation of this type is where it is easy to see how "... it may many hours after birth," might apply.

Remember, our presumption is that a spiritual birth occurs when the essence of a horoscope enters a baby's body. This is during the broader physical birth process. Spiritual and physical births were on several other occasions spoken about together, although when details were given they were separated. Soul births generally were not. Soul births can occur quite a while later after a baby is born as humans understand the term.

Q-11. Give exact time of physical birth and soul birth.

A-11. With THIS particular entity, we find there was—in that as would be called time by man—only a period of four to four and a half hours difference. This mooted question, as may be asked by man, is—as we find—as illustrated here: In the material world life is as of the UNIVERSAL consciousness, as all development through that known or called evolution of life in a material plane, and is a portion of a body from conception to the transition in what is called death. That which enters, as the soul, is that which would use, or be the companion of, that life—physical through any given period of existence in an earth's appearance. As the variations come, these are brought by the activities of those who through their OWN desire attract or detract those that would manifest in a particular body. See?

Q-12. Why is there a difference, and what happened in the interim?

A-12. A physical being, or life, as given, is from inception, and is of an universal consciousness—see? When a physical being, or body, as this body, is brought into being by the birth into the PHYSICAL world, the INTERIM between that is as of THAT period when the decision is being made by THAT soul that would occupy THAT individual body. See?

276-003

With a fairly high degree of regularity and over a period of many years, Edgar Cayce was asked more questions along these lines—some of them just as mooted as the preceding one. In all cases, it was as though no time had intervened between queries, and one question had simply followed the next. The subject was usually soul entry versus physical or spiritual entry. Repeatedly, Edgar Cayce intimated a spiritual entry is when cosmic patterns became fixed in the body. Repeatedly, he said that a period of decision-making preceded spiritual entry. He also said that such decision-making took place at a hovering place. Prior to birth the soul and spirit must maneuver to be at the zenith for the location of the birth event. In order to hover they must be moving at the circular velocity of rotation of the earth. At this position a soul should be able to see the rotation of the zodiac more readily.

In the reading that follows, note the reference to changes even of personalities while the soul is in the process of entering. That almost certainly means that alternative horoscopes were being reviewed for possible selection during the period when the soul was seeking to enter. Astrologically, personality is a function of the sign on the Ascendant. A change of personality would entail the choice of a different Ascendant degree and sign. Logic dictates that the choices of personalities had to be for horoscopes separated far enough apart in time to have different signs on the Ascendant. In a majority of cases those horoscopes would be hours apart: Edgar Cayce continually confirmed that soul births could be hours apart from the physical. Here is one case where he did mention first breath in passing. However, this first breath was for the soul—an important distinction:

Q-26. Does a soul enter a body before it is born?

A-26. It enters either at the first breath physically drawn, or during the first twenty-four hours of cycle activity in a material plane. Not always at the first breath; sometimes there are hours, and there are changes even of personalities as to the seeking to enter.

Q-27. What keeps the physical body living until the soul enters?

A-27. Spirit! For the spirit of matter—its source is life, or God, see?

2390-002

The preceding readings tell us that the soul normally waits for the first breath before entering. The spirit has already entered the baby's body by that time, and it is a source of life. The individuality and personality have been picked. The horoscope has been established. Life is sustained by the spirit during the interim transition period. The soul may enter the body at any time between first breath and a day or so later.

A soul is responsible for making all of these choices. Birth is not haphazard. It is much more of a pulse-of-energy type occurrence coming from on high. The energy packet does not have gradations. It is precise, exact, and instantaneous (or perhaps as instantaneous as the speed of light).

Q-15. Are there several patterns which a soul might take on, depending on what phase of development it wished to work upon—i.e., could a soul choose to be one of several personalities, any of which would fit its individuality?
A-15. Correct.

5749-014

Let's be clear. Personalities in astrology are governed by the zodiacal sign on the Ascendant. Individualities are governed by the Sun sign. A Sun sign typically remains fixed on a given birth day. Only once a month at an instant in time does it change signs. By contrast, one minute change in time can result in roughly a fifteen-minute difference in longitude on the Ascendant. It steps into another sign every two hours, more or less. The tilt of the polar axis and seasons cause wide variations. However, a small change in birth time can cause the sign on the Ascendant to be altered while the longitude of the Sun has shifted by only a fraction of a degree. For a soul to choose one of several personalities means that one of several horoscopes would have to be available with different Ascendant signs. Two or three Ascendant signs are normally available to the soul within a four-and-a-half hour time span, but the number of potential horoscopes are generally greater. Two or three personalities might be available with variations. The individuality would remain constant. This agreement in principle could not be better.

For one enters not by chance but by choice, that it may learn or meet its own self. And when there are those environs through which such material opportunities may perfect themselves, such a soul—seeking—finds expression. These become a part of the whole experience of an entity.

2990-002

Yes, the soul has complex choices to make, and having the will to do so is a "before birth" right. This is a very important point. Willpower is applied by the soul in making the choice, and being able to do so is a gift from the Creator. Application of willpower during reincarnation is permitted for a price.

For it is never by chance that a soul enters any material experience; rather by choice. For, the will is the birthright, the manifested right of every soul. It is the gift of the Creator, yet is the price one pays for material expression.

2462-002

Now a sufficient number of Edgar Cayce's readings have been given to show that spiritual birth most often does not coincide with the end point of physical birth. It does occur most often during the period marked by commencement of labor pains and entry of the baby's body into the physical world. The quantity of these confirmations has been large, because timing is such a major issue. But another reason is that Edgar Cayce kept revealing more little secrets in the process of restating the facts.

In summary, the spiritual birth horoscope incorporates cosmic urges. The soul has a variety of set prospective lives to choose from with different personalities and the same individuality. That series of choices represents destiny to the incarnate being on the earth plane. The magnitude of time differences between spiritual and physical births are variable and, in several cases, were four-and-a-half hours apart. The number of choices available to the soul was not mentioned, but they are the gifts of the Creator. The destiny selected is the specific price one pays for material expression. All of these factors are in mutual agreement.

A deviation from this picture is to consider the timing mistakes being committed by astrologers. Errors in horoscope timing would cause astrological principles known for aeons to be omitted because they do not agree. Parts of astrology would seem to work and other parts would not. Being inventive, man would seek reasons for these errors or omissions. Thus, some astrologers invent new procedures. Some concoct new ways for rectifying horoscope times. Some cogitate on new systems for calculating the prenatal epoch. Some imagine new undiscovered planets, or they retrieve the positions of asteroids. Some dream up new clever mathematical schemes, or they jump to another system that has been proposed by other races. Some introduce midpoints between planets as added angles to consider. Some become exceedingly adroit at explaining away discrepancies. They talk about being born upon the cusp, or they widen orbs of influence, or they just show the horoscope and talk about something else as though the two were synchronized. Any honest assessment of astrology today would have to conclude that all of these conditions prevail. And that overall state of affairs agrees with the assessment of copious errors in horoscope timing that Edgar Cayce pointed out.

5

WHERE HOROSCOPES ARE STORED

IT WOULD BE well to explore where chosen astrological influences come after taking flight to earth and to understand the ways inclinations are expressed.

The endocrine glands have been proposed by writers of astrological philosophy and by others as sites for storing horoscopic information. One logical reason is because their secretions are known to control bodily functions. Horoscopic information consists of a unique cosmic pattern of personal identity for the soul and a series of urges corresponding to milestones in this earthly sojourn. Urges can be instigated by endocrine gland secretions. No proofs for these contentions were offered by previous writers. However, Edgar Cayce's readings and passages from the Holy Bible are in basic agreement. When readings are augmented by the Scriptures in this way, there is good reason to pause, reflect upon the words, and consider acceptance.

This concern over backup information from other sources and proofs is because the contents of Edgar Cayce's readings are intended for everyone, including the most skeptical learned people. Agreements from several sources on any astrological subject add confidence, whether needed or not. A criticism of today's astrologers is that proofs of their contentions are rarely given. When unsure the words become more authoritative. Blind faith is expected while the world is moving from the Piscean to the Aquarian age; this is best viewed as passing from an atmosphere of tolerance for all ideas to an atmosphere of cool reasoning.

Once life readings were initiated, Edgar Cayce was frequently asked to interpret the more mystical chapters of the Bible. Certain chapters made references to the endocrine glands. Cautious reality checks of what he said are appropriate, but nothing has been found amiss. The readings cited in this chapter contribute much understanding. They are unwavering in the vision conveyed.

> 9. There has long been sought, by a few, the interpretation of the seven centers; and many have in various stages of awareness, or development, placed the association or connection between physical, mental and spiritual in varied portions of the body. Some have interpreted as of the mind, motivated by impulse; and thus called the center from which mind acts.

> 10. This is only relatively so, as will be understood by those who analyze those conditions presented through these interpretations; for in fact the body, the mind and the soul are ONE, in the material manifestation. Yet in analyzing them, as given through the Revelation by John, they are active in the various influences that are a part of each living organism conceived in the forces making up that known as man; that power able to conceive—in mind—of God, and to demonstrate same in relationships to others; that in mind able to conceive of manners for the destruction of its fellow man, little realizing that it is SELF being destroyed by that very activity!

> 281-005

The seven centers are the endocrine glands. Associations with physical, mental, and spiritual factors are only relatively so, because body, mind, and soul are one. Yet analysis shows these centers "are active in the various influences that are a part of each living organism." That sounds like planetary influences, although not specifically stated. But then came a warning. When man conceives manners for the destruction of fellow man, the effect of this activity is to destroy self. Wars and campaigns against others are serious affairs, then, because they may work to set back the advancements of all souls involved.

In the Book of Revelations astrological aphorisms were given by the Disciple John. The lion, the beast, man, and the eagle are references to astrology's fixed signs Leo, Taurus, Aquarius, and Scorpio. They are the builders of the world. The twelve zodiacal signs are either Cardinal, Fixed, or Mutable, and four signs occupy each of these intensities. Signs are also divided into four qualities—Fire, Earth, Air, and Water. These qualities are not an ancient list of chemical elements that some modern chemists actually fool themselves into believing. The number seven mentioned repeatedly refers to both the endocrine glands and the original planets known at the time the Bible was written. The number twelve can be associated with signs of the zodiac. The wording of the Book of Revelations is difficult to understand. However, these correspondences are intriguing vis-à-vis what Edgar Cayce said about them.

Q-1. What is meant by the four angels bound in the river Euphrates in connection with the sounding of the sixth angel? [Gen. 2:14; Rev. 9:14, 16:12]

A-1. As has been given, each reference in the Revelation is to some portion of the body as in its relative position to the emotions physical, mental, material; and their activities through portions of the system, as places that represent conditions in some phase of manifestation or development of the entity. Or the whole (to be put in another way and manner) is an experience of man as known to those who were being spoken to by the writer.

Then we find, as in the beginning, the Euphrates—or the good river [Frat.], or the river of the fiat [covenant Gen. 15:18]—is being represented as being sounded now for the beginnings of the changes which have been effected by the activities of those who have preceded, who have acted upon the various influences or forces by the opening of centers and the emotions and the understandings and the conditions of the individual entity.

Hence it represents now, as it were, to the individual—that ye now begin again to make practical or applicable, mentally, spiritually, materially, with that which has been thus far attained.

Q-2. What are the four angels that are bound in the river Euphrates?

A-2. As has been indicated, the four influences that are as the Air, the Earth, the Fire, the Water; being influences now

that are—as understood by the entity, the soul, the individual—
as a portion of itself again.

281-031

Reference to the river Euphrates alludes to the flow of
changes taking place in the body as a result of the new arrival
of the spirit and the new inclinations that begin to manifest.
Inclinations manifest as emotions physical, mental, and material.
Their activities are apportioned to various parts of the body,
and these centers are opened. A distribution of the zodiacal
elements is indicated. Planetary influences through the endocrine glands begin to apply in a practical manner what has been
attained previously. All of the planets affecting the centers occupy Air, Earth, Fire, or Water signs, and their influences are
channeled accordingly.

11. Hence there is then in the system that activity of the
soul, that is the gift of the Creator to man. It may be easily seen,
then, how very closely the glands are associated with reproduction, degeneration, regeneration; and this throughout—not
only the physical forces of the body but the mental body and
the soul body.

12. The glandular forces then are ever akin to the sources
from which, through which, the soul dwells within the body.

281-038

This is a significant revelation, because it affiliates the soul
with the seven endocrine glands. Edgar Cayce said that the glandular forces are "ever akin to the sources from which, through
which, the soul dwells." They are associated with bodily functions, such as reproduction, degeneration, and regeneration—
not just physical forces, but also those of the mental body and
the soul body. These glands are where the soul dwells. The
seven glands he referred to are the gonads, the Leydig (or
leydic), the solar plexus (adrenals), the thymus, the thyroid, the
pineal, and the pituitary. All of them are ductless.

In what might at first appear to be a side issue, he answered
another question about the glands:

Q-5. Which is the highest gland in the body—the pineal or
the pituitary?

A-5. The pituitary!

281-029

This answer might raise a few eyebrows in medical circles, because the pineal gland in a standing body is slightly higher than the pituitary. The question actually relates to the sequence of glands, and that is an important matter deserving attention. Are the two glands reversed? For the moment, further discussion on this subject will be deferred in favor of a few more biblical readings. The issue will be readdressed.

The next reading references the astrological signs and their relationships to bodily functions associated with the glands:

Q-6. In connection with the symbols of Revelations, what are the twelve major divisions of the body?
A-6. Those that are of the general construction and those that are of the keeping alive physical, and those that are in keeping with the influences to the mental, to the material, to the spiritual; and the illustrations are shown in the bodily forces that are opened for those activities in a material plane.

281-030

The twelve major divisions of the zodiac form a three-by-four matrix. Each sign is Cardinal, Fixed, or Mutable, and they individually take on one of the four qualities—Fire, Earth, Air, and Water. Fire signs are for keeping the physical alive. Earth signs are in keeping with the material. Air signs are in keeping with the mental. Water signs are in keeping with the spiritual. The three further divisions cause these inclinations to be energetic or dominating (Cardinal), constructive or acquisitive (Fixed), and enlightening or cooperative (Mutable). These are not the only meanings derived from this matrix, but they are representative and basic.

To a skeptic it must be admitted that Edgar Cayce's words are saying that cosmic inclinations dwell in the endocrine glands, but no scientific proofs have been offered. He talked about glands from which, through which, the soul dwells within the body. However, no methods of measurement have been found that confirm these destinations in the course of reincarnation. No instruments have been developed to measure a soul's options or to detect bodily storage of an astrological framework for living. No tests have been devised to substantiate observations of functional associations except in the most indirect ways.

These bothersome thoughts cause some trepidation that scientific minds will not be convinced from the material given. However, the medical profession has identified functions of glandular secretions, and those can be explored. Other avenues are also available that can shed further light.

Short of having real data, it is possible to proceed with obviously biased assumptions in the background and investigate further. The major reason for these biases is that Edgar Cayce's words are so deep and far-reaching in their allusions. Over many years interrelated associations have been uncovered, and such associations often lead to more revelations. They add to the circumstantial evidence.

For example, one class of association is with colors. Colors have physical properties that can be measured in laboratories. Every color, planet, and endocrine gland has an indigenous position relative to other members of their respective groups. Astrological implications are sealed in these positions, and they correspond in ways known well to the ancients. Colors also match the signs of the zodiac in an intelligent arrangement fitting their order in the universe. Discovery of these interrelationships has resulted in some adjustments to the speculative data that earlier investigators published. Why they guessed and erred is not clear. The most egregious error was in omitting the Sun and Moon. That omission simply cannot be allowed. It must be admitted that Edgar Cayce's words are sometimes issued in convoluted ways that can be misinterpreted; however, his words have consistently been found to ring true.

Q-1. Please discuss more fully the relation of colors to the seven major glandular centers. Do the colors vary for each center with different individuals, or may definite colors be associated with each center?

A-1. Both. For to each—remember, to study each of these in the light not only of what has just been given but that as is a practical experience in the material world—as is known, vibration is the essence or the basis of color. As color and vibration then become to the consciousness along the various centers in an individual's experience in meditation made aware, they come to mean definite experiences. Just as anger is red, or something depressing is blue; yet in their shades, their tones, their activities, to each they begin with the use of same in the experience to mean those various stages. For instance, while red is anger, rosy to most souls means delight and joy—

yet to others, as they are formed in their transmission from center to center, come to mean or to express what *MANNER* of joy; whether that as would arise from a material, a mental or a spiritual experience. Just as may be seen in the common interpretation of white, but with all manner of rays from same begins or comes to mean that above the aura of all in its vibration from the body and from the activity of the mental experience when the various centers are vibrating to color.

Q-2. If so, give color for: (1) Gonads (2) Lyden (3) Solar Plexus (4) Thymus (5) Thyroid (6) Pineal (7) Pituitary.

A-2. These come from the leaden, going on through to the highest—to that as is the halo. To each they become the various forces as active throughout, and will go in the regular order of the prism.

281-030

The sequence of colors given in answer to question two is especially important. Regular order of the prism is red, orange, yellow, green, cyan, blue, and violet. Some might argue for purple or magenta in the lineup, but those colors are in fact blends. The order given follows a regular progression according to wavelength or frequency, one being the inverse of the other. Note especially the reference to common interpretations of white, because white can be approached from many angles with all manner of rays. The associations are red with Mars and the gonads; orange with the Sun and leyden; yellow with Mercury and the solar plexus; green with Saturn and the thymus; cyan with Venus and the thyroid; blue with Jupiter and the pineal; violet with Moon and the pituitary. That sequence with the pituitary gland at the top is correct, otherwise the sequence would be out of order. Furthermore, it may not be well-known among laymen, but all of the endocrine glands come in pairs or in doublet form, except two. In the light of what will be revealed shortly, that is an extraordinary fact that matches the information given.

Belief or disbelief in reincarnation, a soul's choices, alliances with endocrine glands, colors, and the like are not essential for gaining both astrological and spiritual benefits from Edgar Cayce's readings. However, beliefs and benefits are not the same. Becoming convinced requires careful analysis, and all of the elements must fall into place. Additionally, being critical on the part of serious investigators is to be preferred over gullibility. Otherwise a body of valuable information can become contaminated. This is true in scientific fields as well as astrology. The world abounds with misinformation reported and echoed by charlatans. Therefore, being on guard against chicanery is essential in seeking the truth. Nevertheless, when investigating such far-out subjects as these, an open mind would be more helpful than a closed one. A guarded seeking attitude generally gains more than a nondiscriminating passive attitude. Edgar Cayce's readings on these complex subjects provide many opportunities to either misinterpret or to see the light.

Based upon a repetition of what has been reported thus far, beliefs have been added that warrant careful scrutiny. During reincarnation one horoscope matches a soul's choice for its pattern of life. The soul makes this selection prior to material birth from among the available birth times for that location. The soul understands the cosmic characteristics of each time. For humans on earth, perceiving the same information usually requires drawing and interpreting a horoscope. At the proper moment that soul choice is instantaneously entered into a baby's body. An exact horoscope is set precisely for this same moment. It maps the energy of the selection, and tailored influences become fixed in the baby's body. We are led to believe the setting of these astrological influences is in all seven glandular centers. Each glandular center has a corresponding color. Moving from lowest gland to highest, the planet-gland sequence corresponds with colors split by a prism. Another interwoven alignment is with the signs of the zodiac, and that has major significance as well.

Q-3. Do the seven angels govern in order the major glandular centers of the physical body?

A-3. In their order, as they have been set.

281-031

These readings that cover statements in the Bible and glandular centers in the body refer back to the seven original planets. There are, after all, seven endocrine glands. However, the latest planets discovered are Uranus, Neptune, and Pluto. Astrologers view Uranus as a higher octave of Saturn—that is, it works at a different frequency and plane. Similarly, Neptune is considered to be a higher octave of Jupiter, and Pluto is considered to be a higher octave of Mars. Therefore, their influences must be related in some way to the allied planets and glands.

The next reading does not quite make a connection, but other associations do. We shall get there shortly.

> The spiritual contact is through the glandular forces or creative energies . . . Thus we find the connection, the association of the spiritual being with the mental self, at those centers from which reflexes react to all of the organs, all of the emotions, all of the activities of a physical body.
>
> 263-013

Once again the spiritual centers referred to are the endocrine glands. Glandular forces and creative energies are spoken about in one breath. They tie the spiritual being to the mental self. Reflexes from the glands react with all of the organs of the body. All of the emotions and physical activities are affected in a similar manner. The order of the planets has a direct relationship to these glands. Now is the time to bring up the curious anomaly of the pituitary and the pineal glands previously mentioned:

> Q-14. Medical Science calls the glands at the base of the brain Pituitary and 3rd eye Pineal. Why have these names been reversed? Please explain.
>
> A-14. Their activity indicates that, from the angles of this study, these should be reversed.

> Q-15. Meaning we should reverse ours, or that Medical Science should?
>
> A-15. To understand what is being given, reverse them! We are not telling Medical Science what to do! We are telling YOU what to do!
>
> 281-054

If we examine *Gray's Anatomy* for an upright human being, the pineal gland is somewhat more elevated than the pituitary. Yet Edgar Cayce stated emphatically that the pituitary was the highest and that it should be interpreted correctly. With this basis established, we can explore another proposition. Dual planetary rulerships apply astrologically to certain signs and not to other signs. Thus, two planets can be assigned to certain of the glands and their functions. Reexamining the sequence of planets, endocrine glands, and colors by wavelengths, both dual and singular associations can be made (see Figures 2 and 3). The gonads appear to be related to the color red and the planets

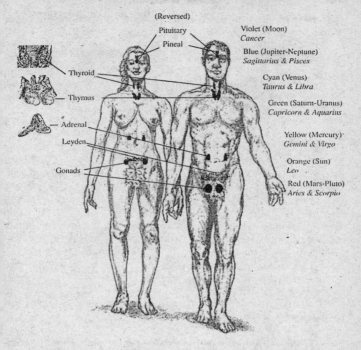

Figure 2. Anatomical positions of the endocrine glands with related colors and planets.

Mars and Pluto. The thymus gland appears to be related to the color green and the planets Saturn and Uranus. The pineal gland appears to be related to the color blue and the planets Jupiter and Neptune. Singular associations remain as they were.

But more details can be given. The gonads, ruled by Mars and Pluto, are the testicles of males and ovaries of females. These are the sexual organs. Spermatozoa and ova are their secretions. They are associated with shades of red. According to Edgar Cayce, each is a "gland of reproduction and the source from and through which impulse acts. Thus it is the source of propagation throughout the experience." There are two separate glands for both males and females. There are two separate plan-

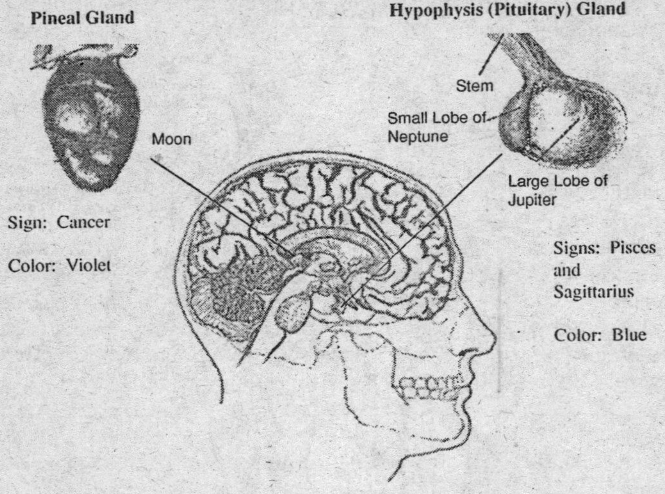

Pineal Gland

Hypophysis (Pituitary) Gland

Stem

Small Lobe of
Neptune

Moon

Large Lobe of
Jupiter

Sign: Cancer

Color: Violet

Signs: Pisces
and
Sagittarius

Color: Blue

Figure 3. The two uppermost endocrine glands in a side view of the human head.
"The highest of these is the Pituitary" was Edgar Cayce's statement. Hence, only
the names are out of order. Physical placements of the glands are in agreement
with the sequence of colors according to those split by a prism. Moving upward
from red, the last two in order are blue and then violet. While not shown, if one
looked down upon the gland labeled pituitary from above, there are actually two
additional bulges on either side. Possibly, these are where information about the
Ascendant and Midheaven of a horoscope are stored.

ets—Mars and Pluto. There are two separate signs—Aries and
Scorpio.

Reference was made to a single Leydig gland, although it is
composed of many interstitial cells. Interstitial refers to occupying closely set spaces in tissues. Edgar Cayce said this gland
was slightly above the gonads:

Q6. The leydig gland is the same as that we have called the
lyden, and is located in the gonads.

A6. It is in and above, or the activity passes through the

gonads. Lyden [See 281-53, R2] is the meaning—or the seal, see? while Leydig is the name of the individual who indicated this was the activity. You can call it either of these that you want to.

281-053

Medical books tend to show Leydig cells only in males and in the connective tissue that separates seminiferous tubules of the testes. They are intermingled and slightly above. However, similar interstitial cells are identified as a part of the female anatomy. The male cells secrete testosterone. The female cells secrete estrogen. In answering a question in reading 281-063 about the power of the centrosome, Edgar Cayce said, "The emotions as related to the CENTRAL forces in eventual activity within the lyden gland itself, or that ability to reproduce within its own self." This is a function of the Sun. The Sun is the central force of life. There are a multitude of Leydig cells, but they are concentrated in one area for both males and females. The Sun rules only one astrological sign, Leo.

The next planet in wavelength is Mercury at the color yellow. The next endocrine glands moving upward are the adrenals, two in number. They are encapsulated flat bodies situated above and in front of the upper pole of each kidney. This is the region called the solar plexus or pit of the stomach. Anatomically, the solar plexus is a nervous plexus situated in the abdomen behind the stomach and in front of the aorta and crura of the diaphragm. A close interaction exists between these ductless glands and the nervous system. Hormones of the adrenal cortex are essential to life and belong to the chemical class known as steroids. It is also interesting to note that the cortex of each adrenal gland is a deep yellow color. Again, that does not happen by chance. When Edgar Cayce was questioned about the endocrine system and arrived at the adrenals, his explanation in one paragraph was:

Then there becomes the first indication of individuality being established in that movement which has come about in its growth, its evolvement; or the gland of the solar plexus, or that YE misinterpret and call the adrenals—as they act with the emotions and the growth and unfoldment of the body itself.

281-051

Hence, there was some misinterpretation on the part of the questioner that he tried to explain. It had to do with calling the solar plexus adrenals. Another misinterpreted question along these lines was answered with a small rebuke:

> Q-4. The life force crosses the solar plexus each time it passes to another center.
> A-4. In growth, yes. In meditation, yes and no; if there remains the balance as of the attunement, yes.
> When we are considering these various phases, the questions should be prepared so that they would not crisscross, or so that there would not be a confusion or a misinterpretation as to what is meant.
> You see, what takes place in the developing body, or in life growth (which we have used as the demonstration, or have illustrated), may be different from that which takes place as one attempts to meditate and to distribute the life force in order to aid another—or to control the influence as in healing, or to attain to an attunement in self for a deeper or better understanding. These questions or statements are such that they will be confusing to some; but if they are asked properly there will not be confusion.
>
> 281-053

Astrologically, Mercury is known as the communicator. It is a planet of movement, meditation, thought, and commerce. Mercury is also considered to be somewhat chameleon-like, taking on the color and hue of other associations. Edgar Cayce is saying that the adrenals control "the influence as in healing, or to attain to an attunement in self for a deeper or better understanding." When use of the wet cell appliance was recommended by Edgar Cayce, one connection was always to be made to the body above the solar plexus. That location communicates with all other areas of the body. However, because emotions are associated with the adrenals, some investigators have thought that Mars applied. The sequential order would be wrong for Mars, and that planet is already accounted for with the gonads.

In answer to still another question about adrenal glands, the following exchanges occurred:

> Q-7. Anger causes poisons to be secreted from the glands. Joy has the opposite effect. The adrenal glands are principally

involved, reacting through the solar plexus to all parts of the body.

A-7. The adrenals principally, but ALL of the glands are involved; as: A nursing mother would find that anger would affect the mammary glands. One nursing would find the digestive glands affected. The liver, the kidneys and ALL glands are affected; though it is correct that the reaction is PRINCIPALLY through the adrenals.

281-054

These readings have been included, because Mercury is a far more involved planet astrologically, physically, and mentally than most astrologers might imagine—let alone the average person not understanding astrology. There are two adrenal glands. They secrete adrenaline when the body is in danger. There are two signs associated with Mercury—Gemini and Virgo.

Moving upward, the next of the endocrine glands is the thymus. The planets are Saturn and Uranus. The colors are shades of green. The thymus is a comparatively large gland situated deep in the neck. It shrinks in size after puberty. Saturn is associated with shrinkage. This gland is composed of two main lobes that are connected. They secrete thymosin and thymopoietin that stimulate the proliferation of lymphocytes. These secretions are essential for acquiring cell-mediated immunity. The two lobes are related to two signs. It is most interesting that the two lobes are connected together and the two signs are adjacent to one another with no separation between them. They are Capricorn and Aquarius. Both signs are thought to be governed by Saturn and Uranus.

Saturn is the planet of caution, constraint, and consumption of time. Uranus is the planet of electricity, forward-looking technology, abrupt actions, and astrology. The combination seems to cover all contingencies for either caution or quick action. Janus, the two-faced Roman god, comes to mind. Both types of action, caution and swift action, are required for complete safety. Together and as necessary they regulate the body's defense mechanisms.

The color related to the thyroid gland is cyan (and indigo). Venus, associated with the thyroid gland, also has two lobes tied together, but not directly. The connection is by a narrow strip called the isthmus. Therefore, we would not expect to find the two signs ruled by Venus to be together. They are not. Taurus and Libra have quite a wide separation.

The two lobes of the thyroid gland are laterally situated in the neck, immediately over the trachea. Thyroid follicles contain nearly all of the iodine in the body. Hormones are produced, including .thyroxine, which controls the basal metabolic rate (BMR) of the body; calcitonin, which controls the calcium level in the body; and various iodine-containing compounds. These regulator functions are in agreement with the astrological viewpoint about Venus. She is a seeker of harmony and balance. Venus is also related to beauty, the skin, and hair.

We now come to the two glands in the head that are alleged to have been reversed (Figure 3). After switching names the pineal gland is associated with Jupiter and Neptune. The color is blue. The pituitary gland is associated with Moon and the color violet.

What the medical profession calls the hypophysis has a stalk with posterior and anterior lobes. It is situated behind the orbits and below the base of the brain. Five hormones are secreted: the thyroid-stimulating hormone (TSH); the adrenocorticotropic hormone (ACTH) that stimulates the cortex of the adrenal gland to increase the production of glucocorticoids; the follicle-stimulating hormone (FSH) essential for the discharge of ova and estrogens in females and spermatozoa in males; the luteinizing hormone (LH) that acts synergistically with FSH to stimulate the cells of Leydig and produce progesterone and estrogens in females, testosterone in males; and prolactine, the lactogenic hormone that stimulates the growth and development of mammary glands. All of this stimulation for growth affecting other glands agrees with the nature of Jupiter and Neptune. Jupiter, in particular, is the planet of stimulation and expansion. The two lobes, while lying side by side, are each coupled directly to the stalk. There is no apparent direct interplay between them. Jupiter and Neptune together rule the separated signs Sagittarius and Pisces.

Looking down from the stalk two main lobes are evident, but there are actually four bulges. Possibly information for the Ascendant and Midheaven are incorporated or stored there as well. The wide variety of secretions indicate more than two functions for this gland. Several Edgar Cayce readings about the pineal gland appear to address some of these additional endowments:

Then the next is the pineal, through which the brain forces make manifest—either in its determining factor there of becoming mighty in stature physically or dwarfed; as may be understood by the face, as may be said, that is held to by the INDIVIDUAL separation and COMBINATION of the activity of the glands in that period of conception. Hence there arises the race condition or contour, or the figure of that beheld by that choice in its activity as it has separated itself from the first cause, or first premise; by the very will of the Father-God in the beginning.

281-051

Brain forces affecting stature, the face, and racial condition or bodily contour are associated with the Ascendant sign. That is why those extra bulges are believed to contain horoscopic information for the principal nodes. The Ascendant/Descendant nodes are one pair. The Median Coelli/Immun Coelli nodes are the other pair. Information for each pair could easily fit these smaller bulges of the pineal gland. They could also be associated with at least two of the secretions.

Ye have gained that the first movement of same physically reaches out and becomes the brain, through which the pineal in its activity brings its physical development; and that it is related to the mind of the body and the environs of the body supplying physical activities to that developing physical entity. Ye know that it reverts then to the brain of the nervous system, to the solar plexus center, and then reflexes through its own MENTAL activity to the physical forces of the still developing body. Ye know that when such a body has developed, when gestation has been completed and it becomes an entity in itself—because of its center through which all physical and mental impulses has passed—it is then cut asunder—and yet functions on. Why? How?

These are not merely pathological questions, but mental and spiritual also.

281-057

"INDIVIDUAL separation and COMBINATION of the activity of the glands in that period of conception" must include functions of both the Midheaven and the Ascendant. This is another reading that has repeated the idea. The face is molded especially by the Ascendant. That is why it exhibits such a distinctive quality for each astrological sign a person is born with. The appearance overlays a skeletal framework established by the Sun. Physical development is a first house operation. Physical development is related to mental development. Both activities during gestation represent changes to and growth of the body. This gland, then, is the center through which all physical and mental impulses pass. Such impulses are not simply pathological but mental and spiritual as well. The pineal gland is cut asunder after gestation has been completed but functions on. Accordingly, the medical profession is quite right in labeling it vestigial.

At last we have arrived at the pituitary gland. The medical profession says that the uppermost endocrine gland is a dorsal projection of the diencephalon, lying above the third ventricle, and is attached to the midbrain by the habenular and posterior commissures. The endocrine function has not been definitely established (by them), and they regard this gland as another vestigial organ. However, it produces two substances, *melatonin* and *serotonin*, that may act as hormones. *Melatonin* is thought to act on the gonads to delay maturation and functional activity. It also acts on the adrenal cortex and the thyroid, and it is thought to influence such cyclic activities as ovarian and uterine changes during the menstrual cycles of women. The onset of puberty may depend on *melatonin*.

Couched in this medical terminology are references to functions that in astrology are attributed to the Moon. Other lunar functions are motion, the mind, and memory, including records of all past incarnations and planetary sojourns. The Moon's color is violet. This color has the shortest wavelength and highest frequency of the visible colors. If one stays in the visible spectrum and closes the loop, one must return from violet like a beeline to the color red. The Moon represents feelings and emotions. It becomes most emotional over the actions of Mars (and Pluto). The hormones of the pituitary gland control gonadal functions, e.g., female menstruation cycles and the release of ova. Hence, the lunar hormones have dominion over Martian glands. That is the straight line connection indicated. The Moon is that mind!

Thus, it is the first of the centers from which arises all that is movement, to bring into being both the face and the preface— or the back, or the reverse—is the experience. It carries with it, what? That MIND! For, remember, ever, the pattern is ever the same—Mind is the builder!

281-051

Another question-answer sequence made interesting comments about the pituitary gland. The querist was reviewing and trying to interpret information from the Bible's Book of Revelations:

Q-23. *Pituitary—heaven?*
A-23. Correct. In all of its activities these open, for the upward lift of the thoughts of man as in relationships to that which becomes—how has it been given?—"He is alpha, omega, the beginning and the end." Hence as we find in its relationships to man, it becomes then the beginnings, the endings, of all things.

281-029

The pituitary gland and the Moon have a relationship with birth and death. Edgar Cayce said that the pituitary and pineal glands form initially in a developing embryo. The pituitary gland is associated with the astrological sign Cancer. There is only one such gland, whereas the pineal gland is associated with the astrological signs Sagittarius and Pisces. In the old astrological doctrine, the planets used to calculate the soul-chosen times are Sun, Moon, and Uranus. The algorithm uses signs of beginning and ending within the circular zodiac. Those two signs are Sagittarius and Cancer. As these first two glands form, they start with the pituitary (Cancer) and with the pineal (Sagittarius). Pisces, the other sign for Jupiter, would more likely be associated with the end of life as opposed to the beginning. So Pisces does not have an integral role in birth. But it is remarkable that these initial gland developments after conception, these uppermost two glands, are tied to the old astrological doctrine and unique spiritual birth times in the manner indicated. Uranus, providing the astrological connections, also relates to the suddenness and forcefulness of the birth event.

Scientists have recently found a switch that says it's a boy or girl. At conception, everybody is female, and during the first weeks after conception female organs start to form. If the egg was fertilized with an X chromosome of sperm from the father, the baby remains female. If fertilized with a Y chromosome from the father, the baby gravitates toward maleness about 35 to 40 days into human gestation. Using sophisticated imaging techniques to explore, on an atomic level, the biological pathway to manhood, scientists have discovered a gene known as the SRY and another gene known as the MIS. SRY activates a male-specific pattern of development. In turn the gene MIS is activated by SRY. MIS causes the nascent female organs in the embryo to disappear. During this period, the pituitary and pineal glands are discernible, more so than any of the other endocrine glands. Whether medical scientists will find a sexual-specific link to the pituitary and pineal glands remains to be seen.

This discourse on colors, planets, and endocrine glands is known to differ somewhat from tables previously generated by other writers. Doubtless they were sincere in their efforts. However, as indicated, the extremely important omissions of the Sun and Moon have now been accounted for. The whereabouts of information storage for the Ascendant and Midheaven has been localized in a speculative, but now reasonable, manner. The dual and singular rulerships of signs by the planets have been synchronized, and the matching configurations of the endocrine glands have been accounted for. Secretions from the endocrine glands are known medically, and they match astrological urges from corresponding planets and nodes. Colors are in the order observed after being split by a prism. Many different Edgar Cayce readings on related subjects have been reconciled. The purported progression upward of Kundalini forces through the endocrine glands without retracements or omissions has been confirmed. Harmony prevails.

As to the influences from astrological aspects, numerology, colors, vibrations—we find that all of these to the entity have a meaning, have a purpose in the experience. But ever know, deep within self, these are but urges—yea, as but weather vanes that would indicate the trend of the mind, as the builder; of the desires, as that which may be patterned with the hopes upon which all may be builded.

1626-001

6

A BIT OF SCIENCE

CAN EDGAR CAYCE'S astrological readings withstand scientific scrutiny? While many scientists might be put off by such a question, making a few technical comparisons yields surprising results.

Medical correspondences between Edgar Cayce's readings on endocrine glands and astrological place holders given in the preceding chapter qualify as being scientific. A number of extraordinary correlations were found. The proposal is that we now look at a few other elements of science, including astronomy and statistics.

Science has produced advancements distinguishing our modern age from the past. Thousands of electromagnetic, chemical, optical, biological, and mechanical products increase the sophistication of our lives, although dangers sometimes accompany them. Accidents in nuclear power plants are prime examples of conjoined perils. However, advancements generally outweigh such dangers. Computers perform millions of calculations and sort huge volumes of data in a fraction of the time that was needed formerly when manual techniques were used. There is a general admiration for the technical breakthroughs that prove themselves to be correct and benefit humanity. Thus, science is generally accepted by the public because of its accomplishments. However, the idea that science can do no wrong is not generally accepted. Many people harbor suspicions that science, or scientists, on occasion go too far in the pursuit of egotistical goals, legal rights, and profits while ignoring the human element.

Correspondences between scientific data and astrological functions do not occur by chance. Furthermore, when Edgar Cayce speaks on *progressive* subjects, he has a way of drawing them back into the reality of a humanistic world. This is helpful for both technical and nontechnical readers. He also has a way of telling us that science creates its own seeds of destruction. That tendency forces it to go through cycles of extinction and revival throughout the ages. Thus, the latent suspicions of the public are justified.

Q-7. Explain how the example of Man's developing and improving his mode of living scientifically on earth, for example in medical work and all other sciences, proves his development and evolution on earth and other planes.

A-7. Man's development, as given, is of man's understanding and applying the laws of the Universe, and as man applies those, man develops, man brings up the whole generation of man. Individuals we find carry out certain elements and laws, and gradually man becomes capable of applying and using those in the everyday life of man. This, whether applied in medical science, in anatomal science, in mechanical science or whatnot, is merely the development, or the application as man applies to Universal laws as are ever, and have ever been, existent in the Universe. As is in this. That producing electrical units of force was just as applicable to the Universal forces in the days of Adam as in the days of the Master, or as in the days of today. Those laws applying to aerial of transmission are just as applicable in one as in other. Man not understanding those. Many times has the evolution of the earth reached the stage of development as it has today and then sank again, to rise again in the next development. Some along one line, some along others, for often we find the higher branches of so-called learning destroys itself in the seed it produces in man's development, as we have in medical forces, as we have astrological forces, as we have in some forms of spiritual forces, as we have in forms of destructive forces of various natures.

900-070

Edgar Cayce spoke ominously when alluding to science's lack of adequacy and direction with respect to the forces of medicine, astrology, and the spirit. These are the areas where scientists are most likely to show arrogance and ignorance regardless of superior mental progress. Among medical forces, not that many years have elapsed since the sick were being bled almost to death. Among astrological forces, vindictive writings have appeared all over Europe. Among spiritual forces, the Inquisition cast a dark spell over mankind.

Actually, Edgar Cayce included all branches of higher learning and warned of the bad seed produced in man's development. Selfishness, greed, and domination over others were identified in many readings as destructive forces. Destructive forces warrant opposition by everyone, because they lessen the opportunities for creative expression. Destructive forces are just as prevalent in universities as elsewhere, judging from news headlines. Campus politics have been known to become particularly noisome in the bastions of academia. Mental giants can be just as deadly in their egotistical pursuits as they attempt to suppress competing creative expressions.

14. For all that is a part of each entity's experience is for a purpose. But if one turns it into the gratifying of self, without consideration of the relationships with others, these bring about fear, doubt, hate, animosity, and those things that wreck the lives of many—creating in all its phases those things that are belittling, harmful—and must eventually bring a dissipation of some phase of the entity's abilities—lessening the opportunities for creative expression, and BUILDING more of those destructive forces in the experience.

1827-001

While not against the teaching profession, Edgar Cayce also saw academic courses in the true light of their worth to mankind. When they were beneficial, he said so. When they were likely to mislead or give false impressions, he also said so. It is easy to see that the following example had almost a foregone conclusion.

Q-4. Is the course in astronomy for which the entity has enrolled with the Massachusetts Division of University Extension sufficiently complete to furnish an adequate foundation for the entity's study of astrology and numerology?

A-4. Very good basis, but not sufficient; neither is the application at present efficient.

256-002

These readings show a degree of respect for science and education but realism with respect to their limitations. Inadequacies in the information dispensed by universities were given only when called for by the nature of the question. The astrological and spiritual parts of academic information are clearly lacking. Those few institutions that do have an astrological course or two teach this subject in an isolated manner. Yet the scientific methods are powerful, and much reliance can be placed upon accurate data gathered through careful experimentation.

By drawing a few comparisons between verified scientific phenomena and related astrological elements, bridges to humanistic factors might be momentarily gapped. This process requires understanding of a little bit of science as well as astrology. Unless the reader is technically minded and knows more about astrology than their own Sun signs, some of the details may be lost. However, an effort will be made to explain each example in laymen's terms. Additionally, equations may cause some people who are not strong in mathematics to feel uncomfortable. But please have patience. Even these people may get a great deal out of this review of observed correspondences. Associations between certain technical findings and astrology are extremely interesting, and they could not be brought to the reader's attention any other way.

ASTRONOMICAL PHENOMENA

Starting with the celestial bodies that Edgar Cayce said were set in motion to provide urges, their study has in recent history been divided into astronomy, the pure material science, and astrology, the tainted prophesying study in the minds of many. Only in the last several centuries have they been separated. Before that time, an educated man or woman had to know both and was expected to have a working knowledge in many fields. In short, wise men in the Bible were astrologers as well as astronomers. An astrologer who did not know astronomy was considered ill prepared and would be looked down upon. To a wise man of old, an astronomer not conversant with astrology was unthinkable. But, if such a person did exist, he would also lack education and be ill prepared for making contributions to humanity. That person might also have been a social outcast.

Edgar Cayce discussed this split between the two groups in a reading on the astronomical subject (or is it not also the astrological subject?) of sunspots. Information pertaining to this dichotomy of learning is fascinating. Hence, the reading is given in its entirety:

TEXT OF READING 5757–1

This Psychic Reading given by Edgar Cayce at the Hotel Warner, Virginia Beach, Va., this 21st day of June, 1940, at the Ninth Annual Congress of the Ass'n for Research & Enlightenment, Inc.

PRESENT

Edgar Cayce; Mrs. Cayce, Conductor; Gladys Davis, Steno.

READING

Time of Reading
4:00 to 4:30 P.M. Eastern Standard Time.

1. GC: You will give at this time a discourse on what are known as Sun Spots, explaining the cause of these phenomena and their effect on the earth and its inhabitants.

2. EC: In giving that as we find would be as helpful information in the experience of individuals gathered here, many conditions and phases of man's experience in the earth are to be considered.

3. When the heavens and the earth came into being, this meant the universe as the inhabitants of the earth know same; yet there are many suns in the universe,—those even about which our sun, our earth, revolve; and all are moving toward some place,—yet space and time appear to be incomplete.

4. Then time and space are but one. Yet the sun, that is the center of this particular solar system, is the center; and, as has been indicated and known of old, it is that about which

the earth and its companion planets circulate, or evolve [revolve?].

5. The beginnings of the understanding of these, and their influences upon the lives of individuals, were either thought out, evolved or interpreted by those of old, without the means of observing same as considered today necessary in order to understand.

6. Astronomy is considered a science and astrology as foolishness. Who is correct? One holds that because of the position of the earth, the sun, the planets, they are balanced one with another in some manner, some form; yet that they have nothing to do with man's life or the expanse of life, or the emotions of the physical being in the earth.

7. Then, why and how do the effects of the sun SO influence other life in the earth and not affect MAN'S life, man's emotions?

8. As the sun has been set as the ruler of this solar system, does it not appear to be reasonable that it HAS an effect upon the inhabitants of the earth, as well as upon plant and mineral life in the earth?

9. Then if not, why, how did the ancients worship the sun AS the representative of a continuous benevolent and beneficent influence upon the life of the individual?

10. Thus as we find given, the sun and the moon and the stars were made also—this being the attempt of the writer to convey to the individual the realization that there IS an influence in their activity! For, remember, they—the sun, the moon, the planets—divine, and they move in same.

11. Man alone is given that birthright of free will. He alone may defy his God!

12. How many of you have questioned that in thine own heart, and know that thy disobedience in the earth reflects unto the heavenly hosts and thus influences that activity of God's command! For YOU—as souls and sons and daughters of God—DEFY the living God!

13. As the sun is made to shed light and heat upon God's children in the earth, it is then of that composition of which man is made, or of that termed the earth; yet, as ye have seen and know, there is solid matter, there is liquid, there is vapor. All are one in their various stages of consciousness or of activity for what? Man—GODLY MAN! Yet when these become as in defiance to that light which was commanded to march, to show forth the Lord's glory, His beauty, His mercy, His hope,—yea, His patience,—do ye wonder then that there become reflected upon even the face of the sun those turmoils and strifes that have been and that are the sin of man?

14. Whence comest this?

15. All that was made was made to show to the sons, the souls, that GOD IS mindful of His children.

16. How do they affect man? How does a cross word affect thee? How does anger, jealously, hate, animosity, affect thee AS a son of God? If thou art the father of same, oft ye cherish same. If thou art the recipient of same from others, they brethren, how does it affect thee? Much as that confusion which is caused upon the earth by that which appears as a sun spot. The disruption of communications of all natures between men is what? Remember the story, the allegory if ye choose to call it such, of the tower of Babel.

17. Yea, ye say ye trust God, and yet want to show Him how to do it!

18. These become, then, as the influences that would show man as to his littleness in even entertaining hate, injustice, or that which would make a lie.

19. Be honest with thyself, as ye would ask even the ruler of thine earth—the sun—to harken to the voice of that which created it and to give its light IRRESPECTIVE of how ye act! For, as given, the sun shineth upon the just and the unjust alike, yet it is oft reflected in what happens to thee in thy journey through same.

20. The more ye become aware of thy relationships to the universe and those influences that control same, the greater thy

ability to help, to aid,—the greater thy ability to rely upon the God-force within; but STILL greater thy RESPONSIBILITY to thy fellow men. For, as ye do it unto the least, ye do it unto thy Maker,—even as to the sun which reflects those turmoils that arise with thee; even as the earthquake, even as wars and hates, even as the influence in thy life day by day.

21. Then, what are the sun spots? A natural consequence of that turmoil which the sons of God in the earth reflect upon same.

22. Thus they oft bring confusion to those who become aware of same.

23. Let not your hearts be troubled; yet believe in God. Then just act like it—to others.

24. He has given thee a mind, a body; an earth, and land in which to dwell. He has set the sun, the moon, the planets, the stars about thee to remind thee, even as the psalmist gave, "Day unto day uttereth speech, night unto night sheweth knowledge."

25. These ye know, these ye have comprehended; but do ye take thought of same?

26. KNOW that thy mind—thy MIND—is the builder! As what does thy soul appear? A spot, a blot upon the sun? or as that which giveth light unto those who sit in darkness, to those who cry aloud for hope?

27. Hast thou created hope in thy association with thy fellow men?

28. Ye fear and cringe when ye find that the spots upon thy sun cause confusion of any nature.

29. How MUST thy Savior feel, look, appear, when ye deny Him day by day; when ye treat thy fellow man as though he were as dross and trash before thee?

30. We are through.

Edgar Cayce pointed out that if the divine Sun, Moon, and planets affect other forms of life on earth, then why not man?

Any thought to the contrary is illogical. Man alone is given that birthright of free will. When used improperly, it causes disturbances. If there are those who deny these gifts of the Creator, then "How must thy Savior feel?"

Anger, jealousy, hate, animosity—those are the sins of man instigating sunspots. And so man's disobedience results in confusions. Denying the Creator and his works causes even greater confusion. Pedantic astronomers probably never considered sunspots in the manner given. Nor have they thought about them in an astrological context. But in the 1920s learned investigators drew parallels between sunspots and historic excitability of people.[4] In 1952, John H. Nelson recorded scientific evidence at RCA to show that communications were disrupted during periods of intense sunspots. Disrupted communications are like the allegory of the Tower of Babel. Later reviews of papers followed on sunspots and sociological and economic phenomena.[5] These studies are scientific. However, the connections with astrology are not openly identified or brandished. Yet the threads are there disguised in terms like cosmic events, cycles, planetary periods, etc.

COLORS

Knowledge about planets, as Edgar Cayce said, "were either thought out, evolved or interpreted by those of old, without the means of observing same as considered today necessary in order to understand." Wise men of old arrived at an original seven-set grouping of celestial bodies that provide urges to the human body. As outer planets were discovered (or rediscovered) during the past three centuries, evolutionary additions were made. Figure 4 illustrates the astronomical order of planets radiating from

[4] The classic reference is "Index of Mass Human Excitability 500 B.C.–A.D. 1922" by A. I. Tchijevsky, Moscow.

[5] A paper, entitled "Economic and Sociological Phenomena Related to Solar Activity and Influences" by Edward R. Dewey, was delivered September 6, 1968, at the Second International Symposium on Solar-Terrestrial Relationship to Physical-Chemistry and in the Science of Life, Brussels, Belgium. Dewey then started an organization called Foundation for Cycles. Many current articles on sunspots and related phenomena appear in *Cycles*, the magazine for members, published at 900 West Valley Road, Suite 502, Wayne, Pennsylvania 19087-1821.

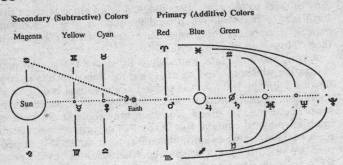

Figure 4. Sequence of planets and associated colors with signs of the zodiac. Violet Moon rules Cancer and Orange Sun rules Leo. Their colors blend to form magenta. The order of the planets radiating from the sun matches the remaining signs in a counterclockwise manner. All outer planets have dual relationships. All planets except the Sun and Moon (which are not planets) share two signs.

the Sun. This is a compressed pictorial representation, and distances between planets are not indicated. The astrological bodies generally accepted today consist of the Moon, Sun, Mercury, Venus, Mars with Pluto, Jupiter with Neptune, and Saturn with Uranus. These are the rulers of the zodiacal signs in normal order. They are Moon to Cancer, Sun to Leo, Mercury to Virgo, Venus to Libra, Mars and Pluto to Scorpio, Jupiter and Neptune to Sagittarius, Saturn and Uranus to Capricorn. Doubling back in a counterclockwise direction, these rulerships continue in perfect order. They are Saturn and Uranus to Aquarius, Jupiter and Neptune to Pisces, Mars and Pluto to Aries, Venus to Taurus, and Mercury to Gemini. Dual rulerships are often referred to among astrologers as being the higher and lower octaves of a sign—although this terminology could be misleading. Another point is that only the Sun and Moon are assigned to single signs—Leo and Cancer—just as they are also assigned to singular endocrine glands—Leydig and pituitary. All of the actual planets rule or corule two signs and doublet or paired endocrine glands.

The inclusion of color assignments in this figure raises several questions. Do they agree with the ones Edgar Cayce gave that are the same as those associated with the endocrine glands? Are they in zodiacal sequence and in prismatic sequence—meaning in frequency or wavelength sequence? To answer these ques-

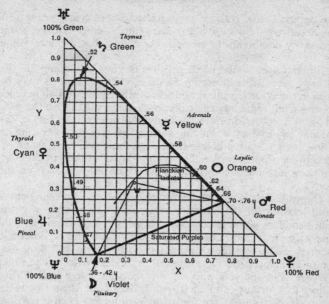

Figure 5. The color triangle. Planets and endocrine glands have been added versus their respective color wavelengths.

tions, it is appropriate to revisit colors from a technical viewpoint.

If a scientist or engineer experienced in the subject of light were approached about colors, the chief reference would be to the color triangle depicted in Figure 5. It has a number of very interesting characteristics. The darkened curve indicates colors visible to the naked eye. Starting with red at the lower right side and moving counterclockwise, colors progress as they do when split by a prism. That is in agreement with Edgar Cayce's statement. The numbers shown alongside the dark curve on the outside of the triangle indicate decreasing wavelengths. As wavelengths decrease, the frequencies of color vibration increase. Colors not on the darkened curve become blends or they are less visible to the naked human eye.

The color white is located near the center of the triangle at the small "w". A line drawn from any visible color on the darkened curve through "w" will intersect the darkened curve on the opposite side. If those two wavelengths of colors are mixed, the result will be white. Many lines can be dawn. Hence, there are many combinations of opposite colors that produce white light.

Edgar Cayce spoke of these lines or rays in reading 281-30, already given. One sentence bears repeating: "Just as may be seen in the common interpretation of white, but with all manner of rays from same begins or comes to mean that above the aura of all in its vibration from the body and from the activity of the mental experience when the various centers are vibrating to color." All vibrating colors have opposite colors that, when intercepted, produce white. The graph illustrates this concept and shows where these combinations translate into auras from the body.

Opposite colors can be readily picked off the darkened curve until looking for the opposite of green. The opposite of green that produces white is magenta. Magenta is just off the straight line going from violet to red. It is actually a blend of violet and orange. These are the colors assigned to Moon and Sun. Magenta completes the threesome of secondary colors. The other two are cyan and yellow. Note how the subtractive and additive colors form triangles of their own if lines were drawn between them. If all six lines are drawn, they intersect each other and create a pattern similar to the Star of David.

To return to the technical for just a moment, three parameters are related. They are frequency, wavelength, and velocity of light. Frequencies of vibration can be derived from wavelengths by the equation $\lambda = c/f$. The numbers on the smooth curve are in milli-micrometers (nanometers or meters $* 10^{-9}$). The velocity of light is "c", or $2.9986 * 10^8$ meters per second. Alternately, wavelength is velocity divided by frequency, making sure to keep the units straight. Any one of the parameters can be derived from the other two. Was it not very thoughtful of the Creator to cause the velocity of light to be a constant? Otherwise, we would have no standard for colors.

> For it is not strange that music, color, vibration are all a part of the planets, just as the planets are a part—and a pattern—of the whole universe.
>
> 5755-001

Each planet has an associated color wavelength and matching frequency of vibration. Starting with Mars and the color red, and moving counterclockwise, the color sequence is the one obtained from a prism. Red is at the longest wavelength in the visible spectrum and the lowest frequency. Violet for the Moon is at the shortest wavelength in the visible spectrum and the highest frequency.

All colors and planets are in agreement with Edgar Cayce's assignments with one seeming exception. When looking at auras, Cayce is alleged to have said indigo was the color for Venus. Now, indigo is not a very well-defined color. It was originally produced from several different plants, mainly of species *indigofera*. Indigo is now produced synthetically, and the resulting products may have changed their frequency of vibration in the process. However, pairs of colors can have sum or difference frequencies in the same manner as radio waves. In radio terminology this is the heterodyne principle. Colors can also have sum or difference wavelengths as well. A technical analysis of so-called beat frequencies (or wavelengths) shows that both cyan and indigo are appropriate for Venus. If we take the shortest visible wavelength for red at .650 nanometers and go straight through "w" and mix it with cyan at .493 nanometers, the difference wavelength is .346 nanometers. That would produce indigo in the visible spectrum. By happenstance the sum wavelength of .558 nanometers is simply a different version of cyan with a tinge of green. Cyans are the colors of copper ores that are tied to Venus. These calculations show that both cyan and indigo are indeed appropriate for Venus. But note that cyan is one of the sequential colors split by a prism. Additionally, it is a known member of the secondary color family. Perhaps the reason for giving the equation can now be understood.

There are forces or pitches above and below the scale, as are applied in the human voice. There are colors above and below the spectrum, as applied by man in a nominal manner. There are the same octaves of force seen or applied in the various elements as go to make up the forces as applicable to elements in any generative force. Many, as seen, have been placed and given a name—without yet having been separated or brought into being by man as a used force.

4665-008
(Essentially the same in 1800-015)

Edgar Cayce associated a spiritual contact between each planet, endocrine gland, and color. Opposite colors and endocrine glands match astrological sign pairs. The order of colors by wavelength matches the sequence of astrological signs and planets while counting up the loop in the color triangle and back down in the other direction. Red and the longest wavelength mark the start of this progression, just as Aries, ruled by Mars, marks a beginning point for moving around the zodiac. These wavelengths are also in the order of the relative locations of the endocrine glands as one moves upward through the human body—not a phenomena of chance.

An astrological and endocrine gland perspective has been added to Figure 5. However, observe the locations of the three outermost planets: Uranus, Neptune, and Pluto. Respectively, they share sign rulerships with Saturn, Jupiter, and Mars. The apexes of the triangle are at peaks in the range of visibility. These three points represent 100 percent saturated colors. They are also the corresponding locations of the three outermost planets. Thus, all planets are shown for each color and wavelength to which they are attuned. The association of Mars with Pluto, Saturn with Uranus, and Jupiter with Neptune has also been made apparent. The additive and subtractive color assignments and dual rulerships have been incorporated in proper order.

When the previously mentioned line is drawn from one of the colors for a planet through "w" to the opposite side of the dark curve, that line intersects the color for another planet. Those opposite planets producing white are exactly in accord with rulerships of the astrological signs. Thus, red Mars for Aries opposes cyan Venus for Libra. The same is true for Scorpio and Taurus. Yellow Mercury for Gemini opposes blue Jupiter for Sagittarius, which is the same for Virgo and Pisces. Green Saturn for Capricorn and Aquarius opposes the straight line of the dark curve. This portion represents a shade of magenta that is a blend of violet Moon for Cancer and orange Sun for Leo. Thus, all of the additive colors have their dual rulerships. All of the subtractive colors have either singular or unshared rulerships. Opposing subtractive colors are not backed by *higher octave* planets. While Mercury and Venus rule two signs, the Moon and Sun do not. They rule one sign each.

The color triangle has been shown to have complete correspondence with the known planets, zodiacal signs, and endocrine glands. While the orientation of the color triangle is technical, a spiritual significance has now been added. It has only three points, and they are filled. All of the other positions in two dimensions are occupied. One may draw a tentative conclusion that if there are more planets in this solar system, astrological influences would have to fit some third dimension of the color triangle. Else the requirement would be for non-visible external colors that cannot be placed in this two-dimensional map.

Uranian astrologers claim to have identified six more planets, although none of them have been observed with telescopes. Thus, they are unseen, invisible, and not on the color triangle. While professional articles have appeared on perturbations of the orbits of Neptune and Pluto, no astronomer has announced the discovery of additional planets in this solar system. A gap therefore exists in credibility, both scientifically and astrologically.

STATISTICS

This is a mathematical discipline used frequently in physics and scientific studies. It accounts for many forms of data that occur by chance. Data may be uniform or nonuniform in distribution, and branches of this mathematical science handle both types. One branch addresses equally distributed probabilities called Gaussian. If a collection of chances is large and can be shown to have what is called a normal distribution (fitting a bell-shaped curve), then appropriate equations can be used to predict probable outcomes. In reality, statistics is a form of intellectual fortune-telling. Professional statisticians constantly fight the problem of attempts being made to apply their equations to data sets that are too small and that, in fact, do not have normal distributions. The use of the word *normal* has interesting connotations: The implication is that all variables are like flips of a coin having an equal opportunity for coming up heads or tails. In the real world that condition is not always met. The coin can be more heavily weighted on one side than the other.

Hence, predictions from this mathematical science are often questioned—as are astrological predictions. Even if that is so, much useful work has been accomplished. Semiconductor properties, for example, have been predicted using statistics. The root causes of illnesses have been predicted using astrology. No one would try to claim that both forecasts were in the same league. A radically different form of intellectualism is required

to make both prognostications. Only wise men and women
would have mastered both forms.

> In direct knowledge one assumes that the all-purpose force,
> or the Universal, is an acknowledged fact, while the material
> minded accepts NOTHING as fact. Hence needs the statistical
> records to prove. This may be seen in ANY turn, and is as a
> truth.
>
> 900-286

Edgar Cayce was quite right on this score. Scientists are material-minded. Those with PhDs also have a credo: to publish or
perish. The scientific method is to accept nothing as fact. Hence,
scientific writers often resort to statistical records to prove the-
orems. When peers do not accept conclusions drawn from statistics, the claim is usually that data was insufficient or biased
methods caused distributions to be abnormal. By contrast, Edgar Cayce said that in direct knowledge, or universal knowledge
(from the Creator), the all-purpose force is an acknowledged
fact. The trick is in recognizing direct knowledge of the universal. It may come as a surprise to some scientists and mathematicians that certain astrological data is of the universal, just as
certain scientific data is of the universal.

Over the years a statistician now and then attempts to apply
this mathematical science to astrology.[6] Generally, these efforts
have failed to convince peers, because the original premises
were not of the universal. Therefore, the input data itself could
be questioned; the results were only partially convincing, and
those who tried to replicate the experiments did not derive exactly the same results. What they obtained instead were different ranges of probabilities or different percentages for artificially
specified degrees of confidence. That is the nature of statistics.
Yet duplicating results is exceedingly important in science, because as Edgar Cayce said, "the material minded accepts
NOTHING as fact."

It is not likely that any scientist would apply statistics to the
velocity of light, for example. That function is considered to be
a constant. Even if they thought there were variations, measurements would attempt to cover the tiniest of perturbations.

---

[6]Michel Gaugelin, for example, in *Cosmic Influences on Human Behavior.* He attempted to relate vocations to Sun signs, and that is not an
astrological fundamental.

Constants of this type came from the Universal Mind. No variations are expected. Therefore, the probability is known to be 1.0. This means 100 percent of all light velocities from whatever the source are the same.

Similarly, in astrology a remarkable and uncanny observation is repeated for every individual. One and only one horoscope matches the timetable of urges for each individual. That timetable was picked by the soul, but it originated with the Universal Mind. The probability of there being such a perfect timetable and match of urges is 1.0. Thus, 100 percent of all souls pick one and only one horoscope. Therefore, properly applied data from soul-picked horoscopes also has a probability of 1.0. What that really means is that statistics no longer apply! Statistics are not appropriate for the true fundamentals of astrology, just as they are not appropriate for the speed of light. Both are fundamentals of the Universal Mind.

By the way, every statistical study performed on verified soul-selected horoscopes with the objective of ascertaining or verifying an astrological fundamental has yielded Chi Square results of zero! Laymen may not know what that statistic means, but mathematicians do. It means the results were always the same 100 percent of the time.

PROOFS

Q-42. Will psychic phenomena ever, or within say 50 years, be accepted and provable on directly scientific measurements; that is on meters (instruments) and mathematics? If not, why?

A-42. When there is the same interest or study given to things or phases of mental and spiritual phenomena as has been and is given to the materialized or material phenomena, then it will become just as practical, as measurable, as meter-able, as any other phase of human experience.

Ye did it before! Ye used it correctly,—even though the whole world was against you: Would you again?

2012-001

This wise reading is given because it discusses difficulties and lack of understanding in making acceptable scientific measurements of psychic phenomena. One day the scientific community may have an interest in nonmaterial subjects, but not now. Astrology is usually lumped with psychic phenomena. On the other

hand, it may encompass the entire subject. The person addressed apparently went against the crowd and made such measurements during a previous incarnation. And he did it correctly.

> He that would find life, other than in its expressions in ma-
> teriality or matter, then must believe that it exists. Then it may
> be with impunity sought; for the aid, for the comfort, for the
> hope, for the faith that it may build in those experiences of
> those who have lost their way or who grope in doubt or in fear,
> those who approach old age—as man counts same. For Life is,
> and its manifestations in matter ARE of an ELECTRONIC en-
> ergy.
>
>   440-020

When looking toward nonmaterial expressions of life, Edgar
Cayce said that the seeker needs to believe. Belief fosters im-
punity of thought while others "grope in doubt or in fear."
Those are the people who may have lost their way. Fear stands
behind much that is negative.

Then he said life and its manifestations are of an electronic
nature. Electronics can be measured. This field of science, as
well as astrology, is ruled by the planet Uranus. That is para-
doxical, considering the differences and likenesses in beliefs,
doubts, and fears.

Meanwhile, those who seek proof for the aid, for the comfort,
for the hope, for the faith that it may build are encouraged.
Those who demand proof about astrology, reincarnation, and
psychic phenomenon to discredit them must be expressing
fears—fear of ridicule, fear of being ostracized by society or by
respected colleagues. Others might have real obsessions about
their own safety. It is easy for these high-minded individuals to
take refuge in intellectual fortresses, and they do.

Edgar Cayce said, "When there is the same interest or study
given to things or phases of mental and spiritual phenomena as
has been and is given to the materialized or material phenomena, then it will become just as practical, as measurable, as
meter-able, as any other phase of human experience." If that
condition prevailed for "phases of mental and spiritual phenomena," then electronic measurements might be professionally
conducted, reported, and accepted. Thus far, only a few experiments have been reported, such as Kirilian photographs that
show electric charges surrounding a body. However, until general interest increases, the majority of scientists will likely con-

tinue taking the easy way out. Edgar Cayce said that having faith in Him can eradicate such fears as they may be concealing.

Q-45. Since I am definitely drawn to occult things, how can I free myself from the fear instilled by an early horoscope which stated that in turning to anything psychic I might open myself to the influences of black magic?

A-45. No better formula may be given than this: Read Deuteronomy 30th, as being directed to thee BY those influences ye helped establish among a great peoples. Then study and analyze John 14th, 15th, 16th, and 17th. Not as rote, again, but as a PRACTICAL experience, as may be the experience of any soul that seeks to make that creative force, God, as manifested there, the rule of the life. No greater psychic lived than Jesus of Nazareth. No greater activity was manifested than by the entity itself in that directing of the household of its own sons; two of which practised black magic and were destroyed. These build that fear. In Him it is eradicated.

2630-001

7

KARMA

RECORDS OF FAVORABLE and detrimental decisions are carried forward to succeeding sojourns, both here on earth and on other planets. There they are assimilated.

Q-11. Have I karma from any previous existence that should be overcome?

A-11. Well that karma be understood, and how it is to be met. For, in various thought—whether considered philosophy or religion, or whether from the more scientific manner of cause and effect—karma is all of these and more.

Rather it may be likened unto a piece of food, whether fish or bread, taken into the system; it is assimilated by the organs of digestion, and then those elements that are gathered from same are, made into the forces that flow through the body, giving the strength and vitality to an animate object, or being, or body.

So, in experiences of a soul, in a body, in an experience in the earth. Its thoughts make for that upon which the soul feeds, as do the activities that are carried on from the thought of the period make for the ability, of retaining or maintaining the active force or active principle of the thought THROUGH the experience.

Then, the soul re-entering into a body under a different environ either makes for the expending of that it has made through the experience in the sojourn in a form that is called in some religions as destiny of the soul, in another philosophy that which has been builded must be met in some way or manner, or in the more scientific manner that a certain cause produces a certain effect.

Hence we see that karma is ALL of these and more. What more? Ever since the entering of spirit and soul into matter there has been a way of redemption for the soul, to make an association and a connection with the Creator, THROUGH the love FOR the Creator that is in its experience. Hence THIS, too, must be taken into consideration; that karma may mean the development FOR SELF—and must be met in that way and manner, or it may mean that which has been acted upon by the cleansing influences of the way and manner through which the soul, the mind-soul, or the soul-mind is purified, or to be purified, or purifies itself, and hence those changes come about—and some people term it "Lady Luck" or "The body is born under a lucky star." It's what the soul-mind has done.

ABOUT the source of redemption of the soul! Or it may be yet that of cause and effect, as related to the soul, the mind, the spirit, the body.

440-005

When a soul makes a choice for working out karma on earth, astrological factors enter the picture. Since a horoscope is the paradigm for potential karmic unfoldment, the time of birth would strongly influence a soul's deliberations. A review of the birth sequence from a karmic angle seems appropriate. First, a choice among races, countries, locales, and families would be expected to match the accumulated karma. The setting of each home and ambience of prospective parents would be important factors to consider for continued learning. Purification of the soul-mind might warrant the reward of an affluent family attributed to "Lady Luck," or it might warrant greater trials by undergoing the hardships of a poor family. After the environs, family and body are chosen; prospective horoscopes would provide the principal information for further decision-making. For tentatively picked parents, there would usually be a few weeks at most of possible birth times and potential patterns of life to review following conception. The quantity of prospects for each birth day could be fairly large, but not infinite. Every horoscope would have its own merits and liabilities. It might be possible for the soul to grade horoscopes on their compatibility with karmic objectives. A choice would most likely be an optimization of all factors for advancement. Those factors would establish the proper continuity and karmic channels for renewing opportunities to proceed along a preferred spiritual path. The horoscope for that time would fit the soul's desires for making progress in another life experience. Such a choice would be a very serious matter, because it would establish one more time-consuming step in the journey back to God. It would also be a most complex choice, because life on earth is not simple. All vibrations, colors, relationships, and planetary patterns would have to fit. They would also have to fit the plans of other soul-minds who are incarnating in groups.

> Hence the entity passes along those stages that some have seen as planes, some have seen as steps, some have seen as cycles, and some have experienced as places.
>
> 5755-001

If the concepts envisioned are correct, then a natal horoscope establishes a foundation for the life and body of a newborn human being that was picked by the soul, providing a motif for working off karma. Its choice consists of an intricate fatalistic plan to reestablish a cycle on earth. The soul has previously traveled, making karmic advancements and retreats. Mistakes must be worked off. Gains may be carried forward and amplified. The soul carries these prior positive and negative experiences with it into the new body that are typically forgotten by the conscious mind in its period of redevelopment.

> Ye may ask—rightly—WHY such urges are in the experience so definitely as is being indicated. Because, as given, of a one cycle. For, remember,—death in the material plane is birth in the spiritual-mental plane. Birth in the material plane is death in the spiritual-mental plane.
> Hence the reason that when those physical manifestations began to be impressed upon the brain centers—those portions of an individual entity that are a constant growth from first conception—there were the impressions to hinder rather than aid the memory of other experiences.
>
> 2390-002

Birth and death mark entries into the material and spiritual-mental planes. They alternate back and forth. Edgar Cayce said that the accumulated experiences from conception were combined with impressions to hinder, rather than aid, the memory of such experiences. Whether this statement applied only to the individual for whom the reading was given or to everyone was not made clear. A tentative conclusion from this and other readings indicates that hindrance of memory about prior sojourns applies to everyone. Yet the levels of submerged influence from unremembered experiences are a matter of strong interest.

In interpreting the application made by the entity in varied appearances, and the influence the same bears upon the abilities, the faults and the virtues of the entity in the present, it may be well for this entity that there be an interpretation of just how much experiences have an influence in the present.

This may be comparable to the experience of an entity as it undertakes its studies, its lessons in school. Not that there is in every day life the remembering of daily experiences in school, yet these daily experiences create the background with which the entity, in its daily contacts with problems, reviews in memory the problems that were part of the experience during such days of which commonly called education, or unfoldment.

Just so in the daily experiences of an individual entity through the various lessons learned, gained or lost in the earthly experiences, it builds a background to which the entity-mind responds as it applies itself in meeting the daily problems which arise.

One may ask, as this entity, "Why, then, does one not recall more often those experiences?"

The same may be asked of why there is not the remembering of the time when two and two to the entity became four, or when C-A-T spelled cat. It always did! Ye only became aware of same as it became necessary for its practical application in your experience!

So with the application of self's experience in material sojourns. When the necessity arises, the awareness as to how, where and in what direction those opportunities were applied, the entity brings those influences to bear in its relationships to daily problems.

2301-004

The horoscope records areas of life where previous aptitudes and skills can be reacquired with comparative ease. Consider child prodigies who adapt so quickly to the rigors of their art. Indicators of their abilities are always present, although the levels of prior achievements may be uncertain. Closeness of pertinent aspects do show magnitudes of interest, and that may be indicative of prior capabilities. However, we can have confidence that horoscopes portray a continuation model for making more decisions and gaining new experiences in those identified areas. The soul might be able to choose either a pathway that is a resumption of a prior life experience or a redirection to face different karmic decisions from further back that require repayment in kind. In any case, the natal aspects of a horoscope indicate both a morphology and a general pattern for living. The signs, planets, vibrations, colors, endocrine glands, memories, aspect closeness, velocities of motion, magnetic influences, and senses must be integrated and synchronized—always seeking a balance. Yet in real life after birth, karma may be misinterpreted.

Q-15. Is my present development on the road to fulfilling my karma?

A-15. MOST individuals in the present misinterpret karmic conditions. The development or destiny as karmic influences—each soul, each entity, should gain the proper concept of destiny. Destiny is within, or is as of faith, or is as the gift of the Creative Forces. Karmic influence is, then, rebellious influence against such. When opportunities are presented, it is the entity's own WILL force that must be exercised—that which has separated it or has made it equal to the creative influences in the higher spiritual forces to make for itself that advancement. Then in EVERY contact is there the opportunity for an entity, a soul, to fulfil or meet in itself or its soul self's association with the Creative Forces from the First Cause, to embrace that necessary for the entity to enter into the at-oneness with that Creative Force. Hence as for the entity's fulfilling, it is EVER on the road. As indicated, during the next three years, during the astrological and the coordinant influences through the earthly experience, the greater opportunity for fulfilling same is before the entity, [903] called in the present.

903-023

If used correctly and with the proper objectives in mind, talents can aid in overcoming bad karma. They may be discerned from the placement of planets in horoscopes and those particular areas where occupations of a particular type will be facilitated. These categories are broad in scope, and the individual may gravitate toward any number of pigeonholes within a given grouping. For example, if theatrics are indicated, the individual can be a stagehand, an usher, a writer of plays, a director, a controller of curtains and lights, a sound maker, a musician, a singer, a backer, an artist in charge of costumes or set design, an actor or actress. Many opportunities are thereby provided for taking opposite sides in karmic retribution scenarios. If one were an oppressor in a previous life, then it is possible to become one of the oppressed in a similar arena. If one were a benign benefactor in a previous life, then it is possible to gain by becoming a better benefactor in the same field. By this means, both indemnification and advancement can be realized. The horoscope simply shows what modes were established by the soul. The development within those modes is a function of exercised willpower using the talents acquired and hereditary influences.

5. In those experiences, then, as come from the influences of the astrological experience of life, as to how the individual APPLIES these IN their experience makes for that as must be called TRUE environ of the entity. As for that which HAS been done in earth, or in OTHER experiences in the earth, may be called true heredity. In that which is to be met through experiences in the earth, and that which brings about the changes in the application of that known and felt and UNDERSTOOD in the experience of an entity in the present as karma, as cosmic influence, as the moving of the spirit forces in an individual's application of its knowledge and understanding of things and conditions—these also are as the use that the entity has made, does make, of ITS ideal. Not ideas, not wishes, not JUST desires—for of the ABUNDANCE of the heart the mouth speaketh! of the DESIRES of the soul is effort made! The flesh is often weak, the spirit is EVER willing! Is the ideal set [If the ideal is set]

451-002

Nowhere else have true environ and true heredity been better explained. Karmic feelings, as cosmic influences, apply to ideals "in that which is to be met through experiences on earth." Progressed aspects show the nature of those experiences to be encountered. They indicate the kinds of forces that will be present and when they will occur. Each planet entering into a progressed aspect has distinctive characteristics. Mars, for example, is masculine and forceful. Venus is feminine and fond of beauty. Mercury travels and communicates. The Sun represents the ego and the constitutional foundation. Jupiter is expansive and shows growth potentials for better or worse. Saturn, by the opposite token, restrains and shows where care and caution need to be applied. Uranus introduces advanced technology and modern thinking. Neptune provides illusions and drama. Pluto efficiently accesses and applies available resources. These latter three planets, especially, cause life to be other than humdrum in a modern age. However, only the simplest of descriptions have been given. Every planet has more intricate characteristics with many variations, complexities, and gradations.

The signs occupied by the planets embellish the planetary forms of energy with additional attributes. For example, Aries adds drive, extra push, and a pioneering spirit. Taurus contributes determination, endurance, and practicality. Gemini sees the big picture and has the ability to communicate major features and conditions that should be disseminated. Cancer feels in control, is family centered, and proceeds in a manner that avoids confrontations. Leo automatically becomes the center of attention and is magnanimous toward others. Virgo focuses upon details and perfection. Libra tends toward sophistication, good appearance, and balance seeking. Scorpio provides ardent intensity and use of assets, always holding something back in reserve. Sagittarius rejects data overloads and gets directly to the nugget of every matter by asking and telling. Capricorn relies upon proven approaches and always seeks advancement. Aquarius takes advantage of reality, as opposed to suppositions, while deciphering the foibles of mankind. Pisces contributes perspicuity, artistic feelings, and awareness of every condition present. Each sign flavors and tones the distinctive energies of the planets.

24. The entity gained through the activity, aiding in the temple service. When there were the various positions set in the Temple of Sacrifice, the entity was among the few that went through the whole course—or that occupied what today would be termed the seat of learning in the various twelve houses

through which it was learned that the sun passed, that might apply to the individual in the material world.

3474-001

The houses (or domains) focus channeled energies into twelve segments of life. Going through the whole course means occupying a seat of learning in each one of them. The first house confines activities wholly to self in the present tense. The second house restricts forces to that which is owned, physically and mentally, for future use. The third house establishes a setting of the immediate environment for local activities, doing things and studying. These events take advantage of what was generated in the past. The scope of the fourth house is personal status and life-shaping influences. It includes one's upbringing, the home, and a close parent. The fifth house guides energies into personal creativity, procreation of children, fun, and speculation. The sixth house utilizes skills and learning for personal accomplishments. The seventh house focuses upon relationships, including business and marriage partners. The eighth house is the opposite of the second, and pertains to the assets of others, including insurance, stocks, bonds, accounting practices. The ninth house establishes boundaries for learning or teaching in educational institutions, applying laws, conducting affairs in foreign countries, traveling, or imparting what one has remembered from these experiences to others through speaking, singing, or writing. The tenth house concerns all matters affecting reputation in a world at large—one's caste, position, rulership, or management of others. Conversely, it shows one's boss or a parent. The eleventh house pertains to friendships, planning for clients, and projections into the future. Such projections can include joy to the public and amusements. The twelfth house represents those real accomplishments that contribute benefits to mankind or leave something worthwhile to posterity. It can also show society's impact upon the self. Houses one through six are the exact opposites of houses seven through twelve. A duality of this kind exists throughout all of astrology. Additionally, the pattern within house triplicities of present tense, future tense, and past tense repeat four times around the circle. One should be aware that every possible event related to an individual fits into one or the other of these twelve categories. Nothing is left out. There is a location for all mental, physical, and spiritual components of life within this framework. Every one of them applies to karma.

Q-32. Will I be able to choose my next country and environment, or does the law of karma place me where I can do best?

A-32. Law of karma and the purposefulness of how well ye serve in the present, how well ye may choose, for it is a choice as well as karmic reactions.

5265-001

The specific aspect between any two planets or nodes establishes either a perturbing or harmonious condition together with a strength and further colorings. Aspects can be thought of as controlled vibrations in the same way that strings of a musical instrument make sounds at set frequencies. Musical instruments also emit overtones and have timbre. So do the aspects for each individual. Progressed aspects add temporal energy. What they decidedly do not do is show exact events that will occur, although a good psychic can often see beyond vibrations. A short reading on aspects by Edgar Cayce is most appropriate:

Each planetary influence vibrates at a different rate of vibration. An entity entering that influence enters that vibration; [it is] not necessary that he change, but it is the grace of God that he may! It is part of the universal consciousness, the universal law.

281-055

The normally used aspects in celestial longitude are angles from a 360° circle that are evenly divisible by integers up to twelve, plus multiples of some of these numbers. The aspect angles formed by even integers are the most intense and perturbing, because they are constantly reinforced by vibratory subharmonics. The aspect angles and vibrations formed by odd integers are easier to take and are generally regarded as being more harmonious or comforting.

We can divide the circle by 2, 3, 4, 5, 6, 8, and 12 to obtain aspect angles of 180°, 120°, 90°, 72°, 60°, 45°, and 30°. Divisions by 7 and 11 do not result in whole number angles. Thus, they drift away from fixed rates of vibration. Division by the integers 9 and 10 are normally omitted by astrologers, because the intensities of their derived aspect angles are considered to be too low. Their reinforcing subharmonics are also weak, but they do exist. Combinations of smaller aspect angles form two others that have been observed to be sufficiently strong. They are 135° (3 × 45°) and 150° (5 × 30°). In both cases relatively strong subharmonics provide the reinforcements. A 15° angle (for the dividing integer 24) is sometimes included, because that angle is a subharmonic for six of the main aspects. Moreover, some astrologers correctly use 105° (7 × 15°) and 165° (11 × 15°).

In addition to these aspects in longitude, there are the parallels and contraparallels of declination. This is when two or more planets are in the same declination angle north or south of the equator. As the earth turns on its axis, a line fixed at the declination angle would describe an imaginary cone that intercepts both planets. The two points of interception would then describe parallel circular planes. That is the reason why these aspects are known as parallels. If we consider that the earth is a rotating electromagnetic mass, then sinusoidal vibrations can be imposed on humans via the surface of the cone. That is the basis for forces in declination.

There is a rough correspondence between celestial parallels of declination and the earths's geocentric latitudes, but they are not alike because our earth is not perfectly round. All astrological aspects have a circular basis in space.

Planets in declination do not swing far beyond the obliquity of the ecliptic (the angle formed between the earth's equatorial plane and the ecliptic plane traversed by the planets). Hence, declinations fall within a band from about 26° South to 26° North with infrequent excursions beyond by such close and energetic planets as Mars.

Thus, when two or more planets are in the same declination angle to the north of the equator, their planes parallel the equator to the Northern side. Northern parallels affect people in an outgoing manner. When two or more planets are in same declination angle to the south of the equator, their planes parallel the equator on the Southern side. Southern parallels affect people in an incoming or personal manner. When two or more planets are in equal declination angles to the north and south of the equator, they are contraparallel each other. Their parallel planes are above and below the equator. Both the individual and other people are affected by contraparallels. The Ascendant and Midheaven have associated vectors equivalent to planets. Thus, they have parallels of declination in the same way.

2. In entering from the astrological aspects, or from the numerological aspects, we find these somewhat confusing—were a parallel drawn, or an application made of that which might be drawn from such purely astrological or numerological

charts. Yet these forces and influences have much, or will have much to do in the experience of the entity during the present sojourn. The more the entity would comprehend the same, the more they may be used as steppingstones in the application of self in its own entity and soul development.

3. In an experience in the earth's plane each soul should gain the knowledge of those forces, conditions or experiences that may influence an entity, a soul, the more. And not only have the knowledge or understanding of such influence but know that the influences are as guides, signposts, conditions. And the use of them may enable a soul to develop the more. For, what a body-mind, a soul-mind does about or with the knowledge or understanding that it has makes development for that soul. For, some beautiful comparisons may be drawn from the entity's own experiences in the earth. For, while the entity was an associate or a brother of Solomon in an experience, what one did with his knowledge and understanding and what the other did with his understanding made for quite a difference in each one's position in that experience and the sojourns of each soul in other experiences.

4. From the astrological aspects we find these as urges rather than impelling, but the inclinations and influences are constantly arising in the experience of the entity; and as to what the entity may do with such urges remains within the ken or realm of the entity to make or to mar its own soul development:
476-001

Even though Edgar Cayce did not specifically address parallels of declination, they have been found to be very strong and very important. A majority of today's astrologers ignore them. Their typical response is, "We get along without the declinations." Neither this statement nor any others offered so far constitutes a valid reason. Hence, the situation is a curiosity—consider that astrologers are constantly wondering why certain events fail to be shown to them by their astrological tools, so they are forever seeking something new to fill these gaps. Something old could do the job, but they usually do not look. It is as though their comprehension cannot go beyond the horoscope wheel that can be pictured as a glyph. Houses, cusps, and planets are shown in degrees of celestial longitude by this wheel, but not the declinations. That means the effects of declinations in houses can be perceived only by translation of planets and major angles into the longitudinal positions of the same elements within the wheel. Need for such translations appear to have created mental blocks. However, records of verified, soul-selected horoscopes show at least 20 percent could not be confirmed without the parallels of declination.

In total, combining both the aspects in longitude and aspects in declination, we have fifteen or more that dispense different qualities of vibrations. These vibrations vary from weak to strong with grades in between. Some reinforce and some just sustain themselves. Overtones are unique, and every angle has its own characteristics. These energy bundles coincide with challenges, conflicts, chances, gains, losses, births, confrontations, meetings, start-ups, new ideas, the laying of cornerstones, and every other known form of event. They superimpose subconscious memories of planetary sojourns.

10. For as there is indicated, it is the MOVEMENT of spirit upon things that do not appear that has brought into being the things that DO appear; not of things that do appear.

11. Thus man's influence upon such or from such is because—as there are the cycles of influence, in the activity through the relationships of what ye call planetary forces or the vibrations about the earth—there are periods when the influence is felt because of the very activity of the entity in that environment, or action, or force.

12. Hence as we find, these become then as intuitive influences; or the higher force of the mental self with which the entity may find contact or be in relationship with by the deep meditative forces.

13. But the influences from the sojourns in a material or physical environment make for the emotions that arise.

14. These may at times be parallel or be in sympathy, dependent upon the activity or the choice made by the soul-entity through the will—that which makes each soul aware of its being at-one with the Creative Forces or God, or of directing for SELF in its activities.

1486-001

Thus, enormous complexities are present for each karmic scenario. Two out of 12 planets and nodes that can be involved in every aspect have 65 possible combinations. Each of the two planets can be in 12 signs—although not necessarily at the same time. Each can be in 12 houses with similar restraints. There are at least 15 recognized angular aspects, although the inner planets (between the Sun and earth) cannot enter into all of them. Then, more than one aspect is normally present for a single event, and so the possible combinations increase again with many nuances. Life is indeed a labyrinthine blend of many factors, and there are many directions available for each of us to take. In fact, there are hundreds of thousands of them obtained by multiplying the above numbers. Thus, each option of a horoscope time provides an enormous number of avenues for a soul's continued development. Not only is the quantity large, but the compositions or makeups of these aspects are large. Hence, sundry bundles of energies orchestrate their temporal availability for everyone. Every set of urges at every signpost is strikingly suitable for providing personalized urges of karmic intent.

The majestic attunement of an earthly reincarnation with this elaborate array of known properties of horoscopes and their progressed aspects is both bewildering and intricate, as indicated above. Yet each plan is imbued with underlying logic. The soul must see all of these heterogeneous mixes and blends of natal and progressed aspects and be able to make intelligent comparisons. The choices must be gradable in some fashion. The advantages and disadvantages would have to be known so that an optimum choice could be made. A vivid picture of what actually happens before, during, and after birth is building.

Yet with all of these combinations of forces at their disposal, some souls may take a long-range viewpoint. They may want to prioritize the order of karmic encounters or be forced to compromise through accidents. Those choices might not result in desired reactions. In addition, the soul in human form may not take full advantage of enervated urges. Opportunities are then lost. People in this latter group might respond less to astrological laws than to other influences or relationships. Karma may then be suppressed or deferred while other laws may be emphasized.

11. While the astrological influences are apparent, we find that these do not in this particular case run true to the ordinarily termed astrological effects; varying because of the application the entity has made in those relationships. Just as that influence termed by some students as karma. This is the natural law, yes.

But there IS the law of grace, of mercy. And this is JUST as applicable as the law of karma, dependent upon the stress or the emphasis put upon varied things.

2727-001

Even when other laws are emphasized by an individual, positions of the planets and stored memories provide what is known to do. So it is that the workings of karma come about sooner or later in many different ways and through many different orientations of the mind. All karmic meetings are personalized, and all prior transgressions must be met. Opportunities can be passed, ignored, feared, or turned into actions. If avoided, they will with virtual certainty return at a later date.

Q-50. What karma do I have to overcome in order to free myself mentally and spiritually?
A-50. KARMA is rather the lack of living to that KNOWN to do! As ye would be forgiven, so forgive in others. THAT is the manner to meet karma.

2271-001

Q-34. Why does she have such a fear of falling?
A-34. This is part of its karma—for it made many others fall far!

3057-001

Reversals of roles accompany many of the karmic situations. "Doing for others as you would have them do unto you" is the modus operandi of these reversals. Every irresponsible act of a past incarnation is represented in the present one. This is another form of fate from which there is no escape. One might wonder, as many have, about behavioral changes that might take place from karmic knowledge being given to us through Edgar Cayce's readings.

Q-15. Explain what is meant by the transformation taking place or to take place in connection with the work of Edgar Cayce?
A-15. In an explanation, let's all understand in their own speech. To some, an awakening to the greater channels of power; to others, more spirituality THAN materiality. To others, the karmic influences have reached THEIR changing point, that

the vibrations may be brought one to another. In transformation
comes a light for those that LOOK for same.

262-007

If one looks for karmic influences that have reached their
changing points, "the vibrations may be brought one to another." Perhaps a beginning has been made in our understanding. But a further wonderment about karma is the need for
planetary sojourns other than on earth.

8

PAST INCARNATIONS AND
PLANETARY SOJOURNS

EDGAR CAYCE POINTED out that urges in one's life are
derived from three sources—the astrological, prior incarnations,
and planetary sojourns. The latter two are not consciously derived from horoscopes by astrologers, although many clues can
be found therein.

We have learned that astrological urges are karmic in nature.
Astrologers may never have made a connection among karma,
past incarnations, or planetary sojourns while delineating horoscopes. They usually just try to make sense out of planetary
placements and angles formed in the horoscope wheel. When
transcending urges are given by astrologers to a client, they are
derived chiefly from interpretations of transits and their aspects.
Transits are the daily positions of planets in relation to natal
planets in the horoscope. They are excellent for timing, but errors in horoscope timing can cause misinterpretations of where
those powers are focused. A much smaller percentage of astrologers actually works with day-for-a-year progressions or
some other form of progressions—such as lunar. But, if a thorough job is to be done, all of the key astrological urges must be
properly calculated and interpreted.

Strengths ought to be prioritized, and the stronger ones really
should come first. Day-for-a-year progressions are far stronger
than transits, and they take precedence. So are prior incarna-

tions and planetary sojourns, according to Edgar Cayce. Thus, transit astrology, while valid, is comparatively weak. It is like the allegory of the three blind monkeys who describe an elephant. An elephant is like a long flexible tube, the trunk of a tree, and a narrow cord. But, of course! Still, there is a lot of truth in those descriptions.

> 2. In entering the earth's experience in the present from the astrological viewpoint, we find the sojourns of the entity in the planetary influences with those of earth's experience influencing the present innate and manifested abilities of the entity; rather than mere position of the planets, or houses, or the varied astrological aspects.
>
> 317-004

If either the astrologer or the entity are to account for these stronger urges from previous sojourns, they must know how to distinguish them. They need to know why planetary sojourns occur in the first place and how to cope with them. What is special about them? What causes a soul to have a planetary sojourn that must differ in some way from a simple reincarnation? Do they arrive in a different manner or from a different direction? Do they retain their planetary imagery?

Then there are more soul-wrenching questions. Are planetary sojourns the real heaven and hell? Is heaven a comparatively pleasant sojourn while the soul learns added useful things? Is hell a comparatively unpleasant banishment for officious acts on earth? Are planets in our solar system the actual locations of heaven and hell? We will want to extract answers from the readings. In answering a question about hell, fire, and brimstone, Edgar Cayce said:

> Q-25. Will we be punished by fire and brimstone?
> A-25. That as builded by self; as those emblematical influences are shown through the experiences of the beloved in that builded, that created. For, each soul is a portion of creation— and builds that in a portion of its experience that it, through its physical-mental or spiritual-mental, has builded for itself. And each entity's heaven or hell must, through SOME experience, be that which it has builded for itself. Is thy hell one that is filled with fire or brimstone? But know, each and every soul is tried so as by fire; purified, purged; for He, though He were

the Son, learned obedience through the things which He suffered. Ye also are known even as ye do, and have done.

Q-26. Is this the period of the great tribulation spoken of in
Revelation or just the beginning, and if so just how can we
help ourselves and others to walk more closely with God?
A-26. The great tribulation and periods of tribulation, as
given, are the experiences of every soul, every entity. They
arise from influences created by man through activity in the
sphere of any sojourn. . . .

281-016

Fire and brimstone are emblematic. He said that the tribulations (of hell) are created "through activity in the sphere of any
sojourn." From what was said before, these tribulations must be
suffered in the sojourns to come. They are in the consciousness
of the spirit.

Q-20. What form of consciousness does the spirit entity assume?
A-20. That of the subconscious consciousness, as known in
the material plane, or the acts and deeds, and thoughts, done
in the body, are ever present before that being. Then consider
what a hell digged by some, and what a haven and heaven
builded by many.

5756-004

A long reading has been copied below in order to understand
more about these questions and their answers. It addresses the
part about coping and reasons for taking sojourns in the first
place. Heaven and hell are not specifically referred to, but the
explanations given increase our understanding. We will learn
more by practical application.

2. In entering the present experience, and in giving that
which has been recorded by and through the activities of the
entity in the earth plane, and in those realms in which there
arise and fall or come and go the experiences of the entity as
an entity or soul, we find:

3. It is well that something be given as to the causes of the
records, or as to the houses of records, that the entity may use

in a practical application those experiences to aid in making the present experience the more worth while.

4. For, as a conclusion may be drawn from that in the material plane, the knowledge of any subject, condition, or knowledge of any nature unless put into practical use becomes of little effect in producing in the experience of an individual any activity worth while.

5. The activities from the astrological standpoint, then, are used as a basis; for the experience of the soul-entity in its activity is continuous. Hence the greater influence, or among the greater influences in the experience of ANY entity, is an indication of the threefold life—or three-fold motivating influence. For there is the material expression (which is of the physical or the earth earthy); there is the mental body, phase or experience of an entity (which partakes of or is an enfoldment or unfoldment of the experiences of the entity in the realms ABOUT the earth—or of which the earth is a portion); and the indwellings of an entity in the interim of its earthly or physical manifestations produce certain activities that make an entity, body or unit act as it does through any given earthly experience. Then, these are of that called the MENTAL consciousness of an entity or soul. What have been the motivative forces in the activities of an entity through any given experience, then, or any period of manifestations in these various spheres, may be used as a criterion as to the expressions that may be expected of the entity; as to its reactions, abilities, shortcomings, developments, when SOME or A particular criterion or standard is used.

6. What then (may be very well asked) is the standard or ideal from which a line may be drawn in such information or for an entity in its development?

7. That which has been set in Him throughout the ages of this expression of the love of the Creative Force for His creatures.

8. For man and woman in their manifestations are given—by the All-Wise, All-Merciful Father, the First Cause, the Mother-God, the Father-God—the opportunity to be one with Him. Hence they are given the attributes of the various phases through which the entity or soul may become conscious or

aware of that Presence abiding with or withdrawing from its activities; dependent, to be sure, upon how that entity or soul uses the opportunities.

9. For without the gift of free will to the soul, how COULD it become aware of the Presence of the All-Abiding Creative Force or Energy called God?

10. Then, as this relates to this individual entity, now called [945], we find the entity born in the present under and in those environs from the astrological aspect of Mercury, Venus, Jupiter, Mars, Saturn.

11. What meaneth this? That during the interims from the earthly sojourns or experiences the soul has been in the environs that have been given the names of the various planets about or within the solar system of which the earth is a part. Thus the planets have their influence as to the various attributes of that we find expressed or manifested in the earth's environs as what we term as carnal or earthly or three-dimensional forms of awareness.

12. But what is termed the dimensional environ of the mental capacities expressed by Mercury enables an entity or soul in the earth's environs to give a manifestation of high mental abilities, high mental capacities. Thus we may observe that such an one is enabled to obtain what we call knowledge, as pertaining to mental faculties, much more easily than those whose environs or indwellings previous to the earthly manifestation at present have possibly been in Saturn, Mars, Venus, Uranus, Pluto or the Moon. But what meaneth these? That these abilities are such as termed good or bad. These EXIST as conditions. And it is what a soul or entity does ABOUT such conditions, or what it uses as its standard of judgement, that produces what is called in man's environment Cause and Effect. The same may be said of each of the other spheres or experiences or phases of the indwellings of the entity; in Venus, Mercury, Mars, Jupiter, or all such that have been the experience of the entity, producing those elements within the MENTAL which is of the body or entity a part.

13. Then, for this entity, we find:

14. Mercury makes for the high mental abilities.

15. Venus makes for the emotional side of the body or entity in the present, that becomes at times rather lacking but at others makes for the great motivating influences and forces in the experience of the entity; that it holds as a duty to self, as a duty to its relationships in its various spheres of activity in a material world. For its environs and activities from this association in Venus have made for not sentimentality, but sentiment is a portion; yet as Mercury is the ruling influence this is done from reasoning rather than from sentiment alone. Yet it makes for those experiences in the present within the entity that have at times brought about the appearance or the feeling of a definite loneliness within the entity; the lack of a friend sufficiently close, a companionship sufficiently close to rely wholly upon.

16. Those are as longings that are being sought within the entity's experience. But as we find, as Jupiter has within the last few months become rather the ruling influence in its sojourners within its environs, as Venus and Mercury and Jupiter are brought more and more into the expression of activity within the experiences of those who have indwelled there, it will bring for this individual entity—in this year or in the next year—a union with such a soul in which the HOME (that is so longed for at times) may be established by the entity. And one whose birthday and associations are near the same year as self's—that is, in 1907–6–5, whose birthday is in the latter portion of June of between that and the 20th to 26th of July—will make for the better companionship with the entity in its experiences.

17. We find also Saturn having been an influence that has made for experiences within the entity's activities in the present in which it has continued to long for changes in its associations. This has caused the entity at times to find itself dreaming; having day dreams, as it were, by longings for that building up as to itself an ideal relationship or condition that would be—as the entity has visualized—the greater activity in which it might engage itself; either for the satisfying of the material desires or to create the character of environment in which the mental and soul forces might find the greater expression. More often have these considered rather the MATERIAL things. But as these changes have gradually passed, more and more does

there come now in the experience that as sought from the mental and the spiritual expression rather than from the purely material.

18. For the earth and Saturn are opposites, as it were; for to Saturn go those that would renew or begin again, or who have blotted from their experience much that may be set in motion again through other influences and environs that have been a portion of the entity's experience.

19. In Mars we find there have been periods and experiences when anger, wrath and sudden conditions or certain things in others about the entity have caused changes, or made great changes in what may have been the experience of the entity. These have been rather from without than from within the entity's own associations and environs, but have dealt their influence in the experience of the entity. And these have come within the entity's experience rather as fears that such might arise in the entity's OWN experience; coming again to the reasoning, as it were, from its close Mercurian influence in its own experience in the present.

20. These, then, are the astrological aspects as we find them from the MENTAL experience that lies INNATE and give expressions in the manner as we have indicated.

945-001

The necessity for planetary sojourns must be because of decisions made here on earth. Some of those decisions ought to be counterbalanced. The chances for wrongful decision-making are fairly high, and too many missteps might overwhelm an ordinary reincarnation. When an important but incorrect decision is made, it must be like a thorn to a soul that has to be extracted. A decision must be rectified so badly that a special sojourn is required. This kind of cleansing sojourn might have a higher priority in the mind of the soul than an ordinary reincarnation.

This entity, we find, took its flight, or position, from the planet of Uranus, with Venus and Mercury controlling the destiny in the present earth's plane. Hence the necessity of the entity's training, especially, in those elements having to do with purity in love and affection, and of nobleness and of goodness for the goodness that comes with that mode of expressing itself in earth's plane, for with the entity under these influences, with the exceptional conditions as come from influences of Uranus, we find the entity's manifestations in the present plane will be exceptionally good or very bad.

143-001

Life is not simple here on earth, nor should it be. Life needs to be interesting, even when the chances are that manifestations will be exceptionally good or bad. Requirements for choosing a course of action on earth are amplified by decisions made in prior incarnations and prior planetary sojourns. Hence, the training of the soul takes many paths.

Confounding decisions made along the way continue to be hidden from view when a new life begins. Any compensation or additional action during the planetary sojourns are also hidden. Cases have been recorded of a few young children who recall remnants of prior lives.[7] However, most of them do not, and sojourns are evidently included in this forgetfulness. The conscious mental slate is cleaned, so to speak. Perhaps this is to provide a fresh start in such a way that life is unencumbered by memories of prior tragedies, fixations, dramatic mistakes, or decisions that need to be corrected or other consequences of judgment best forgotten for the time being. Not remembering the prior life permits a new unfettered outlook for choosing courses of action while the retributive aspects of karma unravel. Yet continuity is also allowed—if not ordained. Recollections of prior life events are apparently buried deep in the unconscious mind. The unconscious mind is assigned to the Moon and the pituitary gland. Under hypnosis these recollections may be recovered—if there is value in doing so.

The astrological aspects, as well as the influences from the sojourns in the earth, are only as signs, omens; producing urges, yes—latent and manifested in a different form.

Astrological influences—from planetary sojourns between the earthly interims of sojourn—are to the mental or innate self, or the deeper visions or dreams, or to that which may be reached the greater through the deeper meditation.

[7] Perhaps the most notable and often-quoted example is *Twenty Cases Suggestive of Reincarnation* by Ian Stevenson, M.D., University Press of Virginia, Charlottesville, Virginia, 1974.

But the influences from material earthly sojourns come as urges from the emotional forces of an entity.

While the entity is emotional, in the deeper sense, we do not find the material urges surpassing the astrological.

These then are urges, and it is the will, the choice that an entity makes regarding its ideal and its spiritual relationships, that governs whether the application of self is toward soul development or only the gratifying of material gains.

1470-001

We may get to more causes of planetary sojourns through the manner in which they are felt. The previous passage instructs that influences from planetary sojourns may be reached through deeper meditation while influences from astrological aspects and earthly interims are only as signs and omens manifested in a different form. These urges or impulses from planetary sojourns are astrological in nature, because every planet maintains its characteristics wherever the soul might be. In a different reading Edgar Cayce described these influences for another individual at some length:

EC: Yes, we have the entity and those relations with the universe and universal forces, that are latent and manifested in the personalities of the present entity. [264]

In entering, under the astrological influences we find the Moon and the Sun—as well as planetary sojourns—affecting the physical as well as the mental and soul being.

These are one when viewed or considered in this material plane, yet—when analyzed (that we may better understand or comprehend)—may well be compared to a formula that may act upon the physical attributes of a body. Alone there may be an influence, an activity, but combined there may be wielded a greater influence upon all phases of the experience of the entity.

Hence we find these influences often misconstrued by those who do not take into consideration the will of an entity, the tenets that may be the impelling influence in the mental being, or that influence which is exerted upon an entity from without itself as it is allowed (or allows self) to be led or guided by such impulses.

With this particular body (in the present), and those influences that are manifested in the material, mental and spiritual affairs of the entity, there is offered an unusual illustration of these truths that have been presented here.

So, in the study, analysis and understanding that may be given or gained from that which is presented, know that this is being given from the actual records that have been written by the activities of the entity through its sojourn in that which may be justly termed reality; a separate entity from the first cause or impulse. And the varied experiences are in the form of matter, mind and spirit; for, as given, the separations must be considered if there would be the more perfect understanding.

As it has been often presented by one school of thought, the dwellers upon the Moon (the satellite of the earth) preceded the abilities for matter (expressed in a form that is known as matter in the earth). And this entity was among those that so dwelt, and is influenced by two sojourns there.

Hence there have ever been in the experience of the entity periods that are governed by the influence of not only the satellites drawing upon the earth and the elements of same but of the mental, in such a manner as to make for physical as well as mental and material changes in the affairs of the entity; when the mental being of the entity allows the influence to dominate rather than dominating the influence.

Also as a sojourner in the environ elemental as well as material, the Sun's activity on the mental has wielded and does wield a powerful influence in the affairs, the activities, the thoughts of the entity. As may be illustrated:

On dark days with little sunshine there is an appreciable manifestation of fear and dread. And especially does this occur when the Moon by its position is on the opposite side of the orb of earth.

As to this influence also, if the entity uses the will in reference to such influences in a spiritual sense, much alteration arises.

Naturally, the question would be: How, when, in what manner, may an entity use such influence as to make for a betterment of those that tend to bring an air or a feeling of oppression upon the mental being?

Realizing, then, that there is an influence from without self of a nature that self may be in accord with or in opposition to; for all entities realize they in themselves are both positive and negative influences, and the first cause or the spirit—must of necessity within itself be likewise, yet more positive than negative, for it attracts with attraction and repels with rebellion of that same activity of which every entity is a part. [See 264-45,

Par. 15-A, 16-A, in re her aversion to flowers and animals.]

Hence the realizing of self's dependence upon that influence is that which makes for the change in the experience of the entity, in becoming conscious—through the mental-spiritual forces in self—of the willingness to be led rather than leading or demanding other than, "Thy will be done in me, use me in that channel Thou, O God, would have me be led."

As to the influences then from the astrological sojourn, these become for an entity (as we have given) as the hereditary influences of the mental being—or impulses; while the material sojourns become as the environmental influences in the mental being.

This entity (as we have given) is swayed more by those two greater lights in the experience, both as to hereditary and environmental, from the astrological viewpoint, than most individuals. Why? Because of that influence which has just been given!

Hence there is an appreciable influence in the ability of the mental body to become analytical in its every aspect, towards every character of influence in an individual's experience, rather than mystical or that which may be termed as rote or formula. For, in its essence, the entity's being is analytical in itself!

From the astrological and planetary sojourn, then, we find as these (For this dissertation might be carried on into infinitum, as to the planetary influences related to the earth and the earth's sojourns of the entity; yet within the earth and the dealings with the material things is there that which the entity has to cope with in the NOW. Yet NOW is the beginning and end!): Mercury, Venus, Jupiter, Uranus; these influencing from the very environ of that which is manifested in their atmosphere (if such a term may be used); for Mercury means mental, as does Venus love, understanding, beauty and the like, as does Jupiter strength, stamen, broadness of vision, temperamental; and these all are from those experiences of the entity in its sojourn through these environs.

One then (from the material plane we are judging) mentally well equipped, yet often called by many one that must be at periods "half cracked" or having very poor judgement; at other periods it is seen, from the activities in the mental, that the entity is one with the abilities to READ people's thoughts, as it were, obtain impressions that are the impelling influences. Yet these judgements at times are rather impulsive than reasoned out.

From Venus' influence the entity is one that is sympathetic, loving, patient, with the abilities of showing kindnesses in unusual ways and manners.

While in Jupiter and from its influence the entity is one that is impatient at times for the greater things in the material manifestations to happen, and with the desire to push or make, or force, or drive, or impel, or induce by some unseen force those things to come about. Lack of patience, which bespeaks of an opposite influence from that just spoken of in the universal influences in Venus.

With Uranus making for those impetuous influences, as indicated from both Moon and Sun as well as from the activities that the entity through its sojourn in the various astrological influences has builded—that bear upon, what? What the entity has done ABOUT its own self in relation to that about it, and allowed to be used as an influence of the more potent influence in the spiritual impulse or first cause! (This applies to every individual, to be sure, but—as given—it is more easily illustrated or demonstrated in the impetuous and impulsive forces or influences in the experience of this entity.)

As to the abilities that are made, in or through these influences, we find that there may be acquired—through the application of knowledge of self—faith, confidence, hope, kindliness, patience, endurance, persistence, consistence, such as to bring for the entity in the present the power, the ability, the wherewithal, to become one that may analyze problems for individuals; or, as may be termed from some circles, a mother confessor to whom those of any faith, cult, clime, may go for counsel; and counsel such as would be helpful to them in their immediate and their developing needs.

                                                                    264-031

Planetary sojourns for this person were as hereditary influences, while astrological were as environmental influences. The nature of the planets themselves were interpreted, and there were no surprises. The manner in which sojourns swayed judgments in certain situations were also given. They add up to a totality of abilities and directions for application.

In still another reading that starts much the same way, planetary sojourns were felt in another way. The implications are that the nature of the individual has a direct bearing on how planetary sojourns are perceived. Characteristics of the planets are again found to be the same as they are in normal astrology—whatever that is:

EC: Yes, we have the entity and those relations with the universe and universal forces, that are latent and manifested in the personalities of the present entity.

As to the activities in the experiences of the entity from the purely astrological entrance into the earth's place, these make for only inclinations; while those apparent from the sojourns of the entity in the various appearances in the earth—and from the mental influences or soul development in planetary sojourns—make for rather IMPULSE to the inclinations that may be manifested in the present experience of the entity.

Then, as to the planetary sojourns that make for the impulses:

The ruling influence we find in Mercury, making for abilities in the mental aspects, in the great visions that come with activities of the entity; with the dreamer, in those respects as related to material things, as related to the mental activities and to the soul development. Hence there are other astrological or planetary influences that are benevolent to even the mental abilities, for often mentality does not mean reason or rationality in a material activity. Hence we find a benevolent influence of Mercury aided by Venus and Jupiter in the application of the mental influence. Hence the vast scope of reading that has been in the experience of the entity; and the love influence that surpasses even that known as attraction or affection, being rather the impelling influence to make for not only mere tolerance but a LOVELY tolerance in the activities of the entity—for this becomes as BEAUTY in its reality. For the activity in the mental, in the love influence, in the Jupiter influence as to vision and scope, is a thing that IS as it SHOULD be in the developing of a soul in relationships to others.

These activities make for impulses; not only urges, as from the affluence of position of stars or various planetary positions, but those that make for abilities in the material forces in the present that are well within—as may be termed—the "rightings" of the self's development, within the spheres of activity that make for staid influences in the experience. Hence they become as these, in personality:

One pleasing; one affable; one congenial; one tolerant; one that is altogether a FRIEND even to the friendless, and making

for friendships that are something beyond mere acquaintance-
ships for reasons of material association.

443-001

This time influences from planetary sojourns were described
as being impulses. Previously, they required deep meditation to
be felt, or they were sensed as moods. Three different ways of
recognizing the influences from planetary sojourns have been
described. Yet, in all cases, influences from astrological aspects,
reincarnations, and planetary sojourns are integrated. Each individual appears to have a personal sensory mechanism that receives the sojourn impressions in a distinctive manner. The
personal sensory mechanism of one individual is not the same
as for another. Considering these variations, astrologers would
have to be more psychic than ever to distinguish among them
and recognize the sources.

In entering the present experience, we find those influences
that may be termed purely astrological being rather secondary—even in impulses—to those from environs through earth's
experiences. Not that the sojourns on the planets have not had,
and do not have in the present, their influence; but these may
be termed rather as moods for this entity, save a few particular
conjunctions of planetary influences when these have had
more to do even then—with the material aspects (as may be
termed) than mental urges. As in 1889, 1898, 1909, 1917–18–
19. True, these periods had influences. In the first, rather as to
relationships with individuals. In the second, or '98, with things
AND with individuals; while in '09, rather the relationships
that were centralized (apparently) in efforts of the entity, yet
were influences more of the astrological nature if looked at in
the present; while those conditions in '17–18–19 dealt more
particularly with material affairs.

Then, as to those things that in the present experience have
to do with urges that make for moods, as may be said (this does
not indicate that the entity is one that may be called moody,
or one of such eccentric nature, yet these ARE as impulses):

One often called hardheaded in some respects, determined
in others; given to full expression of self, not as in a controversial manner so much, yet looked upon at times by associates
throughout the experience as rather one that might BECOME
controversial. Yet, withal, rather given to orderliness; that is
rather exceptional in entities or individuals born in April; rather

given to detail in associations with individuals and with groups, and about things or associations.

These are from impulses arising from sojourns in Mercury (as the ruling influence; hence high mental ability) and in Venus (which makes for a great deal of sentiment). These conditions, weighed with the impulses as given, necessarily make for the characteristics in the entity of being one that is pleasant to deal with, yet able to hold self's own and to carry the points that are set as the policy with or about self.

From planetary sojourns also, we find, there have been those periods in the activities of self in material associations—from Jupiter combined with Saturn—that have made for seemingly unsatisfactory relations, by the associations through certain periods; as in '28, '30, '31; yet these have brought to the entity in the present a period of mental expansion upon which a great deal more material successes (in associates and self) will be built in the next three years—or until the change.

378-012

These readings have been given in some detail, because much can be learned about the variety of influences from planetary sojourns as well as the planetary flavorings. Besides, people are interesting, and every nature has a unique story to tell. Each receives a library of information at birth through the choice of the soul. The information from planetary sojourns is most likely stored in the pituitary gland in the lunar memory bank. Access is not casual but comes forth while pondering one's thoughts or as sudden impulses or as moods.

So far, the causes of planetary sojourns may only be partly clear. They are certainly the result of our own doing. But to digress a moment, a question keeps recurring about the flight path of information from previous sojourns. It comes with the soul, of course. However, is this arrival of historical data from a planet upon which a sojourn was just completed any different from data of a prior earthly sojourn, and is it in compliance with physical laws? These questions may not be answerable, but new probes for more knowledge are intriguing.

Stored historical information must come in initially from outside the earth. If planetary sojourn data arrived directly from the planets, all paths would originate inside a narrow band just a little above or below the ecliptic plane. Only Pluto ventures up to eleven degrees or so from the ecliptic, and that is the furthest excursion of any planet in celestial latitude. The other planets do not wander as far. Because of the tilt of the earth's axis, the ecliptic plane is crossed twice per day by the Midheaven of any location on earth where births occur. One question is whether the planet upon which the soul had its sojourn could be in line with the Midheaven on that day of birth. The probabilities show that this alignment would be very unlikely. However, a soul could arrive at a sphere about the earth, as Edgar Cayce already told us, and maneuver to a zenith position above the prospective birthplace. Thus, it can be concluded that a soul with memory packets of planetary sojourns would be forced to alter course in order to enter a baby's body from overhead. Edgar Cayce settles that question in the reading below.

> In the relation to those of the planets that has, that is and that will influence this body, we find the strongest of these at the moment of the birth or when this soul and spirit took possession of this body for this earth plane. That of Venus and Neptune were the ruling forces for this body, with that of Mars in the 9th house, of Jupiter in the 12th house, of Uranus in the 7th house, see? Septimus almost at its zenith, yet not the ruling factor in this body's actions on this present plane, for with the position of Venus and Neptune this, the influence of Septimus, has become changed by the position of Pisces and the constellation of that of Castor and Apollo [Pollux?]. Hence, the influence that has come in this body becomes more of the ultra forces. For with the change of the position of the residence of the body, [GD's note—from Denmark to America] the environment with the will changed the conditions enacted; and under the same constellations and position of Venus, Neptune, Mars, Jupiter, Uranus coming under their various positions in relativity has made many and various changes in the life on this plane of this body, see? This has also given the various positions, or attitude, towards work for the body in its developing plane. That is, as soon as it has decided that one work was its life work another element would come of the other forces, by the change from other conditions into the life that has positions in life.

> 583-001

This review of astrological strengths shows how a sojourn on Uranus resulted in that planet being the strongest element of the horoscope. This particular individual had many sojourns, and all were evidently in contention for this strongest position.

Technically, souls can come directly to a spherical plane surrounding the earth. Evidently, they then travel north or south on the sphere until they reach the geocentric latitude of the prospective birth. Then they would most likely hover by maintaining a speed of angular rotation the same as the speed of the earth between roughly 78° South latitude and 78° North latitude. This is the zone of population where reincarnations can take place. While probably not impossible, births do not normally occur in the remaining 12° from each pole.

Thus, souls having undergone planetary sojourns can travel to a desired gathering place, sphere, or plane just outside the earth where the gravitational force of the earth is miniscule. When a choice of body to enter is made either before or after this positioning, the review of horoscope choices takes place. At the appointed moment, one soul with its memory packet comes in from above. A planet closest to the zenith has the greatest astrological influence (in either declination or longitude). However, that may or may not be the same planet as the one last visited. The planet of the last sojourn could have a greater influence. With any change in flight from the last planet, there is so much information to transfer that one wonders if all of it arrives without degradation.

In the sojourn in the present earth's plane, we find the entity took its position from that of Uranus, with the elements of Venus, Neptune, Jupiter and Mercury, with affliction in Mars and Saturn. In this sojourn in the relations with other planets, we find the entity having passed through all the stage, or planes, yet returning in the earth's plane for that merited in the earth plane return through Saturn's forces for the again development in the Universal Forces as are applied to the manifestations of soul and spirit entities through the physical or earth plane.

Then, as we see in the present earth plane, while the entity has reached that plane where the mental and the environmental forces in present plane have set many of the conditions for the present sojourn, yet there are many urges to be satisfied, reached, known, accomplished, found, yet, in the earth's plane. Many may be reached. Others may be lost.

294-019

Could lost data be one reason for a planetary sojourn? Is Edgar Cayce telling us this is one possibility?

Such influences from planetary sojourns are as urges. As to what the activities in the experience will be, or as to what the entity does about same (such urges) depends much upon the will and that the entity has made or does make as its ideal—whether mental, material OR spiritual.

And unless the ideal is founded in spiritual things, it must sooner or later turn upon self—and make for stumbling—stones rather than stepping-stones to peace and joy and harmony being sought by every soul in its security here and, yea, hereafter.

1082-003

Therefore, as suspected all along, some of the reasons for planetary sojourns might be tied to not having applied willpower in a satisfactory manner. Others might be tied to inadequate ideals and confusion from information overload. Urges come in all sizes and strengths. Smaller urges might not have been responded to with sufficient élan or compassion. Unsatisfactory responses might best be given another chance, otherwise they can turn upon self—and make for stumbling stones. If this particular reincarnation does not accomplish one's purpose, then a planetary sojourn may be indicated in order to find different stepping-stones to peace, joy, and harmony.

At death the soul ventures outward again, possibly to sojourn on a planet that meets the latest needs. So what about a soul completing its incarnation on earth and going to another planet?

Q-5. Does the soul choose the planet to which it goes after each incarnation? If not, what force does?

A-5. In the Creation, we find all forces relative one with the other, and in the earth's place that of the flesh. In the developing from plane to plane becomes the ramification, or the condition of the will merited in its existence finding itself through eons of time.

In the illustration, or manifestation in this, we find again in the man called Jesus.

When the soul reached that development in which it reached earth's plane, it became in the flesh the model, as it had reached through the developments in those spheres, or planets, known in earth's plane, obtaining the One in All.

As in Mercury pertaining of Mind.

In Mars of Madness.

In Earth as of Flesh.

In Venus as Love.

In Jupiter as Strength.

In Saturn as the beginning of earthly woes, that to which all insufficient matter is cast for the beginning.

In that of Uranus as of the Psychic.

In that of Neptune as of the Mystic.

In Septimus as of Consciousness.

In Arcturus as of the developing.

As to various constellations, and of groups, only these ramifications of the various existences experienced in the various conditions.

0900-010

This passage provides much to ponder. Septimus has been called Pluto. Consciousness is an insightful property of Pluto. Arcturus is a so-called fixed star lumped in with these planets. The Moon is missing from the answer, and the reason is unclear. Possibly, during previous planetary or earthly sojourns, the individual already became sufficiently compassionate in an acceptable manner. But the nature of planetary sojourns as explained above leads to other questions:

Q-17. Is it possible to secure a reading regarding conditions and my sojourn, if any, on that planet?

A-17. If you can understand Jupiterian environs and languages, yes.

0826-008

The message is that planetary sojourns are spent in an entirely different plane and environment than in the physical on earth. Life on a planet is not like a physical life on earth. We would have to understand the environs and languages of each planet to understand the nature of those sojourns. Yet, the questions persisted as did the quest for reasons.

Then, what influences such a journey, such an advent of the soul from the unseen into materiality? Development of the soul that it may take its place, through the lessons gained in physical experience, in those classes or realms of soul activity in an infinite world—among those that have passed in their activity through the various realms; seeking then (as that which first called every soul and body into experience) that of companionship. Hence we have as much hereditary and environmental forces in soul's experience (or the developed soul to such an experience) as we have in the law of the earth, as to that which is hereditary from the parentage of a body—and the environs of the body, as to what is the trend of thought.

Then, what is the environmental and hereditary influence from the soul-body angle for this particular entity shown here, and known as [541]?

The sojourns in the environs about the présent sojourn, or in this particular solar system. Not that Venus, Jupiter, Mars, Uranus or any of the planets about this earth's sun have beings or bodies such as are known in the earth's sojourns; but those that are peculiar to their own realm—their own element or position from the solar light, or the light and heat. And yet with those influences about same by the variation in what is called in the earth the effect of the various influences shed from other solar systems, suns and so forth.

For, much might be given respecting those environs and as to how or why there have been and are accredited to the various planets certain characterizations that make for the attractions of souls' sojourns in that environ. But these are places of abode. As in the earth we find the elements are peopled, as the earth has its own moon or satellites enjoined in its environ, so is it with the other planets. The earth with its three-fourths water, with its elements, is peopled; yes. So are the various activities in other solar systems.

Hence the sojourn of a soul in its environ about the earth, or in this solar system, gives the factors that are often found in individuals in the earth that are of the same parentage, in the same environ; yet one might be a genius and the other a fool; one might be a moral degenerate and the other a high, upright, upstanding individual with an aptitude for influences that may not even be questioned.

Then, such environs PHYSICALLY are needed for the development of the soul.

So the entity here finds these as attributes in the mental forces that lie—as it were—DORMANT or innate in each soul or body manifested in the earth, that may be DRAWN UPON when apparently everything else has failed.

541-001

There have been no doubts that planetary sojourns are worthwhile, otherwise they would not have received so much attention. The best answer about their purpose is to fulfill urgent needs in the development of the soul. Another possibility is that they become the best interim stopovers between earthly sojourns, and they give pause to review the next incarnations on the earth plane. When such missions are accomplished, memories of these planetary sojourns arrive with the soul and they become dormant or innate. Yet they can be called upon whenever a new occasion arises that seeks the kind of help they can provide. Knowing that one has a backup in meeting life's goals is reassuring. It is like having more than one guardian angel!

9
DIS-EASE

DIS-EASE LEADS TO disease if not corrected. The planetary placements and their aspects show the propensities.

Q-17. What is disease and the purpose of the germs produced; as example, my throat and gums?

A-17. Disease arises from, first, dis-ease—as a normalcy that IS existent and yet becomes unbalanced. Disease is, or dis-ease is, a state at variance to the ideal or first cause or first principle. Then, in its final analysis, disease might be called sin. It is necessary to keep a balance.

And those who are in a material world are naturally subject to, and in contact with, sin. Thus the individual entity or soul-entity is to meet, to come in contact with, to overcome, to subdue same. For, what is the first premise? "Be fruitful, multiply, but SUBDUE the earth."

Then, dis-ease is of the earth-earthy.

2533-003

Human beings suffer occasional illnesses and accidents throughout their stay on earth. Some people suffer far more than others. We all have dis-easy periods as well as easy periods. Hardly anyone escapes, because our moods are changeable, leading us through cycles of exuberance and despair. In some people these moods show, and in others they are kept behind poker faces. Keeping aggravated moods pent up can be destructive. Any time hatred, anger, ire, fear, or just plain irritability enter our lives, these feelings need to be replaced with their counterparts or else disease may be the result or some other form of bodily harm. The astrological aspects of dis-ease are the so-called hard aspects—the even harmonics.

Q-48. What within myself brings on the periodic, long-drawn-out illnesses, which seem to check the things I am doing?

A-48. Fear—latent within self; as may be analyzed from that which has been given. Put this fear out, and we will find the healing, the cleansing for that direction ye were chosen, ye have applied, ye may apply again.

2630-001

Saturn is the planet of fear and chronic disease. Those who suffer chronic ailments often have flare-ups within days of an emotional upset. Usually, this upset has a recurring theme like many before. Look for those aspects involving Saturn to gain more insights as to the causes.

Everyone has a different response to drawn-out, Saturn-based physical problems. Some people feel martyred by their long-standing ailments. One type loves to talk about their operations, medicines, and such, because they are among the most important events of their lives. Perhaps this is their form of release. Others suffer in silence or in complaining. The details are to be endured, one way or the other.

Accidents, while not always accompanied by long-term discomforting situations, frequently occur when problematic distractions are present. They often coincide with hard aspects involving Mars or Pluto and the Ascendant. One was thinking about something else at the time. A problem was in the mental background. Thus, both accidents and illnesses can be associated with discomforting situations. Just know that if planets show the conditions for illnesses, they also show how remedies can be made available or applied.

Q-12. Any further suggestions for this body at this time?

A-12. Many suggestions may be made as regarding the physical conditions—for much has been given the body as respecting this very condition that has arisen in the system, as respecting the eliminations as would be set up from the various existent conditions for, with the body creating those forces as were set in the system when these warnings were given, these must be eliminated, and the diet and the excretory system, and the eliminations throughout the alimentary canal, must be kept in the proper condition, else we may expect many of the resultant conditions from excesses that will arise in the system by LITTLE indiscretions that would cause distresses, or disease—not disease—but dis-ease, see? Disease only when allowed to remain in system, see?

136-069

Edgar Cayce faced many struggles in his own life. He was not completely healthy himself. Neither was Gertrude Cayce, his wife. She contracted tuberculosis, and that was quite a serious illness in those days as it still is today (although more controllable). Thus, the Cayce family like virtually every other family experienced illnesses. Edgar Cayce was prompted to give readings on both himself and Gertrude when called for.

EC: Yes, we have the body here—this we have had before. Now, as to the physical conditions and those elements as PRODUCE same, in its entirety, covers a wide range at this particular time; wholly understood, would give a different insight from the concept USUALLY taken as respecting physical conditions of the body—for they are astrological, psychological, mental and physical.

Physically speaking, we find THIS condition apparent—now, APPARENT—understand its meaning!

In the lower portion of the stomach, or the duodenum, where the surface of the walls of same are so exaggerated, elongated, or spread through the various folds so that assimilation may take place from that assimilated from the foods taken, here we find—NOT ulcerations, not a diseased condition—rather the dis-ease, and through these walls of tissue, or the walls of the duodenum itself, POISONS pass—and taken in the blood through the activity of the emunctory and lymph, produce pressure through the vegetative system, that brings distress to the various portions of the body from which radial reflexes come through sympathetic AND through cerebro-spinal reactions. THAT physically.

In the psychological effect, worry—distress in a MENTAL reaction—often brings these activities to a more acute reaction.

In the astrological, those positions of the effect of the planetary reactions through which the entity itself passed in its relation one to another, become more active during certain periods.

Combine these, and you have the condition existent in this body, Edgar Cayce we are speaking of.

· 294-121

In Edgar Cayce's horoscope, his Ascendant sign was Cancer (see Appendix A). The lower portion of his stomach and duodenum are associated with the zodiacal sign Cancer. Its ruler Moon is conjunct Neptune, and Neptune has dominion over poisons. The walls of the duodenum were dis-eased as poisons passed through the tissues. Poisons were taken into the bloodstream through the activity of the emunctory and lymph—Neptunian-Piscean functions these—where they produced pressures through the vegetative system that brought stress to various portions of his body. Moon conjunct Neptune in Taurus means his throat had to have been affected. This susceptibility arose from his natal horoscope. The larynx is located in the throat. At another period Edgar Cayce could not speak. The timing had to coincide with a progressed aspect from or to one of these controlling planets. The astrological picture matches Edgar Cayce's words unequivocally. Yet, in matters of pain, he did not claim that astrology was the culprit.

Hence in thy activity there needs to be the stress upon spirituality in all phases of this three-dimensional being that one finds in dealing with the same.

The consciousness of these is apparent in the experience of the entity. The lacking, or slackness, is in stressing their coordinated influence. For, there must be cooperation,—just as in Father, Son and Holy Spirit. They are one; yet that which is not in perfect harmony in the activities or the awareness of either influence brings that man experiences as—first—dis-ease, disgust, disremembrance in rightful, righteous activity in every phase of his endeavor.

The astrological aspects are not as is sometimes indicated by some students of astrological phases; that because of certain positions the entity is prone to this or that, or must endure this or that. Remember, rather,—as each corpuscle of thy body,— yes, each atomic structure in thy physical self—is a pattern of the universal consciousness, and capable of producing in the physical body such disturbances as to wreck the very purpose of the individual entity if misconstrued, misdirected, misjudged in any of its aspects—so is the influence of a planet.

2396-002

Thus, the susceptibilities are clearly shown by the planets, but an individual does not have to accede to all dis-eases and actually become ill. Individuals in this category have advanced in their decision-making and their progress toward a final destiny. Many horoscopes show square aspects, for instance, or oppositions and contraparallels that never result in illnesses described by the planets or signs in which they occur. The owners of these horoscopes have learned to cope. They have achieved a balance in life that thwarts illness of that particular description. Edgar Cayce managed to convey some of these ideas about harmony in offering cures. He addressed causes—not symptoms—and his track record on cures was quite impressive when the recipients listened and complied. At other times his responses were simplistic, but redolent with truth.

> Q26. Is it indicated that I will ever be handicapped by a serious illness?
> A26. Depends much upon self. For as ye sow, so ye reap.

5349-001

When individuals did not comply with the readings or they had not found a balance in life, the results were often dis-eases progressing toward more serious diseases. Astrological correspondences with dis-ease are so strong that they cannot be ignored or dismissed. They have been studied, recorded, argued, and discussed for ages.

Susceptibilities of the human body have astrological associations with zodiacal signs and planets. For example, Aries has been said to govern the head, face, brains, upper jaw, and eyes; Taurus, the throat and neck; Gemini, the nervous system, lungs, hands, and arms; Cancer, the stomach and breasts; Leo, the heart and skeletal system; Virgo, the gastrointestinal system; Libra, the kidneys and loins; Scorpio, the generative system, rectum, and sinuses; Sagittarius, the thighs and hips; Capricorn, the knees; Aquarius, the ankles; and Pisces, the feet and lymphatic system.

What is more, whenever an illness is localized, these are the signs that correspond or their planetary rulers. Soul-selected horoscopes provide the indications of susceptibility to the disease, and they do not fail in this mission. However, as Edgar Cayce clearly stated, succumbing to a dis-ease or disease is a function of decisions made and attitudes—not these astrological indicators. An illness itself comes about when the response of the person is inappropriate, when the willpower to subdue is not properly exercised, or when the decisions made during the period of stress are at variance with the soul's original goals.

> When a physical body is at dis-ease, the pain or dis-ease is as a warning that some portion is in distress; and the body sends out the warriors within itself automatically to ward off. If there is lacking that which will supply the proper defense, or proper ammunition for the warding off of disorders, then conditions array themselves—as it were—against the better physical functioning of the body. Then organic disorders arise.

639-002

With proper training, the propensities toward organic disorders become obvious in horoscopes. There may be several indications. An astrological diagnosis can readily supplement orthodox medical training. A limited number of medical doctors has discovered this fact throughout history. In the days of Greece and Rome, the planets were regularly consulted. Examples of astrologers during the Middle Ages who also doubled as doctors were Nostradamus and Paracelsus. Today is no exception, although the percentage may be more restricted. Certain modern doctors who will go unnamed have discovered the power of astrology in making diagnoses. Often the astrological information is as good or better than a battery of laboratory tests, although such information will not be referred to in their medical reports. Laboratory tests are excellent at quantifying symptoms—but not always as wonderful at qualifying or finding the sources of physical-mental problems. When an astrological diagnosis supplements laboratory reports, missing holes are filled in. Medically, there is nothing so good as a reliable confirmation of an illness and a direction to the cause backed by statistical data. Astrological signatures of diseases are usually precise, and the physicians who use this information have success ratios higher than their colleagues in pinning down diseases or the sources of illnesses. Again and again, astrology used in the correct manner is a great aid to mankind.

Q-73. Will my specialty eventually be in medical Astrology and numbers or is there some other angle of stars and numbers more suitable for me?

A-73. As we find, it eventually will be rather in the writing, the counselling, the directing. That these partake of the physical as well as the spiritual is to be expected. Do not confuse others, do not confuse self, but in those studies as indicated— and remember, have the ideal and know it is in Him. Have the courage to do and dare, and have the courage to keep that first and foremost.

For what is the gain to have found fame and fortune, to have found self-glory? When the rains of disappointment come there is no ground for faith or hope unless it be in Him.

For His yoke is easy, if His grace and mercy is thine—and this ye obtain only by showing others the way to same!

1402-001

The power of astrology to identify potential illnesses improves when accompanied by right ideals. People with high ideals consider careers based upon their desires to help others in this way. And so advice was given to an individual who was considering medical astrology as an occupation. Edgar Cayce recommended rather for him to do writing, counseling, and directing. Those strengths were doubtless indicated in his horoscope.

Not only does astrology facilitate diagnoses, but it can indicate when the dis-ease will occur. Not being at ease is accompanied by progressed astrological aspects that are stressful—they are the even harmonic aspects. Times of arrival for such aspects can be calculated from accurate horoscopes and placed on a calendar. Or today these dates might be entered into a personal planner or equivalent program on a computer. Being forewarned of a condition that could lead to dis-ease is an advantage. Negative tendencies can be counteracted. These are the earthly tests of life, including encounters with sin. As Edgar Cayce said, too much dis-ease can lead to illnesses. Too much stress can upset needed balances in life and result in sickness. Those of the human race who escape a lot of accidents and illnesses may have acquired more inner peace than the average, but they too can benefit by knowing when stressful conditions will occur.

16. The greater precautions for the health, the welfare of the entity, and warnings, will come during—or should be given for—these periods in October and November of the first four

years of sojourn in this experience. And especially for those things that interfere with the activity of the sensory system, in the throat and ears. In those periods, then, there should be precautions as to dis-ease that would disturb these portions of the system particularly.

17. And there should be precautions also in the fifth and seventh years, in December and January, as to fire. For, in those periods will the entity be passing through the fiery sign for the entity.

18. Hence the colors that will influence the developing years for the entity will be blue and yellow, or shades and tones of these particular colors; with the opal and pearl being those minerals that will attract and influence the entity. For, there will be particularly those periods for the entity when stones or jewelry will be of particular interest to the entity; in those periods when fifteen to eighteen months have passed will this be seen in the activities of the entity, [314].

19. As to the next influence, or those periods when there comes those changes in the physical and developing periods, or in the fourteenth to the fifteenth year—or from the twelve and a half years to the fifteenth year, will be those periods when there may be seen the greater influence upon the entity from ASTROLOGICAL viewpoint—in Uranus. Hence the period of the greater ANXIETY by or from those upon whom the TRAIN-ING of this entity depends.

314-001

A handful of books have been devoted to the subject of astrological disease signatures, and—on a positive note—to stellar healing (i.e., spiritual healing).[8] Edgar Cayce mentioned colors and stones as being counteractive techniques that can be employed. Music and mental fixations on mitigating planets and their signs are other methods. This requires knowing the astrological tools that can be used. They are the opposite planets and signs of the zodiac. Thus, if Mars is the instigator of a problem in Aries, the opposite sign is Libra and the planet Venus.

---

[8]Examples are *Medical Astrology* by Omar V. Garrison, University Books, Inc., New York, 1971, and *Body Disease and Its Stellar Treatment* by Elbert Benjamine, The Aries Press, Chicago, 1945.

Holding Venusian characteristics or Libran attributes in one's mind can mitigate the irritation. This procedure seeks white light as indicated in the color triangle. The same is true for Mercury and Gemini. The opposite sign is Sagittarius, and the opposite planets are Jupiter and Neptune. Concentrating on their characteristics can ease the Mercury-seated pain. And so one can continue with the remaining planets around the zodiac. This approach recognizes and takes advantage of the body as a whole.

Q-10. [585]: Would the conflict between spirit and flesh cause one to be affected physically, to become tired or even ill?

A-10. RELATIVELY so. As He gave, "For whether is easier, to say, Thy sins be forgiven thee; or to say, Arise and walk?" Or again when confronted by that which had become as a disease, as a temperament of the body, as the wantonness of the flesh, He said to the woman, "Where are those thine accusers?—No man, Lord—Neither do I accuse thee; but SIN NO MORE."

What took place then in the experience of those individuals spoken to by LIFE, Light and Immortality? These were concentrated and centralized upon the activity of what? What has ever been the builder, body, mind and spirit? As given, the expressions are in the physical, the motivative force is the spirit, the mind is the builder. What was builded? Those bodies had dwelt as individuals do (as may be illustrated in habit) with the interconsciousness of the necessity of the expression of something within self which brought dis-ease, the natural result of what? An at-variance to the divine law! Hence it may truly be said that to be at-variance may bring sickness, dis-ease, disruption, distress in a physical body.

It is true then that the mind may heal entirely by the spoken word, by the laying on of hands, dependent upon the CONSCIOUSNESS of the motivative forces in the individual body. Yet those requiring material expression to create a balance may necessitate drug, knife, water, heat, electricity, or ANY of those forces that are yet what?

What is the spirit? The MANIFESTATION OF GOD! The CREATIVE Force working in, with and upon what? The awareness, the interconsciousness of the BODY, the mind, the spirit, as separated in individuals! O that all would gain JUST that! and not feel, "Yes, I understand—but my desires and my body and my weaknesses and this or that—and I didn't do it." Who else did? This may be a hard statement for many, but you will eventually come to know it is true: No fault, no hurt comes to self save that thou hast created in thine consciousness, in thine inner self, the cause. For only those that ye love may hurt you.

262-083

Trying to separate spirit and flesh in order to find blame for physical disorders is not altogether productive. Excuses do not solve the problems either. We are the ones who are ultimately responsible, and we have created ourselves as complicated, involved entities. We have an awareness of the interconsciousness of the body, mind, and spirit. These elements are really not conveniently separated, because planetary influences, the endocrine glands, the urges, memories, moods, external effects, etc., are combined or integrated. Besides, hurts can only come from those we love. Edgar Cayce said they do not come from those we do not love.

In considering this whole picture about health, new thoughts intrude. For example, an interesting relationship exists between the sequence of endocrine glands and the sequence of physical rulerships held by the signs. The flow of internal Kundalini forces is upward from gonads to the pituitary. The flow of physical rulerships is downward from Aries and Mars for the head to Pisces and Jupiter for the feet. A few aberrations in the flow of physical associations are present, for example when Scorpio not only has dominion over the sexual organs and rectum but also the sinuses. This doubtless relates to Pluto's dual rulerships over Scorpio and Aries. Similar relationships exist for the other signs with dual rulerships and the remaining outer planets. Aquarius governs the calves, ankles, and leg veins. But Uranus is present for cramps, appendectomies, and other urgencies. Pisces governs the feet and toes. But Neptune also is present when toxins, poisons, or addictions are present that migrate through the lymphatic system. However, the principal flow of sign rulerships is from top to bottom of the physical body.

One can envision a human magnet. The South Pole is at the gonads; the North Pole is at the pituitary gland. Magnetic flux moves upward inside the magnet until it reaches the North Pole. Then the flux field bends over and around externally, flowing downward to the feet. Finally, the South Pole causes the lines of flux to bend back upward and start the internal northerly flow again. Every person has a (Uranian) magnetic field.

2. Now, as we find, there are definite conditions that disturb the better physical functioning of the body. It is true the body

is passing through a period of adversity from the astrological aspect, but as the physical forces of a body are impelled through the elan vitale that manifests itself in that which is assimilated or prepared for a body, that it may function the more normal, these disturbances—then, as we find—rest primarily in the manner in which the glands function with the organs in their assimilation of that which is made for the resuscitating of vital forces in the body. It is true the psychological conditions affect, but the pathological reactions are the more definite, not only in the physical functionings of the organisms but in the manner in which the responses are seen in the mental AND material force of this body, [831].

831-001

Planets relate by rulerships to the signs, but they also have ties to the endocrine glands as repeatedly indicated. Hence, the physical associations of the planets are both external and internal. For example, almost all heart-related posture-related problems involve the Sun. Cataracts, female problems, edema, and sleepwalking are tied to the Moon. Nervousness, deafness, and amnesia relate to Mercury. Acne, eczema, and goiter are influenced by Venus. All surgery, appendectomies, burns, and rashes are associated with Mars or Pluto. Cancer, boils, cysts, diabetes, and obesity accompany Jupiter-Neptune afflictions. Arthritis, atrophy, colitis, and constipation, plus most chronic illnesses, go with Saturn-Uranus. The outer planets have assignations to other infirmities. Hiccups, obsessions, and abrupt untoward events may have Uranus as the instigator. Alcoholism, epilepsy, and drug abuse are connected with Neptune. Pluto is an adjunct to many accidents and intense overexertions. All of these associations are physical. But they are mental and spiritual as well.

3. In the present plane we find the entity takes its position from that of Uranus, with Saturn, Mercury and Mars in the ascendancy. Influences in the early life in present earth plane of Jupiter's influence and of Venus. Hence we have in the present earth's plane one that is in many respects to others often contradictory to self and self purpose. One whose conditions in mental and in every manner of mental conditions have changed from that begun in the developing of the body. Some have been for good. Some have been for retrogression rather than developing.

4900-001

These retrogressions related to positions in the ascendancy can cause serious physical problems. What experience also shows is the regularity and precision of aspects from or to the Ascendant whenever the body is afflicted. Either the Ascendant or the ruler of the sign on the Ascendant is associated with virtually all serious illnesses and accidents that affect the body. That is one reason why they are so important and need to be accurately determined. In addition, Edgar Cayce has revealed the special association of planets with the endocrine glands. Then, there are the unsuspecting effects of the parallels of declination—unsuspecting because many astrologers do not look at them. Control of the body's functions attributed to the endocrine glands may be interrupted when the associated planets are stressed. A stress may be greater when instigated by a slow-moving contraparallel, for example, than for a faster-changing aspect in celestial longitude. The spread of poisons or diseases can be attributed to glandular functions. Very accurately timed horoscopes are required in order to recognize all of these associations and connections. Yet an Ascendant under siege is a sure confirmation of a body under attack. A planet under siege can seriously affect the bodily functions of an organ under the control of a corresponding endocrine gland if action is not taken by the entity to counteract the tendencies. When the illness and the Ascendant-planet aspect coincide, the conditions of stress are obviously accentuated. With the proper astrological training, there should be no mistaking these relationships. With the proper spiritual training, the individual can make the right decisions to overcome identified potential adversities.

An Ascendant undergoing a large number of stressful aspects in the natal horoscope has often been observed in handicapped individuals. It has been noted that all handicapped individuals have an imbalance of stressful aspects in their charts. An Ascendant is the first house node. The first house encompasses that part of life that relates to the self. The human body is a fundamental part of self. When the human body is highly stressed, handicaps can be the result. Human bodies may be overly stressed because of karma that must be reconciled sooner or later.

Q-15. What were the hardships that weren't met?
A-15. Willfulness; that is, the use of self and its activities in the satisfying or gratifying of conditions for the moment, or for the time being, see?

Q-16. How was I handicapped?

A-16. Not handicapped,—only by the lack of that environment for which the entity longed; and circumstance made for more of this than the willfullness on the part of others.

For, the entity being taken by the savages, to many the entity was as a savage, yet to itself only using same to attain or gain the desires for the moment for itself through the experience.

2278-004

One is reminded of Arnold Toynbee's philosophy described in his mammoth work, *The History of Civilization*. Toynbee's thesis was that no civilization could become great unless it was stressed. But that civilization had to be subjected to the right amount of stress. Too much stress or pressure on the population, and the nation would eventually be crippled or subjugated. Ambitions succumb to too little pressure, and the natives become indolent, easygoing, and satisfied with life. An abundance of food, an absence of severe weather changes demanding warm clothing, an easy availability of safe shelter create weaknesses. That is why all of the strong countries in the world have occupied temperate zones where the climate ranges from moderate to severe—or at least a large portion of the strong country was in a zone of that character. The North of the United States has been more powerful than the South for that reason. What applies to nations applies to individuals as well.

Extreme changes in weather conditions are stressful. Cold winter climates require more diligence to survive, more effort to keep warm, more work to acquire food. No great country has arisen from equatorial regions, and no great power has derived from the extreme northern and southern latitudes, where arctic living conditions are simply too severe. Sweden might appear to be the one exception, because that country was once a power to be reckoned with. But Sweden, as far north as it is, is warmed by the Gulf Stream. People in more arctic areas suffer too many setbacks that cannot be overcome. They are like the handicapped.

And so human beings must have stressful conditions if they are to rise from a comfortable, unperturbed, easygoing existence. To achieve prominence requires overcoming adversity. If the pressures are too severe at birth, these human beings may be cripples for life. Perhaps they have a karma to work off that warrants the kind of situation in which they find themselves. Nevertheless, their Ascendants are assailed and in many ways overwhelmed. If the pressures are too light, the individuals do not develop enough character to gain in life. Everything is given to them, and they do not have to work in order to survive. Luck comes their way. Ideally, the odd and even aspects are balanced. The even are needed as well as the odd. A mix of easy and difficult aspects is to be desired, because they provide balance.

Still, an ancient masonic aphorism is that one builds upon the square. Masons do not say that one builds upon the trine. The more difficult square is a 90° aspect, an even subharmonic, a fourth of the circle. A person must have squares to confront untoward situations and build character. A person must have adverse aspects in order to be tested in life and be confronted with the necessity to make difficult decisions. This is the only way to advance. However, dis-ease attends every square. Evidently, illness constitutes a form of stress required by mankind, as Edgar Cayce intimated—so long as the stress levels are not too great.

16. Well that the visions which arise from the latent and manifested urges be not overstressed, but stressed sufficient, as it were, to keep the mental and physical and spiritual body as one, or properly balanced in its relationships to all phases.

1755-003

Eventually, physical bodies succumb to stresses at the end of an earthly sojourn. Even for people who have been comparatively healthy all of their lives, death is invariably shown in the astrological chart by progressions of stressful aspects. These progressions involve the Ascendant or first house, because the soul is exiting the body. The fourth house is affected, because bodily functions cease—the ability to act or do. The eighth house is affected, because the soul and spiritual forces possessed by the body are departing into another realm.

Q-7. Explain the plane of spirit and soul forces, and what relation this plane has to earth. You will start with death, as we know it.

A-7. In that moment—as in birth we have the beginning of an earthly sojourn, little or long, as time may be—as the birth into the spiritual plane begins with the death in earth plane; merely the separation of the spiritual and soul forces.

900-018

Hardly a day passes that the communications media does not announce the death of a well-known individual. Many had their lives terminated by cancer or another serious illness. On all other occasions of sickness, they survived. With virtual certainty every one of them suffered through one or more of the usual childhood and adult illnesses. Very few human beings can say they have never had a cold, influenza, whooping cough, food poisoning, skin rashes, chills and fevers, measles, mumps, or chicken pox, to name just a few examples. Very few have never been cut, burned, scalded, experienced a broken bone, or had an accident that caused minor or major bodily injuries. Almost everyone has been sick on occasion, or wounded or been at disease. Gigantic strides have been made by modern medicine, but hospitals are often filled, and more are being built. Thousands of doctors are on call to take care of every level of illness, including those that are beyond hope. Becoming ill from time to time is a reality of life on earth that has not gone away, and a large percentage of people end their lives with a serious illness. Yet few are the people who understand how attitudes play such a strong part.

13. For, through these attitudes there has been a wrecking of the activities of the sympathetic nervous system with the organs of the body,—by creating—through such—natures that have prevented the normal activity; though the organs themselves do not indicate there is disease,—rather dis-ease, or warnings that there is abuse to their perfect functioning in a body-physical and mental, that may accomplish not only those things that may bring contentment and happiness to the body itself but in the lives, in the experiences of others arouse and bring hope where there has been discouragement, dismay, sorrow, pain,—yea, even dire distress in body and mind.

589-004

Additionally, civilizations seem to go through scourges periodically. They are often shown in long-range return charts or the horoscopes of countries. Lead poisoning from wine goblets took many lives during the Roman era. The bubonic plague of the Middle Ages concluded hundreds of thousands of lives. We now know the carriers were rats. More recently the world is facing acquired immune deficiency syndrome (AIDS). Its toll is steep. While modern vaccines and sanitation go a long way toward combating many types of old and new infirmities, none have been found to date for AIDS, and none of the scourges has been completely eradicated. Tuberculosis and smallpox were nearly curtailed a few decades back, but they are making a comeback. Conjecture about these scourges of mankind can only lead to the conclusion that the individuals involved must have had needs that were fulfilled.

In the interest of humanity, doctors combat these sweeping illnesses, and almost everyone agrees it is the right thing for them to do. That is part of the exercise of willpower in the hands of those who can do something about adverse conditions. Research staffs of drug and biotechnology companies also exercise willpower by working on cures. Many benefits to mankind have been developed during the last decade alone. Hence, the health scene is not entirely bleak. Many people are now working on a way to arrest or cure AIDS.

In spite of this latest scourge, the average person is living longer. Only a few hundred years ago, living fifty to sixty years was regarded as a long life before an illness or battle snuffed it out. Perhaps the current generation is closer to their destinies. Modern medicine and greater awareness of healthful practices have been prolonging life, but the susceptibility toward attack by some old or new form of virus remains. Anyone can still become ill, but today new ways of attacking invaders of the body are being discovered and administered with increasing frequency. Yet the quantity of illnesses and accidents remains about the same as always. These aberrations to our physical, mental, and spiritual bodies persist when the astrological urges dictate. According to Edgar Cayce, the causes lie within us. The causes go back to "doing thus or so without the consciousness of a choice existent."

That element called will—that ability to make environmental and the urge from experimental condition in the life of an entity, whether earthly entity or cosmic entity—is as that which has the greater influence in the building or retarding of that entity towards its ultimate end. Then the astrological condition of a life, an individual entity, is dependent upon the astrological aspects and what the individual did with that experience in whatever sphere it may have enacted its will, that companion of the consciousness to which one must become conscious before the application of will becomes a factor. One may not, then, will to do thus or so without the consciousness of a choice existent. When this is not IN action, then the environmental sphere has its sway. We are through.

900-357

10

FATE AND FREE WILL

A STRONG CONCLUSION has developed from preceding material that what we call fate was a freewill choice of the soul and was captured in the form of astrological placements and aspects.

Although some of his questioners were curious about this subject, Edgar Cayce did not make an issue of fate. The reading that follows is typical, and it did not go into much detail. However, as usual, it made a point. This time the point was about all elements in relative conditions having their bearing upon every element in the earth plane. All elements include the astrological elements. Note that he demurred on what the querist meant about fate and rejected the next question, which really should not have been asked:

Q-7. Is there such a thing as fate? [See Destiny]
A-7. Depending upon what is meant by fate. All elements in relative conditions have their bearing upon every element in the earth plane, and the will of any condition being with mind may act against such condition.

Q-8. When an entity has completed its development, such that it no longer needs to manifest on earth's plane, how far then is it along towards its complete development towards God?

A-8. Not to be given. Reach that plane, and develop in Him, for in Him the will then becomes manifest.

900-020

In many different ways Edgar Cayce referred to astrological aspects as becoming a phase of each and every soul. In many different readings he restated an axiom that the progressed aspects are signposts. These are the day-for-a-year aspects referred to in the Holy Bible. The passing of one astrological day maps the signposts for one year. The passing of the second astrological day maps the signposts for the second year, and so on.

That absent from the material body is manifested in what we call astrological aspects, that become a phase of each and every soul—and are signposts along the individual way . . . all of these are a part of thy heritage, thy innate urge; that arises from, and produces influences in, the material experiences in the present.

1745-001

The nature of these astrological projections confronting a soul needs to be explored in greater depth, because there are many recondite implications with which to contend. Disturbing thoughts of contrarians or nonbelievers should also be answered. For one, astrology still has many doubters. Even among believers a carte blanche position is often taken that astrological aspects impel but do not compel. Edgar Cayce himself frequently talked about willpower being able to overcome astrological urges, but when and how broadly applicable are other questions. Opinions surround virtually every thought about astrological signposts, and they pull in many directions. If an opinion is not strong in the mind of the doubter or critic, then that individual typically poses more questions to elicit convincing answers. "What is fate?" and "What is free will?" are the kinds of questions that have plagued mankind for thousands of years. The heritage of innate urges is often a confusing lot. Many people cannot truly understand such matters while holding doggedly onto personal biases, even when they believe they understand the words.

13. Then, if this be true—those things that have just been said, the natural question that arises in the minds or experi-

ences of those that would study psychic forces—or any of the philosophies that have to do or deal with the principles motivating the influences or activities of individuals in this earth's plane in the present—would be:

14. What has karma to do with this body, then? What is the fate, or the destiny, of such a soul? Has it already been determined as to what it may do, or be, for the very best? or has it been so set that the activities and the influences, the environs and the hereditary forces, are to alter?

15. These indeed are worthy questions, in the light of that which has been given.

16. If there be any virtue or truth in those things given in the spiritual or Christian or Jehovah-God faith, His laws are immutable. What laws are immutable, if truth and God Himself is a growing thing—yet an ever changeable, and yet "ever the same, yesterday and today and forever"?

17. These things, these words, to many minds become contradictory, but they are in their inception NOT contradictory; for Truth, Life, Light, Immortality, are only words that give expression to or convey a concept of one and the same thing.

18. Hence, Destiny is: "As ye sow, so shall ye reap." And like begets like! And the first law of nature, which is the material manifestation of spiritual law in a physical world, is self-propagation—which means that it seeks self-preservation and the activity of the same law that brought the thought of man (or the spirit of man) into existence—companionship!

19. What, then, is karma? And what is destiny? What has the soul done, in the spiritual, the material, the cosmic world or consciousness, respecting the knowledge or awareness of the laws being effective in his experience—whether in the earth, in the air, in heaven or in hell? These are ever one; for well has it been said, "Though I take the wings of the morning and fly unto the utmost parts of the heavens, Thou art there! Though I make my bed in hell, Thou art there! Though I go to the utmost parts of the earth, Thou art there! Truth, Life, God! Then, that which is cosmic—or destiny, or karma—depends

upon what the soul has done about that it has become aware of.

20. What, you say, has this to do with this soul, this entity, that—as we have given—is well balanced and attuned as to that it will do; by its own activating forces of its will, its desire—that arise from its experiences in the mental, the spiritual and the material world? Because it is thus making its destiny, its karma! For, HE will stand in the stead. For, by sin came death; by the shedding of blood came freedom—freedom from a consciousness, into a greater consciousness.

21. So, in His promises do we live and move and have our being. Be patient. But know much may be done.

                                                    ˆ276-002

Edgar Cayce did not try to sway the minds of others on the subject of fate and free will by harsh invectives. He simply gave his consistent answers to their questions. The rationale was always consonant with the pursuit of spiritual development. That spiritual development requires every individual to exercise free will versus acquiescing to the sometimes flippant orders and impressions forced upon them by others. While some people need to be prodded more than others in order to get them to act, those acts should be their own decisions. Every individual should preferably march to his or her own drummer, rather than necessarily following the various opinions held by others. An opinion, as Webster's dictionary defines the word, is: "belief stronger than impression, less strong than positive knowledge; a belief; view; judgment." To move beyond the weakness of contrary opinions that are not well-founded is a worthy goal.

However, in pursuing this subject of fate and free will, logic imposes some constraints. Edgar Cayce's statements must be correctly interpreted. If his words are not interpreted correctly, one could come away believing that man can exercise free will at all times for all occasions. That has not been found to be correct or entirely realistic. Edgar Cayce squelched that idea himself.

Q-8. Each soul is a free-will agent in a material world, with the choice before it in its own experience. Are there not times when the will is overruled by higher forces? May this information be given?

A-8. Yes. It is overruled. Through the destiny, that ye must learn—but take the first steps first. Learn that thou hast to learn, then it may be given.

262-070

Free will can only be employed most of the time on the earth plane. It cannot be employed for those things that are fixed or preordained. It cannot be employed when matters are out of control. Yet the soul beforehand might have chosen these fixed situations using free will—before birth, not afterward. Free will in such cases was exercised, but at a different instance in time. And that is where Edgar Cayce's words become complete in their meaning. What was free will at that pre-birth moment is no longer free will at a later—after birth—moment. This collection of thoughts could be mildly disturbing when initially considered. But if we accept viewpoints about spirit, soul, and body that were expressed in his readings, then it is possible and desirable to differentiate these contested influences. In doing so, the astrological factors become considerably more abstruse.

Then, ye wonder—can such be possible in threescore and ten years in the earth? Also ye wonder—doth the time of birth, the place of the environment, make or have a part in destiny? Do the days or the years, or the numbers, all have their part? Yea, more than that! Yet, as has been given, all these are but signs along the way; they are but omens; they are but the marks that have indicated—for, as given, He has set His mark, and these are SIGNS, not the destinies! For the destiny of the mind, of the body, of the soul, is with Him.

262-075

Setting His mark is another way of saying fate. These settings are not destiny. They are but signs along the way. Decisions in response to these signs contribute to destiny.

In continuing the thoughts being analyzed, it might be worthwhile to deviate a moment and review a bit of history. The great unsettled astrological controversy of an earlier era with heavy religious overtones was between fate and free will. This conflict surfaced in the early days of Christianity and extended into modern times. The issue eventually became a problem to the church, because it conflicted with ideas held by many, but not all, of the early popes, bishops, and priests. St. Augustine crystallized ideas during his reign. The position of St. Augustine against soothsaying, oracles, magic, and fatalism was the most telling among the church fathers, because he was an authoritative figure who had stated a position around which his subordinates could rally. Today intelligent human beings might be in agreement with the specific bans issued. However, they did not settle the question of fate versus free will. The church fathers generally wanted a submissive, believing populace without the complications of fate. According to their understanding, fate would remove options of parishioners to exercise free will, to sin, and then to be saved. Fate, according to their thinking, would reduce the need for clergy. Therefore, it was to be opposed.

During the centuries of religious history that followed St. Augustine, lower-ranking priests did not always agree with each other on the subject of fate and free will. The Reformation became, if anything, a period when there was too much free will for the Roman Catholic Church. History shows that some members of the clergy took opposite sides of the issue. Although hotly debated and fiercely defended over the years, they did not really solve the fate versus free will controversy.

At present, this conflict remains a thorn in the side of some sects. The issues have not been resolved, and in the last few centuries the debate has just become tiresome, perhaps, and subsided. Modern thinkers using advanced technologies and the latest knowledge taught in universities have not shed an overwhelming amount of light on the subject either. However, Edgar Cayce's readings shed a lot of light. They suggest that elements of both fate and free will are present concurrently. Moreover, they are readily understood when astrology and reincarnation are combined and properly considered. If the information he imparted had been known centuries ago, the great debate might never have taken place.

Among the finer points in Edgar Cayce's life readings is the doctrine that says each soul has free will to make a choice and select creative forces manifested in materiality. Each soul is endowed with self-will whose forces have the capacity to become law (fate). The choice of forces becomes as a law that is not in effect until the human being has come into materiality.

An entity, or soul, is a spark—of the Whole, the First Cause; and thus is a co-worker with that First Cause, or Purpose, which is the creative influence or force that is manifested in materiality.

Each entity, each soul, is endowed with self-will; that which is the force that makes it able, or gives it the capacity, to be the law, and yet complying with a universal purpose.

Thus, whether the activities or consciousness are in the material expression or in the universal cosmic expression in the spirit, these are ever a part of the entity's expression—for either development or retardment.

As may be seen, then, the activities or entrances of an entity in materiality and out of materiality are not so much governed by the stars or planets as they are by what the entity has done respecting the law of its relationships to same!

Thus it may be said, as the entity of soul—a soul—is part of the Creative Forces, the positions of the stars or planets do not influence the entity so much as the entity has influenced, and does influence, the affairs of a universal consciousness!. . . .

For, indeed each entity, each soul, is in the process of evolution towards the First Cause. Much becomes evolution—much may become involution.

2079-001

As a coworker with the First Cause, each soul has the capability of exercising free will to become the law, or to seal fate. Yet it does this while complying with a universal purpose. Before birth, the soul can select a particular cosmic expression for an earthly sojourn. Once selected and spiritual birth occurs, this astrological expression becomes established as a law. Even though the planets and aspects are fatalistic and operate like a law, the maturing soul-spirit in a human body can exercise free will in response to the urges they produce. The free will at this stage does not have to act in accordance with exact direction from the law. Its acts of free will, however, would be in consonance with the astrological law. In other words, astrology provides considerable latitude as to the manner of expression. However, that expression functions within the boundary conditions allotted.

"Whether the activities or consciousness are in the material expression or in the universal cosmic expression in the spirit" refers to free will of a human being in the material earth plane and to free will of a spirit expressing astrological influences. Thus, a horoscope chosen by a soul represents one of several options using free will to select a time for spiritual birth. Spiritual birth is mapped by one perfect horoscope chosen by the soul. The horoscope is perfect because it matches the human being exactly. It times urges exactly. Although the order of spiritual and physical birth could be reversed, physical birth normally comes later.

Q-75. Did I enter this plane through free will or was I drawn here through some combination of relative forces for a particular development?

A-75. Yes and no; that is: When the environs, the activities are visioned by the entity seeking a channel for expression, wherein there is visioned (in the environs in which there is free-will) the opportunity for the working out of that needed, ye enter.

Hence it is not only the creating by the activities of those through whom the soul enters, or who are the channel through which the spirit or soul enters, but it is the choice of the soul for seeking expression in that environ.

1641-001

There are two separate and distinct periods for exercising will-power. In one period the soul chooses an environ and birth time. This establishes the earthly personality, sex, and collection of situations arranged for the working off of karma. In the second period the soul has taken on the body of a human being, and cosmic expressions provide urges for decisions to be made leading toward its destiny. Fatalistic opportunities are presented according to the selected astrological road map. Certain of these opportunities are carefully chosen by the soul to provide a means for working off karma that may be called bad or unpleasant.

Astrological insight shows that after coming into materiality, an entity can make personal decisions about actions to be taken in response to stimuli. Yet the horoscope reflects a singular individuality and a singular personality. There is no initial deviation from the characteristics under which one is born. The physical and mental natures that the person receives at birth are fixed. The parents and place of birth are fixed, and after this event, cannot be altered. One can rationalize, these are fatalistic or as a law laid down. If a soul truly can make a choice prior to a birth, as Edgar Cayce's reading has just indicated, then the fatalistic parts were, in fact, acts of free will! They were selected and executed by the soul when the spirit entered the body.

Once physical birth takes place, these soul choices cannot be immediately changed. Only behavior can be changed. Behavior is a reflection of the control a human being has when making decisions. That control is where free will enters the picture (again). Being impelled to exercise free will is a fatalistic occurrence decided earlier by the soul. Not being compelled to respond or responding in a personalized manner are acts of free will on the earth plane.

One can behave in such a manner as to change characteristics received at the time of birth. The physical features can be altered (such as by plastic surgery) or the personality can be redirected through training. Building a healthier and more desirable body can become a conscious activity. As in *My Fair Lady*, speech can be altered. Beauty can be created or enhanced. One of the most common ways for beautification to take place is to change the hairstyle. Whether male or female, everybody can grow, advance, and improve through free will.

> So the basis of not only the complexions of body would be changed as to be more in a healthful and thus in an activative force to beautifying of that which is to man his crown of strength and to woman her head of beauty; for to man hair in the head is as strength—to women is as beauty.
>
> 636-001

Additionally, it is relatively easy to modify the effects of environment (and the sidereal energy) by relocation. But one starts with what one is given (or what the soul has chosen). Moreover, the calendar of upcoming events marking when those options in life might be undertaken was laid out through this choice. What the words in Edgar Cayce's readings convey is that it is far better for an individual to think and act upon principles at each milestone than to simply endure the forces and perhaps not respond or follow the dictates of others.

Hence, astrology establishes a fatalistic timetable for the impingement of distinctive and intricate forces that will affect the life. The nature of these forces can be calculated in advance of their happening. The soul can predetermine which forces to choose, and the astrologer can reproduce the timetable showing when these forces will act. The astrologer can, that is, if working from a correctly timed horoscope. All such forces operate only within certain categorical departments of life. The planets indicate the kinds of forces present (seven in the original allegories, but now ten). The aspects indicate the harmony or disharmony of the forces and their strengths (twelve in longitude; three more in declination). The houses indicate which departments of life are going to be affected (twelve). One might consider progressed aspects to be mainly, but not completely, predestined.

The timetable in the Tropical system of astrology cannot be changed. It is wholly fatalistic. The Sidereal astrology timetable can be modified and adjusted by moving to another place to live, but then that timetable remains in place until another move is made. Frequent moves cause frequent changes to Sidereal horoscopes, and the strongest changed aspects are mainly to the angles.

> 2. Many are the changes, many have been the alterations in the astrological aspects of the entity, through the application of will as respecting the entity's relations in the astrological, as well as through environmental conditions and relations.
>
> 2670-003

It is these astrological forces that prod the individual and create situations for working out one's karma. The choices of how to work out these experiences are with the live human being and his or her free will. That is why knowledge of these blueprints for a living organism facilitate selection. The schedule of when forces will be present becomes fixed at the instant the soul makes its move. More than one birth time and horoscope are available for the soul to choose. More than one associated schedule of milestones is available. The whole package becomes a matter of choice, just as selecting and verifying the horoscope by an astrologer can be a matter of choice. However, the choices are not infinite. The available times are pre-fixed by the First Cause!

What is not known is whether the soul must comprehend all of the infinite details of each discrete horoscope before making a choice. When several souls are progressing together, however, it would seem that the main definitions and interwoven places would have to be understood by all. That is a very complicated matter requiring precision. The probabilities are very high that no relaxation in comprehension level is permissible. In the final analysis a soul using free will must somehow know the prospective pattern of life completely. This knowledge must be coordinated by the Universal Mind. Any other mind would be woefully inadequate for this task.

Q-31. Is there a special problem of karma causing certain members of my family, for at least four generations (including myself), to be Leo-born?

A-31. Not necessarily. Yet one who has in this family so lived that he wants to be or desires to be, can be. For remember, the soul is co-creator with God and Leo demands, and if you keep on demanding you will keep on having to face the truth.

5259-001

Edgar Cayce could be sardonic both in and out of trance. Facing the truth can demand a large variety of decisions under not necessarily the best of conditions. For example, most progressed aspects allow the human being to exercise free will after birth. However, situations are encountered when the best-laid plans of the soul might not allow for such responses. In a few cases, such as when accidents occur, the time may be too short to act. When an out-of-control car on a narrow road is fast approaching, free will may try to stop the action. In a split second a collision may occur. Some might argue that the individual did not have to be driving on that day and on that road, even if it was the normal route to work. The truth of the matter is that free will did not have a ghost of a chance under those circumstances, with one possible exception. That exception would be foreknowledge of the possible accident that astrological or psychic insight might have indicated. Otherwise, the chances for avoidance were slim to none.

But there are far more opportunities to take positive actions than to react to uncontrollable accidents. Speculation about people is even more interesting. Since many people live on earth together, it would be expected that souls have relationships with other souls. Considering the sequence of steps taken by souls before and after birth, the complexities of fate and free will would have to expand—in many cases becoming joint responsibilities. Any soul may have been masculine or feminine in prior lives. That hardly matters, and a wish might be harbored to change sexes. Or two souls may simply want to continue reincarnating together, both sexes remaining the same or exchanging places. By being born in one general area, meeting, and becoming friends, such individuals can continue their relationships

Q-8. The sex has not been changed, then?

A-8. Has not been altered, as far as the physical forces are concerned.

140-036

There is considerable evidence that souls congregate. Furthermore, there is no apparent reason why spiritual growth cannot take place jointly for even closer relationships. Do we now understand that the fate of being born as companions was really the result of free will being coordinated by more than one soul? Being born as brothers and sisters in the same family is one form of a closer relationship, although births would occur at different times. Ample evidence has been given by Edgar Cayce to show that family members in one life often reincarnate into the same family group in the next life, although roles might be changed. A husband might become a son, or a wife might become a daughter or vice versa. These switches provide unique opportunities for expiating karma. Their opportunities for using free will and advancing toward a final destiny would necessarily become intertwined.

For a moment, let's turn to what is that termed as the Akashic Record, or that which may be said to be destiny in the entrance of a soul into materiality. For remember, matter moved upon— or matter in motion in materiality—BECOMES the motivative force we know as the evolutionary influence in a material world. An entity or soul is a portion of the First Cause, or God, or Creative Energy; or the terms that may be had for the MOVEMENT that brings matter into activity or being. Hence souls in their varied experiences—whether in the earth or materiality or the various spheres of activity about the earth (termed the astrological sojourns and their influences, where there have been the fruits of what? Spirit! As the motivative forces in a contact)—are again and again DRAWN together by the natural law of attractive forces for the activity towards what? The DEVELOPMENT of the soul to the ONE purpose, the one cause— to be companionate with the First Cause.

Then as the entity here contacts in materiality those of its own body, those of its own sympathetic condition, it is for the development of each in its associations one to another toward that First Cause.

As to each of the children, then, as we find these have been leading one another, leading self, the ego to these varied activities.

903-023

Family members have a special togetherness with each other that must be ascribed to fate. Children play together, grow up together, and learn together. They may fight, compete, or help one another, but the ties are strong. In ideal families parental relationships are close, and the mother and father provide a major portion of training. Today, when the percentage of family units are declining, there is cause for concern. Fate might not be applied in the same way. It would appear that backward steps are being taken in the pursuit of destiny by some of the world's inhabitants—or destiny is not a paramount concern to them. More sojourns are indicated. Sometimes everyone else besides the immediate family is an outsider. No one else can be trusted, but that is a function of individual decisions and experiences. Home is where the start is made. Edgar Cayce said exactly the right things about home, and all should understand the deep implications.

> For the home is the NEAREST pattern in the earth (where there is unity of purpose in the companionship) to man's relationship with his maker. For it is ever-creative in purpose, from personalities and individualities co-ordinated in a cause.
> 3577-001

There are possibilities for joint relationships other than usual family members. If more than one birth occurs at a particular hospital and a number of soul-chosen times are clustered rather closely together, each baby will capture one of the astrological times available. That might happen if there are a sufficient number of prospective birth times to go around for that place and day. When the quantity is limited, especially in large population centers, it would seem that several babies might have to acquire one or more identical horoscopes. This is conjecture only, because the special type of data required for proof have not been collected by this investigator. It has been collected by others. Thus, the indications are that two or more babies from different families adopting the same horoscope is not only possible, but probable. If true, the babies would be astrological twins and share most of the same characteristics. Reports have been written that indicate they lead parallel lives. Each baby in these situations has different parents, except for twins. Yet the evidence suggests they inherit the same timetable of progressed aspects and share the same experiences whether living nearby or apart. Edgar Cayce also gave similar reports.

50. For the entity then was a mate or a twin, that was often mistaken for the Prince himself; though not even of the same

family, yet of such a mould, such an activity as to be oft misunderstood, misdirected in some ways and manners—until the
union of their purpose and activity made for the preventing of
turmoils arising in the experience of Su-Son.

1610-002

Q-55. My twin sister, [2268]?
A-55. This has been a very close association,—and much to
be worked out together. In practically each sojourn or experience, a very close association.

1789-007

Twins can provide an even closer relationship than any of the
other possibilities. Over a period of more than half a century,
the number of available incarnation times for both twins and
single babies varied from one to thirty-six during the quarter of
a day centered two hours before their physical birth times. The
average number of spiritual birth options for that period was
eight. There could be more than thirty-six, but no larger quantity
has been encountered. If agreeable horoscope times were relatively close together, no problem would really exist. The two
souls could choose to be born as fraternal twins, provided the
cosmic patterns were acceptable. But, if the choices of horoscope times were sparse, joint reincarnations as identical twins
might be the best course of action available. These two souls
would probably insist upon parallel developments. In that kind
of situation, only one horoscope might be acceptable to both for
continuation of their journeys in spiritual development. So they
are born as identical twins. There has to be something special
about sharing one horoscope, because it is an unusual occurrence. Yet it would be an understandable situation when viewed
in the light of what Edgar Cayce has told us. Their similar be-
haviors would be jointly fatalistic to uninformed spectators. Yet
both souls choosing to reincarnate together would be acts of free
will. To add to the complications, acts of free will include those
of prospective parents.

Q-8. Astrological conditions indicate my next and last child
will be a baby girl. Is this true? and is it possible that there
could be twins? If so, when would be the proper time for conception to take place?
A-8. The astrological influences for SELF indicate such. For
the PROPER relationships to be established, for a CERTAINTY

of same, would require the relationships with the mother and the astrological aspects THERE. In the creation of INFLU-ENCES, as we find, these may be altered by the actions of the INDIVIDUALS as related to ANY ASTROLOGICAL aspect; for that within each individual's development is the application of the will. As to this BEING a twin, this—we find—may be POS-SIBLE, but would depend upon the many variations, as indi-cated. The best time, as we would find, would be that the BIRTHDATE would be in February or March.

1925-002

One important conclusion is that identical twins might be able to share the same horoscope, but they absolutely cannot be born at the same physical time on earth. Their births or first breaths could not be the same. Observations show that identical twins are born fifteen to thirty minutes apart. There is no reason to believe their horoscopes are different. If unenlightened astrol-ogers only understood, the existence of identical twins refutes any first-breath theory!

Fraternal twins are special too, because the relationship be-tween souls must be closer than for ordinary brothers and sis-ters. All fraternal twins studied had separate horoscopes, although their physical birth times were usually around a half hour apart, the same as for identical twins. In these cases, it appears that at least two potential horoscope times were avail-able and acceptable for continued parallel developments.

Q-14. When twins are conceived the ideal of each parent is expressed.

A-14. This may or may not be true.

Q-15. When triplets or more are conceived it is the result of confusing ideals in each parent.

A-15. Remember, it is physical first, mental next, and spiri-tual next. All are dependent one upon the other.

281-055

Another condition that consumes the minds of astrologers, because they do not have positive answers, is caesarian births. The whole matter of timing a horoscope becomes perplexing, since an artificial birth time is not the same as a natural one. Yet empirical records show that differences between spiritual birth times and the times when a surgeon operates are larger than average, often amounting to three or four hours. Quite a few twins are caesarian births as well. That adds further complications to astrologers. These souls may sense that the birth must occur as soon as possible, in time for both to be born. Both have to enter before the doctor intervenes. These are interesting speculations, although Edgar Cayce really did not say much about such matters. He spoke more often about causes and therapy.

Q-21. What is the cause of Caesarian births?
A-21. This is produced by other disturbances. This wouldn't occur here with this body.

Q-22. What should be the care, the precaution, against?
A-22. The perfect relaxation and the position of the womb or the uterus during the stage of pregnancy.

2072-006

Spiritual birth times for one location of birth change daily. A baby born one day at a certain time would be born on the preceding day at a slightly shifted time, or on the succeeding day at a small change in the other direction. This observed phenomena has implications with respect to babies who are taken before their normal terms. Their horoscopes would be changed. Their fates would be changed. This implies that artificially induced labor causes small, but definite, alterations in the physical characteristics and personality of the individual being born. The timetable for experiencing tailored forces would be altered. Induced labor is another form of willful interference with respect to what might otherwise be a natural process. Additional urgency might be forced upon the soul for making a decision in favor of a modified phase of karmic experience in a body with an altogether different personality than the one originally planned.

It has already been disclosed that a horoscope time for each day is governed by physical positions of Uranus, the Sun, and Moon, with Cancer and Sagittarius as reference signs in the circular zodiac. Only these three planets govern the times, and not any of the others. Only these two Tropical signs are baselines. No other signs are involved in this manner, and the signs are definitely not Sidereal in nature. They are from the Tropical zodiac. These three heavenly bodies form the directional vectors for the day. Each alignment of a directional vector is thought to act like a pipeline for instantaneously fixing a horoscope. The mechanism of actual horoscope fixation, as stated earlier, is unknown. But spreading of these cosmic forces into the seven endocrine glands has already been speculated upon. Invariably one of the calculated times coming into alignment has been found to match a perfect horoscope for the newborn life. A perfect horoscope matches every one of the entities being born together. None of them gets shortchanged.

What comes to mind when reviewing these particulars is Edgar Cayce's frequent references to planetary sojourns. One might ask, "Do twin souls or allied souls depart directly from the same planet where their sojourns were taking place when deciding to be reincarnated?" Probably. "Can logic prove a stopping place must be available for both souls at some location outside the earth as Edgar Cayce said?" Probably not. "Do these considerations of joint soul births give further significance to the idea of a stopover?" Each soul might more rapidly execute entry into two adjacent bodies from the nearby position. If two souls shared a horoscope, the shortened distance from the takeoff spot to each baby might be absolutely essential. No changes in the selected time of their identical horoscopes could be acceptable. "Is the reconnoitering point also to accommodate joint decision-making with other souls who will become closely associated?" Maybe. "Does moving the location to keep it in line with the chosen babies in some other way facilitate the gathering of the immense amount of information upon which joint decisions will be made?" We cannot know for sure.

Therefore, answers implied by several of these questions must again be labeled speculative. Fraternal twins, identical twins, and coincidental birth twins have occurred, and their lives have been studied. Marrying on the same day, buying clothes the same day, moving on the same day are examples of facts uncovered. Nearly the same or exactly the same cosmic patterns would be necessary for these actions to be synchronized. Of this, there can be no mistake. The evidence, therefore, reinforces the idea of a joint place of departure. By hovering in line and over the head of each child, joint decisions with the Universal Mind and other souls would be facilitated. Will is the force applied by each soul when building toward a union, and will can be altered as necessary.

2. In entering, we find the entity coming under the influence astrologically of Mercury, Jupiter, Uranus and Nep-

tune; Venus in the foreground, as it were, in its varied
aspects. These influences, with the application of self in the
present experience, have been altered somewhat by the application of will, that developing factor in the entity's (as in
every other entity's) experience; for with the will those influences are made either applicable in the experience or they
become altered as the influence varies with that influence in
the PRESENT experience by the environment, as well as the
shading of those in the innate or hereditary forces. These
may be one, even as all force, power, or every spirit activity
is of one source. The individuals, in their use or application
of that development within themselves, build toward that
union or they separate from same.

1924-001

Understanding bits and pieces of this overall scheme urges
astrologers to be more accountable when casting horoscopes.
What is being determined is not just a configuration of planets, but a picture of each soul's choice among a number of definite options. Fate is determined and free will is exercised.
Fortune-telling is emphatically not an objective in casting such
horoscopes. The importance is much, much greater. Absolute
causes and potential effects upon destinies had to be reviewed
by each soul upon entering. This realization has lead to an astrological approach that relies primarily upon selection of a
precise time (to a fraction of a second) as opposed to groping
for a rough time in hours and minutes, proceeding through
rectification (possibly to an assumed minute) and then trying
to ascertain whether or not the adjusted time yields a horoscope that is satisfactory. Understanding leads to a responsibility for picking the soul's precise fatalistic choice correctly.
In fact, the choice of a discrete horoscope for a discrete time
emulates the soul's action, but from a different perspective.
Honing one's skills in determining which of several horoscopes
is correct replaces less determinate methods, or those that require more roundabout efforts. The chances for error are also
significantly reduced. The essence of this approach is to focus
discrimination skills upon astrologically delimited human characteristics and detailed recognition of functionality for selecting a predetermined horoscope that will behave as a law.
Visualizing the ingrained karmic pattern and the manner in
which planetary sojourns materialize, and associating these

details with the being that has come into existence is an inter-mingled challenge and responsibility. Visualizing two or more ingrained karmic patterns with their cross links is even more challenging and rewarding.

11

FAMILY AND FRIENDS

HOROSCOPES CHOSEN BY souls are outstanding in showing where mother, father, brothers, sisters, children, spouse(s), friends, and partners are located and the nature of each relationship.

The soul not only picks the individuality, personality, a timetable for karmic unfoldment, and predilections affecting physical health; it picks all family members, friends, and partners. This marvelous collection of indicators is in addition to the planets that describe the individual's pattern of life and milestones—all in the same figure. Not any horoscope will do. Only one of those available to the soul can and does show all of these individuals in proper alignment. The parents and other relatives born before the soul enters have to be properly shown in the chosen horoscope. Moreover, all future relatives, friends, and marital partners must be indicated. These other personalities might be born before or after the birth of the particular soul. This would not matter. The entire group must be integrated. The fact that they are for every birth is sensational.

Q-50. For what purpose did the entity come to this plane at this time, and why in this particular family?

A-50. That the relationship has been such, with the family associations—or those that are responsible for the entering of the entity into the earth plane, that they may make for the abilities to ENABLE the entity to find self the better.

The entity may be an aid to them, as they may be an aid to the entity; a complement one to another.

At this time the entering was for the purpose of giving that which the entity has that many need; the opportunity for self-expression, the opportunity to lend aid to others is before the entity.

984-001

Many choices through willpower in later life may be available. That is, one can select or reject many different friends. One can find a spouse from among many different people. Willpower is exercised to enact these associations, but those choices must fit the pattern shown in the horoscope. Broad latitude in making these choices is granted. An open interpretation of the planets and signs allows one to see that many different matches between individuals are possible. Yet in particular ways the planets in the houses must represent the natures of those people who come into the life of the individual soul.

2. In an astrological aspect, you will find these have altered much through the application of the entity's will regarding associations and relations, MAKING much of the environment for self.

772-002

All of the above is a remarkable assignment for a soul to manage. It is remarkable that all coalescing souls can be kept straight. Only by the will of God could that be done. Moreover, the astrological signatures must be reciprocated in every horoscope. Pure logic tells us that only one horoscope for each person could possibly incorporate all of these indicators and urges for the involved souls to choose. The remaining choices of horoscopes for each particular place of birth and period of time must belong to other souls preparing to enter.

Astrological lore postulates that one parent is shown by the fourth house, the other by the tenth house. Children are indicated by rulers of the fifth house. A mate is characterized by the seventh house. Close associates or partners are also in the seventh house, but friends are in the eleventh. Brothers and sisters are in the third house. If these interrelationships with other souls are to be coherently established in the selected horoscope, then the soul must be aware of all the latest affinities in making its choice. Foreknowledge of the kinds of relationships to be expected in each house and for each moment of birth must be possessed. That is, parents, brothers, sisters, offspring, friends, future spouse(s), partner(s), and associate(s) have definitions in prospective horoscopes. The selected horoscope for the soul being born into this physical plane must show all of these bonds in the proper light. The indicators in each of the aforementioned houses must be attuned, and the nature of each related person must be unmistakably characterized by some prominent feature. The aspects must show the nature of compatibility between each soul. Every related horoscope must mesh in all of these ways. Overall, that is a tall order. The fact that multiple horoscopes exist that coordinate all of these variables is astounding. However, remember that the Universal Mind established the conditions.

Q-56. Do I owe the members of my family anything and what?

A-57. This is a very uncertain question. There is a duty, an obligation that ye owe SELF in the relationship to EVERY member of the family; as EVERY member owes same to thee; to make the associations constructive and each better for having been thrown or drawn together.

For nothing happens as by accident, but that the glory of the Father may be manifested in the doings and the relationships of each individual as one to another.

1432-001

With respect to karma, the groups of souls involved would be expected to have karmic patterns that fit each other. Mothers and fathers have their own personalities; furthermore, each parent has karma to work out. Investigations of their horoscopes in relation to their children's horoscopes are uncanny in what they reveal. Together, they provide needed opportunities for the advancement of all of the evolving souls.

Q-13. Does the incoming soul take on of necessity some of the parent's karma?

A-13. Because of its relative relationship to same, yes. Otherwise, no.

5749-014

Thus, it would appear that a soul in concert with the Universal Mind is faced with making a precise choice of relationships through the single horoscope picked. Characteristics of those souls already living on earth must be known to the incoming soul. Matching of these characteristics to the available times of birth and attending horoscopes must be made correctly. In addition, such a choice portends coming children, later-born relatives, spouses, and companions. Each relationship must fit the proper house as a place holder.

However, the specific soul to occupy each position in the future would not necessarily be a prerequisite. It may be that a number of souls could fill each position, so long as the proper qualities and distinctions are maintained. Many nuances must be weighed and balanced. Nevertheless, they are among the intricate factors that must be considered in each soul's choice of a time to be born. The sheer volume of these considerations is another one of the reasons why finite times are available for a birth to take place and not an infinite number of times. The aggregate choice is a complex enough task as it stands.

If one thoroughly contemplates this picture, understanding the way it is repeated for every birth, then a specific finite horoscope time must be one of those available for the soul to choose that fits in every way. A gradation of moving times would be inconsistent, if not impossible to imagine. Even hour births would be highly improbable, and close to thirty percent of all horoscopes cast by astrologers are for even hours. About seventy percent of all horoscopes cast by astrologers are for even quarter hours. It would be most improbable that one of those crude times could provide the correct alignments being required by the entire group of souls, including those not yet in the earth plane. Yet, as monumental as this task has to be, some leeway might exist through switching of roles in the same exact horoscopes.

Q-16. What associations or connections have I had with the members of my family in previous appearances?

A-16. These have been indicated in the experiences and expressions of those that have been given as to the period of activity when they came together. These were then closely associated in the activities during that particular experience. Not always the same relationships as in the present. Some experiences are reversed, as has been indicated in the experience of the entity—as indicated in the experiences for those of the family relationships in the present. But these become such that, as indicated in the present, there are the needs for that advice, that duty, that relationship which exists in the present—as an OUTGROWTH of those periods of activity. And these become then the REAL reasons—if there is as a reason—rather because the brother was then the sister, or the sister rather then as the relationships of the companion or as an overseer or as an advisor, but rather than in the present the relationships are such that if the relationships are related to Creative Forces, as they are expressed in the fruits of the spirit, and these exercised in the relationships, the development of body, mind and soul becomes in its proper relationship in the present.

338-004

Edgar Cayce clearly indicated that role reversals or interchanges of soul relationships can occur when progressing from one incarnation to the next. There have to be reasons why a particular soul in its latest relationship now fits one of the indicated houses, rather than a different house for a previous incarnation. Some of these reasons are most likely karmic in nature. Buried in the language of more readings are additional explanations.

Q-56. How was I associated with my present family in previous incarnations; first, my wife, [2175]?

A-56. As the father of the present wife in the experience before this, and didn't always make it easy for any—owing to associations with others!

Also in the Palestine activity ye were closely associated as the companion or husband of the one who is the present wife.

Again in Atlantis, the associations were rather as acquaintances and helpful influences one to the other,—yet questions oft as to one another.

Q-57. My daughter. [2308]?

A-57. In the period before this we find an association, as well as in the English land.

Q-58. My daughter, [1566]?

A-58. In the Egyptian period close associates, as well as in the experience just before this.

Q-59. Why was I separated from my parents at such an early age?

A-59. These are experiences that may best be known by the paralleling of some of the associations. For, there are conditions—especially in the soul experience, not from the physical. For, remember it is the soul choice, the soul vision in which there are choices made for entrance into material experience,—so that little of the channels, save as a channel, enters into the developing or retarding. For, as to soul—"Who is my mother, my brother, my sister? He that doeth the will of the Father!"

Q-60. Any other advice for the entity at this time?

A-60. As indicated, great possibilities, great responsibilities lie before the entity. Choose thou well. Take one step at the time. Be SURE that the way leads, in choices made, to the way which HE, thy Brother, thy Lord, hath chosen. For He withholds no good thing from those who love the Lord!

2301-001

Thus, former friends can become sisters or a previous child can become a parent. This complicates house locations for each associated entity, and somehow the soul must keep track of them with respect to new prospective horoscopes it can select. Those emergencies in time come to mind when a soul must abandon an orchestrated pattern and rapidly switch to another one. The administration of such a switch must be a nightmare. If a number of souls are progressing together, then choices of horoscopes for their next lives must by re-synchronized and made acceptable to one or more of those concerned, if not all of them. An integration of desires has to be maintained for any change in birth time. An integrity of principles must be maintained throughout the period of sequential rebirths. That integration can only be attributed to the Universal Mind.

Hence we find from the astrological great friendships have existed and do exist in the experience of the entity; oft becoming a stronger or more of a tie than those influences of material or family relationships.

One who is enabled through these very abilities to make friends, and has experienced both those influences of losing them when not desiring to and not being able to get rid of some when it desired to!

These become then a portion of the experience of the entity

to be dealt with in constructive ways and manners.

1522-001

Hence, friends reincarnating together must have their births coordinated, including those who have already been born. A parent in this present life, or individual with some other earlier-born relationship, may not have a subsequent say in the choice of a soul coming into this current life plane. They are already in the earth plane and no longer have all of the prerogatives of souls between earthly sojourns. However, it would appear that their own choices of horoscopes must fit a mutual plan. The pattern for offspring of parents was established with their choice of horoscopes as they were themselves born. Likewise, an older close associate or other family member would have chosen a horoscope to fit the new relationship with its latest soul birth. Thus, it is entirely possible that a soul realizes prospective new relationships that accompany the soul choices of others as they become sequentially aligned. In many cases, great patience would have to be exercised if priorities had to be deferred.

This, then, has made for that opportunity—as it were—for the entrance of this soul in these environs, these conditions; that it—through an All-Wise, All-Merciful Creative Energy (or God)—might be given into the keeping of those that have within themselves that ability to raise within themselves that which will prompt, does prompt them to give of themselves, of their abilities, of their own patience. For, as He was given to all, "In patience possess ye your souls."

731-001

We learn from such passages that unselfishness, as well as forbearance, become part and parcel of the process of group betterment. But some people are born into poor, even destitute, families. Some are born into wealthy families. Some people are born into dangerous or fearful existences. Some are born into comfortable, protected surroundings. Often the irreligious, not knowing about the justice inherent in reincarnation, point to this seeming lack of fairness. These nonbelievers are upset by the apparent diabolical plots of life that are constantly unfolding. However, pleasant ones are unfolding too. Often, it would seem, the choice of an economic or sociological environment is a matter of karma. Karma earned and karma to be worked off establish the particulars. The fortuitous situations in life can become evident to those who would look and see. The strained situations in life can likewise become evident. Both kinds exist for good reasons.

It is not an accident that an individual is born into a family where there is fortune or fame or position or power, but rather that the soul has merited, does merit—the OPPORTUNITY for expression in that environ.

So with this entity then those urges and those influences that are roundabout from the activity of the entity in the earth, the activity of the entity through its experiences in the interim, have been rather what the entity has done, does do in the present (as to its FUTURE development), regarding that IT, the entity, has set as its ideal.

Then as He gave, study to Know Thyself, the INNER self; what motivates self in this or that activity!

For there are indeed those things that seem right to a man, but the end thereof is death. The end thereof is separation; the end thereof is confusion.

THESE are when there are self-aggrandizements, self-indulgences. Not that man in his evolution or in his development does not arise to those influences that make for the greater opportunities, but what does he do with them?

1167-002

Not only does a soul warrant good fortune in the present life through past accomplishments of merit, but often conditions or tendencies toward others are carried over from a previous incarnation. Again and again, karmic ties are intertwined. Coincidences happen so often that they must be noticed and recognized for what they are. Coincidences may be only those happenings for which reasons have not yet been discovered by the frail minds of man. Without reasons the intuitive instincts hold sway. They emerge as feelings.

Q-50. Why have I always felt one apart from my family—brother and sisters?
A-50. Because ye were once cast out by some of those.

2624-001

In giving the interpretations of the records we find that the experiences in the earth before this, as well as the two other outstanding experiences, are such that amulets or things that

arise from honors conferred upon individuals close in association or affiliation, or in the family, become a part of the entity.

These become innately, manifestly, either experiences that
may become stumbling-stones or used as stepping-stones for
greater opportunities.

For, know that in whatever position an entity, a soul finds
itself, it is that the greater opportunity may be had for fulfilling
the purposes for which each soul enters a material experience,
and that the greater opportunity arises from and through that
condition, that experience.

In giving the interpretations, these are chosen with the desire
that this experience may be a helpful one to the entity in its
seeing itself, and in the desire that the entity analyze its purposes, its desires, as in relationships to its fellow man, that the
experience may be filled with greater joy, greater harmony, and
that the glory of that for which the entity enters may be made
more and more a part of the experience.

For the desire of the heart and the mind and the body should
be, "Thy will, O Father; that Thy purposes may be fulfilled in
me and my feeble efforts."

We find that the astrological aspects give expression through
the innate feelings of the entity—the dreams or the desires.

And those that arise from the emotional, or the material sojourns, are a part and parcel of the whole of the entity's experiences.

1582-002

Again and again, we are told that a soul-chosen horoscope
gives expression not only to the feelings of the entity toward
others, but also specific past, present, and future relationships.
Each member of the family, each associate, and their relationships to the entity are shown by particular houses. Houses three,
four, seven, ten, and eleven are the main ones that indicate these
other souls in the group that are progressing together. The first
house is reserved for the self. The nature of each individual, self
as well as others, is shown by the planets within those houses,
or by the ruling planet(s) of the sign on the cusp, or the aspects
of occupying planets to any other planet in celestial longitude
or declination or another zodiacal sign within the house. Should
the signs in one house be intercepted, then the rulerships increase and the relationships may increase, whether planets are
within that house or not. One would expect activities of the
affected house to be compounded as well. Therefore, a broad

variety of possible relationships is often indicated. This variety may ease the problem of finding places for associate souls. Moreover, a large variety may be necessary for families having a large number of children, friends, and relatives. These individuals are definitely not alike, but their places must be indicated in all of the horoscopes. They form some of the ingredients in a soul's repeated choices for each incarnation that must be correct. Not a single house is allowed to describe a relationship that does not fit!

3. Coming in those periods when there were the changes not only in the astrological aspects but in the associations and environs which the entity chose for its entrance, we find that there has been, there is, there will be an influence upon those associated with the entity. Also there have been those influences which have made for a development for the entity in this experience; development meaning in the soul or the spiritual associations and activities.

4. As to the astrological aspects, we find the entity coming under the influences of Jupiter with the benevolent influences of Venus. Thus the urge in the activities among peoples of various associations, classes or groups or characterizations. Yet the entity deals an influence upon those whom the entity contacts. And with the benevolent influences in Venus it finds that in charity and in love these activities have made for the more pleasant associations in the present; making for the home life, the associations in the home yet with many homes represented. In other words, the activities deal with the influences in many homes. These are as the choices, as it were, of the entity in its appearance in the earth in this particular period, through these particular environs.

5. In Uranus we find those influences making for interests of the mystical or imaginative nature, having to do with the activities in peoples' lives, in the associations of others, in the abilities within self for depicting and interpreting for others those things that may be or are of the imaginative nature. The entity is an interpreter of art, song, verse, and of those things that may make for experiences in the affairs of individuals rather than eccentricities. Yet these having an experience in the entity itself, others oft call the entity rather unusual than eccentric. However, at times the entity is considered by others

as being rather stubborn or hardheaded. These have grown, as it were, rather through the experiences in those activities brought about by the Jupiterian and Venus influences; though more and more they have become tempered with mercy and justice.

6. From the activities through the astrological sojourns of the entity, then, there have been brought influences in the inner self that are innate—and that find expression in those things indicated as being a portion of the entity's experience in the present.

379-003

After a birth, parents, family members, and associates can be delineated from the proper houses by a competent astrologer working with an accurate horoscope. When the horoscope is inaccurate, an astrological review might pay lip service to these relationships, or the subject might be avoided when the signatures do not appear to fit. This is where the careful validation of horoscopes adds credence to the fundamentals of house relationships. Only accurate horoscopes show all of these fellow souls. Only accurate horoscopes show the nature and type of person each companion soul represents in the current earth sojourn. Only accurate horoscopes show all of the remarkable coincidences. The timetable of meetings and appearances are also indicated. Otherwise, omissions and misinformation creep into this elaborate picture that cannot be accepted by those who care.

Q-32. Is it accidental or significant that my sister's first child, born in 1942, should have the birthday of a little brother of ours who died in 1913?
A-33. It is significant.

5259-001

Examples from accurate horoscopes are appropriate. The third house shows brothers and/or sisters. In one horoscope the third house contains no planet. Virgo is on the cusp. The ruler of Virgo is Mercury. Mercury is in Sagittarius. The brother of this wonderful woman has a Sagittarius Sun and Gemini is on his Ascendant, ruled by Mercury. Meanwhile, her Moon, governing emotions, is in Gemini. The closeness of this sister and brother is fantastic and unusual for any family.

The husband has Pisces on his third-house cusp with Aquarius intercepted. Pisces is Jupiter-Neptune ruled. His sister has a Sagittarius Sun and Aquarius is on her Ascendant, certainly not an unexplained coincidence.

Q-45. Please explain the simultaneous dreams experienced at various times by me and the entity [849].

A-45. As there were the sources of the one thought and purpose through the close associations as brother and sister (and they were brother and sister in spirit as well as in the fleshly understanding), we find that in the state when the physical consciousness of each is laid aside, the SOURCES of their impelling influence become the same.

1857-002

The fourth and tenth houses indicate parents in soul-selected horoscopes. In one example, Virgo was on the tenth-house cusp. Virgo is ruled by Mercury. Mercury is in Aries. The father had an Aries Sun. The father also had Gemini ascending, ruled by Mercury. Pisces was on the son's fourth-house cusp. Pisces is ruled by Jupiter and Neptune. The mother had Sagittarius rising, ruled by Jupiter and Neptune.

In another example, Mars is in the tenth house in the sign Taurus. The father had a Taurus Sun sign. Libra is on the cusp of the fourth house. Venus rules Libra. The mother's Ascendant sign was Taurus, also ruled by Venus. These types of indicators are commonplace but unfailing in what they portray.

Q-28. My father [. . .]?

A-28. Again in the Egyptian we find the closer associations, for the father was then the father in the EGYPTIAN association—or the father in the flesh; while the relationships in the Persian brought a different character of association but such that it made for the associations as the father again in the present, see?

Q-29. My mother [. . .]?

A-29. These associations were very close in many of the entity's activities. They drew rather one upon the other in the Egyptian, in the Persian, in the American; that is, they were DEPENDENT one upon the other for their relationships in the earth.

993-004

The fifth house shows children. A family with accurate horoscopes had five children. Places for these five children had to be present in the horoscopes of both the wife and the husband. The wife has Scorpio on the fifth-house cusp with Venus, Sun, Saturn, and Mercury therein. Mercury is in Sagittarius. These four planets have many aspects, but the closest are to Neptune and the Moon. The husband has Aries on his fifth-house cusp with Mercury therein. Mercury closely aspects five planets in his horoscope plus his Scorpio Ascendant. The planets receptive to being place holders for children in both horoscopes are Uranus, Jupiter, Neptune, Moon, Mercury, and Mars. The first child has a Cancer Sun with Sagittarius rising. The second child has a Capricorn Sun and Sagittarius rising. The third child has a Taurus Sun and Aries rising. The fourth child has a Scorpio Sun and Virgo rising. The fifth child has a Pisces Sun and Sagittarius rising. Moon, Jupiter-Neptune, Saturn-Uranus, Mars-Pluto, Mercury, and Venus collectively describe these children.

Now, one might argue that most of the zodiac was represented in this large family. But the facts are that Gemini, Leo, Libra, and Aquarius were not represented in the lineup of Sun signs and Ascendant signs of the offspring.

In addition to the indicators described, every child had at least one planet in their own horoscope making a qualified exact aspect with at least one planet in each of their parent's horoscopes. A qualified aspect is subjectively defined here as being within 0° 04' of an exact theoretical aspect angle. The exact aspects of the first child were to Mercury in the mother's chart and to Mercury in the father's chart. The exact aspects of the second child were to the mother's Ascendant and the father's Moon, both being conjunct with one another. The exact aspects of the third child were to the mother's Pluto and the father's Mercury. The exact aspects of the fourth child were to the mother's Sun and the father's Moon. The exact aspects of the fifth child were to the mother's Saturn and Mars, to the father's Saturn. Are any further supporting comments really necessary about these interrelationships? Could mere human minds make these selections without the aid of the Universal Mind? As strong as some humans are mentally, and as great their intelligence, methinks not!

With such powerful astrological associations, there is no question that the parent's responsibilities are more important than ever:

Q-42. How can I be of most service to my children?
A-42. Be their inspiration.

Q-43. How can I make my greatest contribution to humanity?
A-43. Through thy children.

2936-002

The seventh house shows marriage or marriages and other close associates. Perhaps the example couple are anomalies in a twentieth-century society. They have only been married to each other one time and feel very fortunate that they can keep it that way. There have been no divorces for either party. The husband has Taurus on the cusp of the seventh house and Mars is in that house. There is a close aspect to the Moon. The wife has Capricorn on the cusp of her seventh house, and its ruler Saturn is in Scorpio. It is conjunct Venus. The husband has a Taurus Sun, and Scorpio is rising. The wife has a Scorpio Sun, and Cancer is rising. In addition, the husband's Moon is conjunct with his wife's Ascendant. The wife's Sun is conjunct with her husband's Ascendant. This is only the start of the mutual aspects. It is a marriage made in heaven. It was confirmed astrologically before the marriage took place. It was set up by the Universal Mind and implemented by the two souls when they had the chance much earlier, before the birth of either.

The eleventh house shows close friends not in partnership. Perhaps you will recall that Edgar Cayce had Pluto in his eleventh house (see Appendix A). Pluto represents extremely capable people. David E. Kahn was as good an example of a Plutonian friend who can be found to illustrate this type of soul association. True to an astrological fundamental, the eleventh house of an accurate horoscope always shows friends.

One of the spellbinding characteristics of astrology is that thousands of such examples are constantly turning up. However, those who work with verified horoscopes are the only astrologers who find so many. Meanwhile, every kind of question continued to be asked of Edgar Cayce.

Q-73. Will I, or any of my immediate family, reincarnate with Mr. Cayce in 1998?

A-73. This is not to be given, or things of such natures, but is to be determined by the desire, the need, the application of those who may desire to do so.

2285-001

12

INWARD DECISIONS

ASTROLOGY PROVIDES TWO broad directions for making decisions that can benefit everyday lives: inward and outward.

Edgar Cayce repeatedly described the plan for every human being to live, gain, or lose by personal decisions, reincarnate as needed for further advancement, and eventually master spirituality as the soul works its way back to God. Astrology compartmentalizes these decisions within twelve houses. The twelve houses can be divided into two halves of six each, equivalent to the yin and yang of Chinese philosophy. They are inflowing and outflowing, personal and social, me and you. This is a very profound arrangement, known to many people throughout the world. Edgar Cayce did not bring up these divisions directly, although the two parts were often implied. He did have much to say about decisions to be made fitting each of the houses. By studying these subdivisions of a horoscope in more detail, individuals may learn much to help them live better lives and achieve success. Success, by the way, is measured not so much in earthly gains as it is measured in further advancements along a spiritual path.

That an often misunderstood or erroneous astrology was a part of the plan for mankind came across many times, starting with the first of the life readings requested by the man Lammers. These life readings included statements on the proper role of astrology. Lammers was exultant with the answers he got. The unexpected responses were recorded so that eventually others could share the knowledge imparted.

After Lammers fell on hard times and the sessions with him ended, many life readings and horoscope readings continued to be given. References to astrological matters were routinely delivered. Of course, many of these readings pertained to the self, that is the self of the querist. Most of them were not really selfish questions. People wanted to know why they were here on earth, and they wanted to know more about the decisions they were supposed to make. All of the personal questions answered in the readings can be related to the querist's physical and mental bodies, possessions, abilities, activities, home environment, parents, plans, creations, business gambles, children, work, or health. While questions were not asked in that order, they filled the spectrum covered by astrological houses. Therefore, examples from this large group will be addressed according to the sequence of houses. The inflowing questions apply to the first six houses. Many of the answers were coupled with more mysteries that Edgar Cayce revealed.

FIRST HOUSE

The first house contains information about the existence of a human being and its physical and mental body in the present tense. The personality is there. Aspects related to first-house affairs usually set the stage for involvement of the complete self, such as travels, moves, participation in sports, dancing, aerobics, and actions. Injuries or illnesses that impair bodily functions may be shown, as well as uplifting experiences. This is the place where the "I am" of life is found.

Q-8. Explain persona, its form, character and evolution.
A-8. Persona, that radiation through the individual in the earth plane as received by its development through the spiritual planes, as we would have in this: We find two entities in an earth plane, of same environment, of same hereditary conditions. One with a personality, or persona, radiating from every thought or action. The other submerging every other persona it may contact. Different degree of development. Persona comes from development, then, either in earth plane or spiri-

tual plane. The persona [is] acquired physically, the persona [is a] natural development.

This condition we find comes nearer to the radiation in astrological condition, for partakes of the environment of spheres or universal action in the developing entity. Hence we find persons born under certain solar conditions have that condition of persona that radiates in the same direction, while the individual conditions as brought to, or given off from such persona, may be of entirely a different nature, for these are of the different developments. As we find, that would be illustrated in conditions of individuals born in the material world, on the same moment. One in East, one in West. The different environment under which the persona would manifest would partake of that environment, yet there would be similar conditions in the earth plane to each entity.

900-022

Persona is simply the Latin word for a specific person. Edgar Cayce said that persona is a function of prior spiritual developments, environment, astrological conditions, and how the individual handles this combination. The results are a totality of all these experiences as they exist at any moment in time. Thus, location or local environment can make a difference, although a whole variety of conditions would also apply. One's existence on earth is oriented toward its purposes for being here.

Q-45. When did I first exist as a separate entity?

A-45. Would this add to thy knowledge? The first existence, of course, was in the MIND of the Creator, as all souls became a part of the creation. As to time, this would be in the beginning. When was the beginning? First consciousness! There is no time, there is no space. Hence the injunction, first know thy spiritual purposes. Ye know thy ideal. Now correlate same with thy application of thyself in the material associations, and ye will find in same peace and harmony, as well as the ability to carry on.

2925-001

An injunction was given that applies to all human beings. We should know our spiritual purposes. If we do not already know them, then they should be developed. Having ideals is very important. One does not have to write them down. But if that would help to provide focus, then do it. Some people find there are advantages in keeping a diary. Others use planners effectively. Owners of notebook computers sometimes apply them in this way. One of the key benefits is that all of these methods furnish an organized, time-oriented place to write things down and help one concentrate on upcoming tasks and appointments. They do not just remind. They converge and direct energies. The best of the planners and software equivalents have sections for setting down long-range goals where ideals can be recorded. It pays to devote time to these long-range goals in life. Those who do make a habit of attaining them. Those who do not often just drift in life. "Which is better?" is a question that should not have to be asked.

Q-15. What directions can you give me for the "pivot" or turning point that my life has been undergoing these months, with the planet Neptune.

A-15. As indicated heretofore, do not attempt to be guided by, but use the astrological influences as the means to meet or to overcome the faults and failures, or to minimize the faults and to magnify the virtues in self,—as may be used through such periods in a propitious way and manner. But through the channels indicated for the present may the greater steps be taken for equalizing and bringing about the better influences in the experience of self.

Do that.

815-006

Here Edgar Cayce is reprimanding the querist to use astrological influences but not to be guided by them. It is so important that personal decisions be reached through exercise of willpower for character development. Following an astrological influence is not exercising willpower in the best manner for advancement. Taking advantage of the forces provided by the astrological influences in one's own way is another matter. In the example reading Neptune is the planet supplying energy. Neptune offers drama and illusions. The querist should not simply succumb to these influences by entering a dream world, but should take proactive advantage of them by creating something dramatic or special with flare.

Q-7. Is there any other information that this body should have now?

A-7. The body should keep close in touch with the spiritual side of life; with sincerity to the spiritual side of life, if he is to be successful, mentally, physically, psychically and financially.

The safest brace is in the spiritual nature of the body; sincerity of the work done or obtained through any channel with which this body is connected is governed by the masses through the action of the body towards the spiritual.

254-002

Astrology is probably the safest brace for understanding the entire nature of any body. Sincerity of the work done or obtained by the individual for whom the reading was given would be governed by the masses through actions toward the spiritual. Since true horoscopes are derived from spiritual entrance, keeping in touch with the spiritual side of life can be augmented through the channel of studying same. Actions of the body toward the spiritual are reflected in one's first house and progressions affecting planets ruling that house. The Ascendant is the powerful node leading off this house. Its angular position in the horoscope and ruler are included. Now services in concert with the masses would tend to appear in the twelfth house of a horoscope. However, one's body and soul immersion in spiritual matters pertains to the first. Understanding such ramifications of astrology is always fascinating.

SECOND HOUSE

Money, possessions, talents, and the things owned in life belong to the second house in astrology. Making money is the number one concern of a huge number of people during their waking hours, although there is some danger in it.

26. There's no security in worldly possessions. For the earth is the Lord's and the fullness thereof, and the silver and the gold. If ye use same for self-indulgence or self-gratification ONLY, ye do so to thine own undoing. And ye are not alone—this is man's failing, and the devil's way of handling man. For it brings glory to his own ego to possess, or to be looked up to.

2970-001

Mental, physical, psychic, and financial success requires use of second-house assets. These assests are possessions acquired after birth, especially when growing into adulthood. All such acquisitions are oriented toward the future. Possessions are held so they can be used in the future. Astrology can be a powerful aid in this regard. By examining the planets in, and the ruler of, the second house, the best vocations to bring in money can be ascertained. These same elements show directions for producing the greatest gains. But decisions made in pursuit of wealth are all important. Decisions made in spending wealth are also important. The purposes make a big difference. How or why money is earned and spent have a strong bearing on destiny. Many life readings were devoted to financial gain and the reasons why one approach would be better than another. If such undertakings were to obtain the things necessary for sustaining life or to help others, they were condoned. If selfish reasons were the chief motive for increased wealth, that was not so acceptable. In fact, such motives seem on some occasions to cause disruption of the information flow or suppression of energies.

Q-52. Whom should I seek to contact in order to better my financial condition?

A-52. FIRST contact self from within! And then, as there is the application of self, those CHANNELS may be opened for self.

For, as is or should be known, those that are in the earth in the form of material expressions or possessions are LENT! And if ye are in accord with the divine influences, and apply thyself, the way is opened; rather than to say seek John Smith or John Henry.

956-001

To advance spiritually as well as materially, we really need to understand this passage. None of us really owns anything except transcendentally. We are given temporary ownership by the Creator. How we handle these borrowed possessions impacts any betterment that can be obtained. Attitudes toward material objects that express accordance can open channels. Selfish expressions can close them. Thus, possessions can become either pleasures or sources of upsets and irritations.

Knowledge of astrology provides special insights that integrate well with this idea. The principal role of astrology is to map the tendencies chosen by the soul. Hence, certain tendencies can indicate a line of work that will produce financial gain. Certain tendencies can describe those categories of life where money can be best applied. Decisions that are consonant with the idea of lent possession can produce pleasure. Decisions motivated by selfishness can produce agony. Hence, a combined knowledge of the astrological signatures of wealth and accordance with the divine influences can be extremely enlightening.

Approaching that which is owned as a loan from the Creator places the concept of wealth in an entirely different perspective. If this concept were in mind when striving to become rich, the purpose would not be to buy what one wants. The purpose would be to apply accumulated riches in ways that would be approved by the Creator. Learning and applying astrology can facilitate this objective. The insights given make it possible for more people to handle their assets well and to have greater peace of mind.

By the opposite token, demands for money and how to use it once received are sometimes the basis of domestic disturbances. A wife wants more pretty things and drives her husband insane to satisfy her desires, or she abandons her domestic responsibilities to have material possessions for herself alone. He spends for the adult toys he wants, and the family comes second. The me generation wants more and more for self. The most selfish owners of anything seldom attain much spiritual advancement. Observe the agreements to share fifty-fifty in marriage that never work out that way. Then it is often amazing to watch members of otherwise respectable families hover like vultures when an elder member passes on, and their competing greeds for the estate clash. An old saying goes, "Money is the root of all evil." This saying came from reasons of the type described.

Mental upsets can occur when such negative attitudes are present. Freud conceived the idea that knowing the causes of discomforting situations can establish a psychological basis for remedial action. The horoscope can show causes of possession-related problems as well as many other types of problems. Freud understood this very well. He knew that horoscopes can also show ways to apply corrections and benefit from the lessons learned. The mental health of large segments of the population might improve if the participants really understood astrology and the messages Edgar Cayce gave. Possibly, much unhappiness could be eliminated, although that would depend on the levels of development attained by those involved.

Some families handle wealth very well, judging from the way they establish trusts for giving it away after the game of accumulation has been won. There are many very good wealthy people in this world as well as very good poor people. Edgar Cayce's words did not discriminate in this regard. What he did do was to refer to the meek instead.

30. Rather know that the meek, the patient, those that are of one mind in Him SHALL—SHALL—inherit the earth, the possessions thereof!

31. Learn ye what to do with them. For if you say, "Had I much, I would give to the poor; had I plenty I would be kind to the unfortunate," and you do not do the same with your mite, you would not do it if you had much! What said He? "She that cast in the penny gave more than them all." So you are only fooling yourselves if you are not giving, doing, being, even thy little!

254-095

Many readings asked about astrological aspects in making the best investments for maximum profit or the potential success of business dealings. They will not be repeated here, because the messages were for a particular time, place, and person. Much has changed in the world since then. What has not changed appreciably are the variety of schemes for obtaining possessions. Each of us needs to make sure ours are worthy. In the final analysis what we intend to do with possessions loaned to us matters the most.

THIRD HOUSE

Reading, writing, arithmetic, practicing, learning, personal doings and movements in the vicinity of where one lives are in the domain of the third house. All of these preparations for living and personalized actions occur within the local environment. They are mental, physical, and spiritual undertakings by the live body that utilize God-given talents and God-lent assets while acquiring knowledge, experience, and maturity. A truism is that all third-house matters originate in the past. When we study lessons, they were written or taught from prior knowledge acquired by others. Or we may learn from the lessons of our own past behavior. Familiarity derives from this background of conscious and subconscious remembrances. Intelligence that already exists may change or become further developed in one's mind. New inner communications within self are forever being placed in the library of the Moon.

Truth is growth! For what is truth today may be tomorrow only partially so, to a developing soul.

1297-001

The third house of a horoscope and any planets therein show the paradigm of learning. They can provide guidelines for the types of information best remembered or the methods of remembering. They can show the best ways to excel in developing one's writing, speaking, arts, crafts, playing, or singing. In addition, Mercury is the planet of communication who is generally involved with such matters. Mercury configurations read with third-house planets are important in utilizing astrology for understanding this area of life. Brothers and sisters are included, by the way. Those are the individuals, in addition to the parents, with whom communications are first conducted and usually continue the longest.

8. In those influences in Mercury, we find the application, or that as shows for the mental abilities of the entity in the application. While these may oft be termed by others as wonderment and awe, yet with those influences in the Mercurian influence—with that that makes for the eccentric forces—brings, as in these influences in Uranian, that of one well-doing, well-being, often arriving at conclusions, often arriving at the answer to problems in life—secularly, mentally, materially, spiritually—not understood by others, by that innate influence of justice as MUST come. There MUST be, to the entity, the pay to the last farthing. Hence there is often seen in the activities of the entity that which makes for an obedience to those to whom the entity feels there is a tie or any bond of duty, that which may be SOMETIMES mistaken for law. Do not lean too far forward or backward in such relationships, yet let thy yeas be yea and thy nays be nay.

9. In the experiences through which the entity has passed in the earth's plane, we find these as but a SCHOOLING for the abilities in the present, and the application in which they may become those of lessons, those of truths, those of under-

standings in the hearts and minds that the entity may contact,
or that which may be left by the entity for the study, the development, of other minds.

933-001

Conclusions, answers to the problems in life, schooling, and
understandings of the hearts and minds that the entity may contact do little or nothing unless expressed. One must master how
to speak and write in order to convey lessons learned. This is
the only way they "may be left by the entity for the study, the
development, of other minds." Lessons may very well include
those learned during planetary sojourns, as well as the formal
education received while growing up.

For each entity in the earth is what it is because of what
it has been! And each moment is dependent upon another
moment. So a sojourn in the earth, as indicated, is as a lesson in the school of life and experience. Just as it may be illustrated in that each entity, each soul-entity, is as a
corpuscle in the body of God—if such an entity has applied
itself in such a manner as to be a helpful force and not a rebellious force.

2823-003

Integrating the messages contained in Edgar Cayce's life readings with an understanding of how to study, as found in one's
own horoscope, can illuminate pathways for improvement and
right action. Decision-making with respect to these studies becomes more purposeful through the use of astrology. Having the
ability to know one's signposts in day-for-a-year progressions is
a further benefit. There are proper times to prepare for the
greatest potential success, proper times to act, and proper times
to rest. The resting periods might best be used in contemplating
how to benefit one's fellow man—practically, quietly, and without fanfare. Some dangers could be avoided. Some ventures
could be enhanced. But, with certainty, one reaches a destina-
tion more easily with a map than when having to travel strictly
on instinct. Such is the case if one knows how to read that map
correctly and grows during the journey.

In the studies, then, know where you are going. To find that
ye only lived, died and were buried under the cherry tree in
Grandmother's garden does not make thee one whit better

neighbor, citizen, mother or father! But to know that ye spoke
unkindly and suffered for it, and in the present may correct it
by being righteous—that is worthwhile!

5753-002

Without astrology or a comprehension of Edgar Cayce's messages, there are many who just live for the moment. Reasons
for living can be unclear. Degrees of satisfaction with what a
person is doing can be highly variable. Often, people in this
category are nine-to-five jobholders and find nothing inspirational in their work. Yet one's occupation can have branches
that lead to other goals for advancement. Immediate interests
can establish purposefulness. Taking classes can fill comprehensive needs. Acquiring new skills can establish confidence and
broaden outlooks. These third-house activities can brighten
lives, and they offer opportunities to meet other like-minded
people.

Those who backslide usually find the pursuit of happiness to
be elusive. Some individuals meet uncertainties, unhappiness, or
traumatic circumstances that they attract by taking refuge in assumed family superiorities, aloofness, or irritable behavior.
There is a hidden danger in such comportment if, or when, it
becomes a substitute for right treatment of others. It would be
especially well for these people to listen to what Edgar Cayce
said about such behavior. It would also be well for them to learn
what can be done when astrology is learned.

Q-27. Would it be well for me to make a study of astrology?
A-27. Well for everyone to make a study of astrology! for, as
indicated, while many individuals have set about to prove the
astrological aspects and astrological survey enable one to determine future as well as the past conditions, these are well to
the point where the individual understands that these act upon
individuals because of their sojourn or correlation of their associations with the environs through which these are shown—
see?

Rather than the star directing the life, the life of the individual directs the courses of the stars, see? for was it not
given when His star appeared? Is it not shown in all the
studies of the positions that the earth occupies in its course
through the spheres that every condition is as cause and effect? but that the scale has gradually been on the increase
for the individuals as they passed through their various ex-

periences in the cycles of position? This is not intended to indicate that (as some astrological reports have been made) there is a definite period when individuals enter a cycle, or that every two thousand or one thousand, or five hundred or twenty-four hundred years an individual re-enters the earth; but as a race, as a whole does the twenty-four hundred year period hold good, see? for in each period does the earth, do the planets, do all of those about space again revert to that it would begin over again.

The individual activity is a thing of itself, see? for, as may be illustrated in Life—as of an individual: It may be said that the line of thought in the present is towards a change in the Aries age from the Pisces, or from the Aquarius, or to those various activities, see? but it doesn't mean that every individual changes, for each individual has its own development. As we look about us we see the various spheroids, spheres, planets or solar systems, and they have their individual activity. Look at the soul of man and know it may be equal to, or greater; for it must be man's ability to control one of such! Vast study, yes!

311-010

Astrology is a vast study indeed. It is studied in the third house. The implications of man's activities are fierce if we consider that our decisions can alter the courses of the planets.

FOURTH HOUSE

We have just traversed and explored three domains of existence—being, earning, and learning. Let us now enter three domains of effectivity—influence, creativity, and accomplishments. Concepts incorporated are authority, home life, prestige, eminence, importance, inspiration, projections, implementations, and accomplishments. This second group of three houses comprise what we stand for or represent to ourselves. They indicate the results or effects of our being, just as the body, things owned, and preparations may be thought of as causes.

The fourth house kicks off representation in the present, starting with the home. The home is where authority or lack of same starts. It shows the dominant relationship of at least one parent, usually the mother, because in the traditional sense she exerts authority during the early stages of life while father is away at work. It shows upbringing. The home is the first place where character is molded. Ultimately, it relates to family positions throughout life. Influences may be either positive or negative, but it was chosen by the entering soul for a reason. Planets in the fourth house and signs give the qualities of this domain.

8. One, with those influences in Jupiter and in Venus, finds many loves come in the life in the younger days, and centralized in the one in the latter day, giving then much to the family and being that of the exceptional mother in the home, being able then to give much advice to those in or under the care of the entity.

780-006

The previous example reading with its astrological indicators portrays an expansive and harmonious home life in youth and in later years. This person is very fortunate. The next example may not seem to be as fortunate, but perhaps the opportunities are just as great.

Q-24. To what extent have childhood home influences incapacitated the entity for a normal, happy marriage?
A-24. Just as much as the individual entity lets it have. For when ye were a child, ye thought as a child, but when ye became a man ye should have put away childish things and not blamed others for same. For each soul is an entity, body, mind, soul. If it will use its will, in applying the fruits of the spirit to those conditions about it, the entity may attune itself to the infinite. If it attempts to abuse such, the entity pays the price. Just as ye may see about thee. As a tree grows you may bear it and use it and grind it in the shape desired. So may an individual entity, as it is trained, grow. It has those complexes but it also has its own individuality, and apple trees don't produce peaches, neither does a son of Satan produce saints. But ye are the son of the Almighty, the Creative Forces, even as Satan. Whose side are you on? Ye alone can determine! Will ye?

4083-001

Planets in the fourth house show the nature of home life, whether favorable or unfavorable. This is where influences upon the individual are strong, where character is molded. Those influences can have all of the shadings and variations of the combined planets, signs, and aspects. When no planets are to be found in the fourth house, its ruling planet and sign command. When planets are present, these basic indicators are amplified. Every planet has many possible modes of expression. Two more examples are found below:

7. We find in Venus that there have been disappointments in the home and family relationships, yet much that the entity may call beautiful. These the entity cherishes a great deal, and these the entity should apply in the life of self and in the lives of others.

3197-001

13. As to the influences in the experiences of this entity, then, from the astrological aspects we find these have been met in most of the activities in the present experiences. For these become in Jupiter that of a protective influence, so that the relationships, the dealings, the activities of the entity tend to be—while of an individual nature—rather with the MINDS of others as a whole, as a group; though individual in application.

14. Hence in any field of service or activity in which the entity may give the greater hope or knowledge, or aspect of human experience or endeavor, becomes an outlet for the self that gives the assurance that ever "Thy spirit beareth witness with my Spirit as to whether ye be the children of God or not."

15. Not in an abstract manner, but in the definite giving forth of self, as in the abilities of building—first a home.

1458-001

Any planet in the fourth house should be applied in the life of self. One of the great applications is in building a home, but many are the interpretations. Some astrologers err by reading too much into the positions of such planets. They may be guilty at times of trying to force events to agree with predictions. Here Edgar Cayce explains another adverse fourth-house position wherein the planets are kept in proper perspective.

Q-35. [Left out of original copy] Thru astrology and palmistry she seems fated to lose her father easily. How will this be and when, or is it untrue?

A-35. As we have indicated, that may appear—but astrology and palmistry are only indications. What caused the loss of the father, or the self to the father, in the experience before? RASHNESS! Then, let ALL keep their head, keep cool—even in those periods of disturbance.

3089-001

Losing her father was not a foregone conclusion. The adverse astrological aspects did not necessarily mean that fate of a parent was sealed. Causes can have many effects, and keeping cool during disturbances is often the best course of action. Keeping cool bolsters confidence. Losing cool does the opposite. The aspects did show disturbances related to the home. That situation occurred. The exact results of the disturbances could have manifested in many different ways, and the exact results could have required a choice. The precise fulfillment of the astrological aspect in a situation of that type would have to wait for a decision.

Now, all of these must be considered, would the entity bring now to self that of the better conditions. Would the entity pay the price, give self in that way and manner as to bring about the advancement, by being away from family, then do that. Would the entity consider the home the higher consideration, and the money the lesser condition and consideration in the end, do THAT. The entity must act from its own will forces. Conditions have been set before the entity. As to HOW they will be acted upon is with the entity. Hence, free will in Man— for, as has been said: "Before you this day is set good and evil. Choose THOU."

779-014

Citizens of every land need to recognize that their start in life on earth came through the desires of a father and a mother. Family life shapes and molds the child. In this generation with the integrity of the family unit in decline, there is much to be concerned about. The needed fourth-house influences may be deteriorating.

8. Remember, He has given thee father, mother, home, opportunity, possibilities that are within thine own grasp now.

And the meanest, the littlest man in the world is one who is unappreciative of what has been done, what is being done. That is why man, when he forsakes God feels so low, becomes so little in his own sight.

2780-003

The home is where many possibilities are within grasp. Children who do not have much of a home life are often envious of those who do, but the more fortunate children brought up in good homes may not be completely appreciative or aware of the responsibilities they have. Establishing a home is a significant responsibility.

Q-9. What are the warnings to be seen in the love of home, and the love of family relations?

A-9. As has been warned as respecting relations and family relations do not let thine GOOD be evil spoken of; nor do not allow the relationships to become such as to make self or the relations as selfish, or as bigotry in ANY sense. These the warnings, as has been given to those in care, as well as of self and self's relations see?

282-003

And so every astrological house can have its positives and negatives. In the case of the fourth house, as for all of the others, looking forward to a reciprocation in kind is a powerful and meritorious objective. One's position on such matters is always important, even when that does not seem to be the case.

Q-14. Please give me any other advice that may be helpful.

A-14. It would be well that each entity—as self, considering here—ever look forward to that experience of building a home. The entity will experience (while do not entangle self from a financial angle) in the preparations, in the layout, and in the care for that as being contemplated, the greatest constructive force in the experience of the body that may ever be had.

For HOME represents that of permanency, to the mind, to the body; in peace, in harmony, yet in doing good for goodness' sake—which brings within the experiences of all, when the speculative influence is left out—a home, a fireside; mother, father, home, family; that becomes as the overflowing blessings in many, many ways.

416-011

FIFTH HOUSE

The fifth house is the springboard of creations that grow and inspire, coming to fruition at a later time. The range of creations includes plans, inventions, investments, gambles, children, sex, and fun. This is the house where even a joke can be hatched and retained for telling again, creating lasting joy. And so it is also the house of enjoyment. But more importantly, it is the house where the projections of spirit may be found.

> And the purpose of each soul's entry into an experience is not only to apply the material and mental self for the enjoyment of what may be called the material pleasures but these if they are of and making for constructive influences to individuals as to the manifestations of Creative Energies, or of God, then does a soul, an entity, manifest and experience the greater blessings of a manifestation in the material world.
> For unless the Creative Forces or the divine within each self find an answer in the lives of others that gives expressions for a channel of manifestation of those influences, little does life become to such individuals. For sooner or later it must pall upon them. Thus interesting self in the lives, the experiences of others in a constructive way and manner that is tempered or directed ever through the impulse as arises from the spiritual self and import, brings peace and harmony that those who have not been active in such CANNOT, DO NOT know.
>
> 1238-003

A life without exercising creativity palls. It becomes dull and insipid. The fifth house of the person cited above expresses the effects of creativity upon self, hence, sad results if something is not done to take advantage of abilities. Answers can be found in the lives of others. The closest lives are one's own progeny. Every kind of question was asked of Edgar Cayce about those little darlings.

The following was an astrological reading as much as it was a quest for knowledge about another child. Edgar Cayce reported that an Aquarian or Pisces Sun sign would be best. Imparting this type of knowledge seemed to be effortless, because he had an inexhaustible source of astrological intelligence to call upon. Furthermore, he was not adverse to answering questions of virtually any personal nature.

Q-11. What is nature of experience and urges which have acted to produce the behavior of self in sexual matters, and how is this to be properly adjusted throughout?

A-11. These ye can analyze by the ways and manners indicated. This is a part of nature itself, yet it can be controlled according to that held as the ideal of the individual entity. First the concept must be in that which is of the same nature of sex itself which is creative. Then as to whether this shall be abused or used in those directions that have been set forth and indicated, as to what you would like for others to be if there should be the choice of a mate with whom there would be the creating of a channel for another soul to enter the earth. Act in relation to the opposite sex as ye would have the opposite sex act toward thee, if you were to be chosen as a companion.

3198-003

Same sex relationships cannot create a channel for another soul to enter the earth. Hence, a tremendous opportunity for advancement toward destiny is lost through such a fifth-house decision. Neptune is frequently the source of delusions in such matters. A fifth-house Neptune can allow misplaced emotions unless the will is used to overcome such tendencies. But once again, a placement of this type need not lead to such life choices. The Neptunian influences could be directed into personal dramas and hopes for a more idealistic future. This would be gratification of a different type.

Q-70. What trend of thought or tangible plan must I follow to rest myself at ease mentally so that I may remove ever-present doubts and apprehensions as to the future?

A-70. As indicated, in those fields of service that bring to others a hope and an understanding—though you may do it in fictions or in fun. And as you study for this, not only the assurance for the material conditions but for the mental and spiritual forces will be aroused to activity. Hold to that as given; first, know thy ideals, and the author of them—and whether they are able to keep that ye may commit unto them in any condition. This brings the greater assurance and must be, as has been indicated, of SPIRITUAL inception.

For, good alone lives.

1574-001

The scope of this house may be difficult for some to grasp. It holds enjoyment, and it holds children. Then every bit of speculation, gambling, and betting can be found there as well. It illuminates a way of imagining what will be in the future. Planets within this house shape those urges to make things come true. The thread tying all of these elements together is one's own spirit coming to the foreground, making those projections. The projection can be something trivial like mentally picturing the drawing of an ace or rolling a seven. The projection can be more important expressions of ideals that one hopes will be fulfilled by offspring, or the projections can be a plan to increase wealth for the worthy cause of supporting a family or more. Sometimes much more, and that can lead to widespread happiness.

5. As we find these are the astrological aspects, which come as those latent forces or influences that are intuitional, or intuitive. And the body has the abilities in intuition to the point where the psychic faculties of the body, or the soul forces, may give expression in the material, or manifest in material ways and manners, to an advantage—if the ideals, the purposes, the SOURCES that are held to are constructive and not merely as explorations or as curious or wondering where it would lead.

6. Rather let self be directed by that which has been builded in its relationships to Creative Forces.

1444-001

If the purposes are constructive, the finest expression can be realized. If the purposes are for the satisfaction of curiosity or wondering where explorations entirely for personal gain might lead, negative manifestations can be the result. Sexual exploitations without real human bonding can fit this category. It is a form of pleasure, frequently short-lived and without constructive motives.

17. Then we find certain astrological aspects as a part of this entity's experience. As to what he does with these depends

upon self, and the standard or measurement by which the choice is made.

18. Thus the warning to every soul, and to this soul: KNOW thy ideal, and the AUTHOR of it—spiritually, mentally, materially.

19. You manifest in a material world, yes,—but prompted and guided by that which is the IDEAL of the soul, mind and body. There is the ideal of each.

20. WHICH, what, do you gratify?

2462-001

Q-32. How should I conduct my life henceforth so as to extend my usefulness and my enjoyment of the activities of this life, as far as possible?

A-32. In that direction of the purpose for which each soul enters a material experience. It is not for the gratifying of self, but to the glory and honor of God. These should be the activities, then; as in appreciation of that opportunity, and being of such a help to others as to maintain at least some consideration of self in same. For, as ye treat your neighbor, as ye treat the least of thy brethren, ye are doing to thy Maker. Then so live that it will be to the glory of God and to the honor of self.

3083-001

Edgar Cayce's points are not just repetitive religious ideals. Repeatedly, he emphasized the importance of having a plan of conduct in one's life. This is the way to move forward, instead of just wandering from one pleasure to what is hoped will be another. New pleasures can become elusive, although humor has the virtue of being expressed to others. For an individual who had Uranus in his fifth house, he said:

19. In Uranus we find the extremes,—the tendency to withdraw within itself at times—as has been the warning—and others attempt to express in humor something that is not felt, to see the reaction upon others. Yet this may ever become the saving grace. For, humor—or to be able to see the fun, the ridiculous, in the most sacred experiences to many—is an attribute so well manifested here, but so seldom found in many individuals.

2775-001

For another person with Uranus in the fifth house, he said something quite different and gave another type of warning:

> 15. Turn rather within. Know that whatever experience ye have in the material sojourns for a purpose. Know that it is not by chance that ye are in a material or earthly consciousness in the present. For know that all activities of the mind, of the body, must be based upon SPIRITUAL things. This does not mean goody-goody, but the PURPOSE, the ideal,—unless it is founded in that which is constructive, which is CREATIVE, this experience may become—under these extremes—a torment throughout.

> 16. Yet if thy ideals, if thy purposes, if thy desires are set in that which IS creative, we may make a glorious experience of this sojourn in this material plane.

> 17. The natural inclinations which arise from the Uranian give an interest in the unusual, in the mystic forces and influences, in the spiritual things.

> 18. Cultivate them. For know, though thy body, thy mind, thy soul be as the triune, they are one; with each endowed, by the Maker, with each attribute of the various phases of the experience.

1754-001

And so the effects of creativity are shown by the fifth house, and they can produce glorious experiences during this sojourn on the material plane if so willed.

SIXTH HOUSE

The importance, authority, and clout of an individual exist in the present (fourth house) to use new concepts, new offspring, new projections, new ventures or pleasures with the intent of bearing fruit in the future (fifth house). When executed, there is application or service to or by oneself (sixth house) that makes use of these prior existing and generated assets. Therefore, work is accomplished based upon past causes and the accumulated destiny to that point in time. For one individual, Edgar Cayce gave counsel for application by means of a horoscope reading:

> 10. From the Jupiterian sojourn we find not only the benevolent but the adverse forces. For, while Venus WITH the Jupiterian brings the enjoyment of the beautiful in ways that would pertain to a universal consciousness or activity, the adverse in Mars indicates that wrath or anger or temper, or such, may bring those things that will cause the influence to be in a reverse manner, as it were, in relation to the entity's APPLICATION of abilities in these directions.
>
> 1990-003

Here was a direct interpretation of the client's horoscope without the usual guiding principles or suggestions that ought to be followed in perusing this person's line of work. However, answering specific questions and giving advice were sometimes combined and sometimes separated. The next example separates these two thoughts. A specific question was asked about a potential health hazard that might affect the querist's ability to perform work. Health of the physical body is an important factor with respect to accomplishments. Therefore, it is very much a part of sixth-house considerations.

> Q-19. How may I as a student of astrology understand and interpret the new turn of the constellations and their effect on the physical body?
> A-19. This would require a reading IN ITSELF! For these would go into those changes that have been given by the mystics of old, as to how and when—at certain periods—they are to pass. This began on the twenty-sixth (26th) of September this year.

> Q-20. Any further advice that would benefit me at this time?
> A-20. In the mental and spiritual attitudes, the inclinations are for an active service in the use of the spiritual and mental understanding. Keep these as constructive for SELF as for others, and we will find NOT that it may produce or would produce selfishness but rather selflessness in the experience of the body. For constructive forces are always POSITIVE. The mental reactions create negatively through doubt or fear. But KNOW in what thou hast believed, and know it is able to keep that thou committest unto it against ANY influence that may be in

thine experience. For the earth is the Lord's and the fulness thereof. He has not forgotten! For Life itself in every form bespeaketh HIS PRESENCE, His mindfulness of those that would do His biddings!

1100-008

Positive and negative forces, as well as selflessness, are reflected in attitudes. Some people look upon work as a hardship, and that is a negative. They do not view work as one of the great pleasures of life but as an interference or imposition upon their time. This business of health, physical fitness, attitude toward job, and the ability to perform are intertwined. The huge preponderance of physical readings that Edgar Cayce gave were frequently attuned to the sixth house astrologically, because so many people who came to him were sick.

2. Yet, as we find, there should be kept the suggestions that have been given for the proper consideration of the physical activities of the body and the diet; not as an obligation or a hardship but as a necessary influence for betterment to the general physical conditions of the body.

3. If the attitude is held that it is a hardship, that it is a condition which prevents the physical body from enjoying itself, the aid that might be received is more than half undone.

4. Rather it should be the ENJOYMENT of the body to adjust itself physically that the betterment mentally and spiritually may have the better temple for activity in this material plane.

464-014

Many questions about service were combined with astrological or horoscope readings. Therefore, it was inevitable that questions about careers in astrology would be asked sooner or later.

Q-2. To be an exponent of Astrology, is this my proper Life work?
A-2. This is indicated at least as being a part of the Life's work. Writing on such subjects and aiding others in their spiritual and mental development should be a portion of, or may be combined with this as, a life's work.

Q-3. I dislike immensely the commercializing of my astrological knowledge; is there any way I could contact the proper
parties and funds so that I could give my whole time to research
astrology?

A-3. Only through the making of contacts where this might
be used as a feature, or from the radio, or some such means
for the immediate commercializing of the activity to supply—
through such an association—sufficient amount. This may be
either with the manufactures of perfumes or toilet articles—the
making for the association towards those tendencies in that
direction; or it may be an association in such ways and manners as to make for the ABILITIES of the body to carry on in
such research work.

778-002

Actual work performed or services rendered as they affect self
fall into the sixth house. Any circumstances that affect the abilities of a body to carry on work are to be found there as well,
but service to self includes the activities of servants and employees, so they are included too.

Q-8. Are employees properly taking care of income and ex-
penses, and should they be kept in employ?

A-8. These have been, in most instances, most satisfactory.
This, again, depends a great deal upon the attitude of employer
to employee, for where much is required, where confidence is
placed, where the activities physically and mentally are in and
of a cooperative nature, there is seen that, that as is GIVEN that
is received. In the same attitude, then, as the employer holds
to the employee, and the employee holds to the employer, we
find that reaction as is in keeping with the attitude, active and
passive, as respecting each; for when one becomes supersti-
tious of, or fearful of the actions of such an employee, that the
actions become in a manner as expressive of an attitude, then
dilatory action, the inabilities become manifested, and the
weaknesses become accentuated. When there is the whole-
hearted, not as of working for—but working with, or toward a
common end for all—not necessary, under such, that the social
environs be made equal, no—but that the one purpose as may
be held, for an individual knowing that in the success, in the
correct attitude, in the holding of an ideal—as business, as
social, as religious, as the principles of life—as ONE—these
may be made so cooperative that the success is assured. These

may, in such a way be worked out—and ones acting in such a manner as to become unsatisfactory, then reason with such an one. Then, not heeding to same, change.

2189-003

The advice here is virtually a short road map for good labor relations. The message is really, "Do unto others as you would have them do unto you." This theme is repeated in many ways as questions were asked expressing concern over personal accomplishments, spiritual attunement, and relations with others.

Q-4. How can [257] group proceed with the opening of the plant at Chichester, N.Y., to be successful with it and still allow [257] to develop his spiritual self to the satisfaction of his Maker and those surrounding him?

A-4. This would indicate, from the questioner, that there is a difference in being a material success and in developing spiritually and mentally in a material way. The question itself is based improperly. For, as has been given, to gain the whole world and lose the own spiritual self or soul is naught. Then, the policies, the activities, in every way and manner, must be in keeping with that which is constructive, that which is activitive in that way and manner, if there would be a mental, a spiritual, a material success.

To be sure, there may be material successes in sharp practices; there may be material successes in taking advantage of one another in varied activities; but—the Lord thy God is ONE! and this applies in business, in mental, in the spiritual life, and should be construed so—and they that attempt to make them separate do so to their own mental and spiritual undoing, and sooner or later a material and mental failure.

Q-5. In what way, so far, has his ego prevented the proposition from progressing to the point that his will desires it to reach?

A-5. It has not! The warnings that have been given were not to allow the anxiety, the desire, to make for the allowing of improper or unseeming promises, or for the depending upon purely material things for gain—without the proper consideration of all phases of life.

Here: In the experiences of those in a material world where financial gain is had, where fame to an extent is given to individuals, it is oft seen that they are not at peace with themselves, with their fellows or with their God. There may not be outwardly in the individual experience failures financially, or other than a whitewashing of the mental individual activity, yet there is oft seen in such households that which has been expressed in this manner: "Yes, their money is needed to care for that afflicted one, that disconcerted one in their midst."

God is not mocked; whatsoever a man soweth, that shall he also reap.

And, as has been given [257] oft, too gracious, too beautiful, too sincere has been and is the INNATE desire of this entity to be spoiled by the desire of material gain or fame at this time. Hence the warnings—Know, O Israel, the Lord thy God is ONE! If each soul would understand what that means, he may pattern his life, his associations, his dealings with his fellow man, in such a way and manner as to make not only harmony and peace within his own home, his own mind, but all who contact the body-entity will know same for the beauty of his dealings with his fellow man in every way and manner.

Man should learn—[257] should learn—it is God that giveth the increase. Man as he labors, as has been given of old, is worthy of his hire. To take advantage, then, of an employee because of circumstance, because of surroundings—or for the employee to take advantage of the employer because of any condition that arises—must be met in the experience of them all.

For it is the law; and the law shall not pass away until it is fulfilled to every whit and every tittle in the experiences of each individual!

Hence the warnings given, that there be the building within self of that as would be not merely an axiom but as a living experience. For the Lord thy God is a living God. Man's soul, man's activity, is a living experience. Begin to build constructively in the beginning, if you would have the success in all phases of the endeavor.

257-182

Those employees who have taken property from their employer and those employers who have taken or withheld compensation from their employees should be aware that the obligations incurred are laws that shall not pass away until fulfilled to every whit and every tittle. Were you aware that those office supplies and obstructed payments were so karmic in nature? You do not need to answer me, but it might be a good idea to answer yourself.

Q-22. How long will the entity continue in the present work?
A-22. Until it chooses to change! As given, there are those forces being set about wherein these changes may come— these definite conditions as appear from those of forces from abroad and from near. Application of self as respecting these is of self's will, and not of that as is read in stars.

778-001

13

OUTWARD DECISIONS

HOUSES SEVEN THROUGH twelve are the exact counter-parts of houses one through six. Each inward-looking house has an opposite outward-looking house that shows how decisions cause impacts between self and others.

Just as the lower hemisphere of a horoscope projects inward, the upper hemisphere projects upward and outward. Each lower hemisphere house has its opposite in the upper. They are linked in their purviews of life. White light shines between these du-alities when properly attuned and balanced.

SEVENTH HOUSE

This is the house of mates, partners, and associates opposite to the first house of personal being. The relationship is soul to soul. Marriage means the taking on of a soul mate. A business part-nership is really not much different in terms of souls working together. The partnership relationship in any case may turn out to be constructive or unconstructive. Hence, both parties are faced with taking a chance. If the chance fails, they may become adversaries or they may drift apart. If the chance succeeds, the parties are bonded together as a team. Each soul becomes a companion with another soul, laying the foundation for becoming closer companions with their Maker. Therefore, all decisions involving commitments to others in both directions are serious matters and important to both destinies.

Q-19. Is marriage as we have it necessary and advisable?
A-19. It is!

Q-20. Should divorces be encouraged by making them easier to obtain?
A-20. This depends upon first the education of the body. Once united, once understood that the relationships are to be as one, less and less is there the necessity of such conditions. Man may learn a great deal from a study of the goose in this direction. Once it has mated, never is there a mating with any other—either the male or female, no matter how soon the destruction of the mate may occur—unless forced by man's intervention.

826-006

Edgar Cayce was asked hundreds of questions about prospective mates and business associates that fall into this seventh-house grouping. They were always asked with a degree of uncertainty behind them. The young especially are almost always apprehensive about this major step in life. Both sexes are concerned about who to marry, usually starting at an early age. And that is well. Yet marriage during previous sojourns may have been a more serious undertaking than it is today. During previous times most people for better or worse were married for life. In contemporary society marriage and divorce seem to be on an easy-come, easy-go footing. Divorces (in the United States) now exceed long-term marriages by more than 50 percent. Even so, Edgar Cayce's answers reflected old-school thinking more than the new.

Q-32. How shall I go about finding the kind of man I want?
A-32. Better find the kind of man you can be the best mate with! And if you are thinking of self alone, you are chopping up the wrong tree.

3655-001

Astrological information was frequently imparted with the answers. They gave clues as to what category of prospective partner should be sought after preparing themselves rightly. To one

female below, he essentially said look for a Taurus-born male.
To a male he said look for a Libra-born girl. There is no doubt
that he was seeing the signs associated with the seventh house
of each querist.

Q-40. If there is a "soul mate" for me, where shall I look for
it?
A-40. As ye study to show thyself approved unto God, a
workman not ashamed, rightly dividing the words of truth and
keeping self unspotted from the world, it will come into thy
experience,—and ye shall know it,—for the birth date would
be in May.

2023-001

Q-66. Could you describe the best type of mate for me?
A-66. One born in October—not born in May or in the
months before your present calendar year of October would
be the better. Let it be one with whom there is not necessarily
so much agreement, but that the ideas and ideals of each are
a complement of the other,—but by all means let her be born
in October!

2285-001

Of course, Sun signs are not the only astrological consideration for mating. Marriage or business partner prospects are indicated by planets in the seventh house, their aspects to other
planets, the ruler of the seventh house, and the sign of the Descendant. These indicators portray the types of potential relationships. An astrological sign or planet categorizes the type of
person to be sought. The better relationships for a soul mate
are usually found among signs to corresponding Sun, Ascendant,
Midheaven, or Moon. However, as indicated above, it is not
always essential that the aspects be harmonious. Partners do not
have to have continual agreement. They can have ideas and ideals that complement each other, and that combination can form
a very strong team.
When Aries is the sign for a partner, the individual is usually
pioneering in spirit, aggressive, and a self-starter. This individual
may also assume me first in all matters. When Taurus is the sign,
the individual is usually strong, determined, earthy, and desirous
of beauty and harmony. Taurus can be morose and stubborn at
times but will know quality. When Gemini is the sign, the partner will typically be busy with the hands and will love books.

Gemini may be very casual, if not deceptive, with their words, but they also enter into many scintillating conversations and see the big picture very well. Cancer is the family man or woman. Normally, emotions are controlled, but they can run deep. A characteristic of Cancer is to avoid confrontations if at all possible, otherwise the emotions may very well come out. On the other hand, Cancer is a power to be reckoned with. Leo is the sign of royalty, and its natives assume that they should be the center of attention, catered to, or in control. Very generous at times, but the boss of Leo who does not meet ideals can be the subject of vituperation. Virgo seeks purity in many ways, one of them being a propensity to account for every detail. Hence, they are among the accountants and chroniclers of facts. Virgos can have a very acute sense of right and wrong, thereby causing them to be extremely critical. Libra aspires toward sophistication and always putting the best foot forward. Appearance matters a lot. However, they can easily take positions far left or right of center in attempts to balance the scales that never seem to be balanced. Additionally, they can be very indecisive at times. Scorpio is the resourceful one, always maintaining deep reserves. Scorpio mates can soar or keep their noses to the grindstone. Often having secretive, magnetic personalities, they can be the best of facilitators for good or for bad. The Sagittarius mate asks all and tells all. They are usually philosophical idealists that see into the heart of every matter. When ideals are not met, they can abandon ship quickly. They make good mediators. Capricorn soul mates are traditionalists with strong ambitions, never willingly taking a backward step while climbing up the ladder of success. They like the old tried-and-true. Every step must be surefooted. Aquarius is the individual who takes up for the underdog. They have a keen insight of human nature and can use this advantage in many ways for meeting both selfish and unselfish objectives. Aquarians tend to be independent thinkers and can have fixed, uncommon likes or dislikes. Finally, the Pisces soul mate is the perspicacious one who may appear to be swimming in all directions at once. They are sensitive, deeply emotional, and most forgiving, seeing many sides to every situation. This sign is the culmination of the circle of the zodiac, where mankind is often served by great tolerance of others and the total accumulation of acquired knowledge.

As Edgar Cayce showed many times, milestones chosen by the soul could be read and interpreted. Marriage, of course, would be a major milestone. From experience it has been

learned that seventh-house aspects include an additional set beyond the normal even-and-odd angles between planets. They are
the progressed Descendant longitudes and progressed Descendant parallels of declination. The progressed Descendant longitude is in the same degree but opposite sign of the progressed
Ascendant. The progressed Descendant parallel of declination
has opposite polarity from the Ascendant. That is, if one is
North the other is South, and vice versa:

> 20. There will be great attractions for the entity to the op-
> posite sex. Hence there would be the warning that there be not
> an early marriage for the entity, for this would bring the Saturn
> as well as the Uranian influences in those activities through the
> Venus forces,—which will occur in the experience through its
> seventeenth to eighteenth year of experience in this sojourn.
>
> 2015-003

What Edgar Cayce advised this person was that progressed
aspects of Saturn, Uranus, and Venus would come into play at
ages seventeen and eighteen. The configurations of the so-called
hard aspects did not bode well for marriage; thus, it would be
better to wait for more favorable signs. An unfavorable Saturn
would indicate a stern, penurious taskmaster, while an unfavorable Uranus might lead to a wild, hippy type and a great deal
of uncertainty as to livelihood. Always the comforter and steady
adviser, much counsel was given:

> 22. In the astrological aspects we find those very conditions
> that have been indicated from the experiences have been man-
> ifested. For not only has the entity lived and does live in this
> experience but has lived and does live in many of the material
> experiences of the entity in the earth. Thus no wonder confu-
> sion comes, unless there is held to the one mighty purpose—
> LOVE DIVINE that so overshadows all else as to be that alone
> that makes an experience in the earth worth while; even though
> the entity has experienced those periods when so much
> shadow has made it not worth while. And only the will has
> carried it on, because of that hope which has sprung anew.

> 23. DO NOT let things RULE, but give them—as to self, as
> to others—their proper sphere, their proper place, in the ex-
> perience of others.
>
> 1402-001

As might be expected in this modern age, the negative questions about marriage were asked nearly as frequently as the positive.

> The body physically is made up of many atomic units, yet when one is not in accord with another trouble ensues, and when murmurings or dissensions arise from within, dis-ease—and finally DISEASE—sets in. When a body of individuals (with the mind the builder again) sets forth to gain from that same Universal Energy, or Forces that build, and in the physical, the material, the mental, the spiritual plane, are in accord in mind and in action, the WORLD may be TURNED AROUND, see? for, as it has been given, faith may remove the mountain, see?
>
> 996-011

Readers should note the number of people who are ill and ask themselves whether they get along well with their partners. A good case can be made that a majority of the people who suffer diseases have been or continue to be embroiled in family disputes. Many times one condition simply follows the other from dissensions to dis-ease to disease.

> 15. Then in the choice of a companion it is seen that it becomes necessary to choose one whose purpose in such would become or BE as one with the entity's; and not such an one that would tear down such a place. Choose one who also seeks for a home; not rest, not convenience alone, not that which is an excuse for the activities of satisfying the bodily needs, the bodily ambitions for fame, fortune, position, or the exploitations of its worldly knowledge, but that at such a fireside, at such a place, in such a home, there might be peace and harmony and an understanding of those influences that make for the creating of that which becomes as the material or earthly representation of that called a haven, a heaven, a place of rest; a place where the turmoils of the world, the cares of the days may be for the moment laid aside and there be visioned rather that hope, that promise which has been ever in the hearts of men since it has been given, "Be ye fruitful, multiply, establish thyself in the earth; for thou art lord of the earth and not lord of one another." Never has been the command to man to lord over his brother. For indeed he is his brother's keeper.

> 16. Those influences then that arise from the sojourns in

Venus make for a loving, a sympathetic, a patient entity. Yet these qualities or virtues (as may be termed) have oft been stretched to its own breaking point, that MIGHT and POWER of possession and of "MY this and MY that" have brought those periods when it has sought within itself—to make rather that activity as penance—which has only debased self; but atonement is an activity in the relationships to its fellow man.

17. These make for quite a variation in the experience of man's mind and soul and body; for atonement and penance are as far as the poles of the earth in their influence in the experiences. For no one may buy himself into the good graces of his friend, his foe, much less of his God. But as ye sow, so shall ye reap. And with what measure ye mete to thy fellow man, to thyself is it measured to thee again.

18. For the Lord is not slack in His judgements. Neither doth He forget those that would do good, though they be hindered in their material efforts.

1230-001

Q-37. Would you recommend a separation from her husband?

A-37. It would be a necessary separation while the treatment is going on, but as for the separation for good—this should be determined most with their own selves when conditions are changed; for with those disturbances in the physical and mental being of a body, when disease or dis-ease of any nature is existent, there is a different outlook upon life—and the duties and the associations, and the surroundings—than when normal or nominal conditions ensue. To make decisions under conditions when stress or strain is existent is unwise for anyone; or to insist that such be done, save as the measures that may be brought about for the more perfecting of the conditions that SURROUND a body for the improvement of a mental, physical and spiritual outlook; for ALL should ALWAYS be considered. Do that.

911-001

The prescriptions for business partners and married couples was much the same. That word of caution about not making decisions when under conditions of stress or strain applies to every interface between human beings. Those partners who get along well have less to worry about in such matters.

EIGHTH HOUSE

The eighth house is the counterpart of the second. Possessions of a soul are in the second. Other souls' possessions are in the eighth. But, in addition, the eighth house shows inheritances, economics, investments, insurance, banking, savings, and a variety of other enterprises concerned with the management of money or material things for other people.

> Q-49. From which side of my family do I inherit most?
> A-49. You have inherited most from yourself, not from the family! The family is only a river through which it (the entity, soul) flows!
>
> 1233-001

As always, Edgar Cayce set matters straight and gave a correct rendering of every issue. He also made his points in many unique ways.

> 20. Then as for material gains,—investments in things pertaining to same may be considered by the entity as those that should have due consideration given to them; or as pertaining to air, as well as earth. earth, air, water,—NOT fire.
>
> 1662-002

This is as astrological a piece of advice for one client as can be found anywhere. What Edgar Cayce said was that investment matters could come under any zodiacal sign profitably except for Aries, Leo, and Sagittarius. Of course, material gains to self alone are second-house matters. Material gains affecting brokers, investment houses, buyers, dealers, and sellers are shown by the eighth house. Positions typically show the interplay between both sides. He gave many more readings in investments and other eighth-house matters. They usually contained added useful information—all read from horoscopes that he could see in trance.

> 7. The influences from Mercury, with Uranus, make for the high mental abilities; and an individual, person or entity who

may read character easily; thus adapting self—in the mental, the associations and the environs of associations—towards an executive, or as one who may direct the activities of others in their associations with individuals, especially as to such things as COLLECTING—whether money or things, or those things that would deal with the individual life or affairs of individuals—even moneys. As insurance, banking, or the like. All of these come under these influences.

630-002

10. From Jupiter as well as Uranus AND Saturn, things pertaining to the earth—as of properties, real estate OR the like—should be channels in which material gains may oft be expected. As for things having to do with investments of any nature pertaining to CHANCE, these are not good in the entity's experience—for long times, at least.

2662-001

In giving his advice Edgar Cayce not only pointed out the astrological indicators, but he gave reasons why they did not work at certain times. Cycles caused unworkable plans to be workable at other periods. These changes are synchronized with the rotations of the planets about the earth.

3. In coming into the earth's plane in the present, we find the entity coming decidedly under that condition of the cusps, and in the sign Pisces, with the influence then as is seen in Uranus, Jupiter, Venus, Mercury, and influences from Mars and Saturn; adverse influences in Moon and Neptune. Hence we have from these many varied conditions, some very exceptional qualities, some very ennobling conditions in the life. The Moon being in that adverse condition, we find the entity has found that there are apparently periods in which everything (as would be termed in earthly parlance) is lucky that the entity touches; other periods wherein everything "goes to pot" that the entity has anything to do with. These are especially as pertaining to investments, and if the entity were to take the time he will find these are those of any conditions that have to do with pleasure seeking in the evenings. These have been failures. The influences rather then are that, at certain periods when Moon is at variance with the various elements that enter from the astrological viewpoint into the life, the entity tends toward investments of that nature. Will's force and more of that

ENNOBLING, rather than that of obtaining dollars for the pound of flesh, or irrespective of the result that is to come to other hands.

2855-001

Philosophies were dispensed as seen fit. Also timing. Given that many investments were being made for both noble and less-than-noble purposes, the philosophies could be very different between people on what appeared to be the same subject and at different times. Noble purposes usually benefit other people, such as·mate and family, and they emphasize the eighth house more than the second. Purposes not quite so noble might also be indicated by fifth-house gambles for purely selfish gains. These are just a few of the reasons for differences in the messages given.

Those calling upon Edgar Cayce for market help usually wanted to know when to time their purchases and sales. Answers frequently were astrological in nature, although the planets and signs were not always given.

Q-12. Is this the opportune time to make the investments which I contemplate making next Monday?
A-12. This an opportune time·for making investments that are to be held for a period. For those that are to be changed soon, NOT an opportune time. Where investments are such as are being considered, these are well.

3871-001

Investments to most people become very important decisions. Another eighth-house category requiring advice is insurance. Edgar Cayce once attempted to sell insurance himself, but that occupation did not last long. Meanwhile, perhaps because of this experience, the following reading became somewhat esoteric.

4. In giving that as may be helpful for this entity, it would be well that the activities through the varied experiences be interpreted—at least in part.

5. Let these be first understood, then, and there should be found a response in the inner experience of the entity. For, as we have indicated, this is the practical application of those helps and truths as related to protection—or insurance, as it is termed today.

6. To be sure, man and divers are the manners in which many of those individuals throughout time have altered the purposes for which such protections were first indicated or put into an organized form by the entity. Many corporations, organizations, have taken advantage of those conditions, in which they have used such and have dissipated the real purposes for which this was first instituted and organized. And thus it has brought many problems, even to those who would sue in the correct manner, or who would follow the ideals and purposes for which such institutions were first established or such work was first created.

7. In those experiences, as indicated for the entity, there was the reviving of ideals, the instigation of purposes wherein there might be the protection for home, for life, for all the problems arising in the experience of man through that period of activity.

8. The entity conceived the idea, or ideal (rightly), of there being combined groups for definite purposes to act in stead for those conditions where—through accident or through any activities that brought about turmoils—there was the separating of the head of the house, or members of the family, of the destruction of home by accidents in nature or of any incendiary nature. These were combined not as for monies, as is considered today, or that payments would be made of any medium of exchange, but rather that—as there were those separations of homes from state, and there were groups allowed to make their own fireside, their own kingdom, their own activity— there were the needs for some such grouping, or organization, that would stand in their stead; unless they were again to become wards or dependent upon gifts, or charity, or love, or work of the state.

9. Thus there arose those combinations of groups, of individuals, who pledged themselves as a group to stand in the stead, where there were those conditions arising that prevented the activity of those upon whom such homes, or such a group, or such individuals depended for aid.

10. This then brought about first the assurance groups that there would be protection for the young, or those dependent. This was NOT, as today, for gain, but that there might be given

the material opportunities for the activity of the young, the aged, the infirm, by those groups set or organized for fulfilling of those offices.

11. Such, then, should be the principles of the activities in the present, and in such a manner may better be presented to individuals or groups,—not as investments but as protection. For, these may be put upon such a basis. And when such is considered in that light, every individual realizes the needs of such.

12. Thus it again becomes, as in the beginning, a matter or fact of making individuals aware in their consciousness that there ARE such groups, such organizations that take these condition into consideration.

13. In meeting the needs of such today:

14. The problems of life, to be sure, are one thing; those as of home or property another—as of the protection from destruction by fire or storm or the like. The entity may aid in formulating groups for this VARIED difference.

15. To be sure, in life there is the mortuary or mortality expectancy. There is that increase in this rate in any given group, and in the formulating of policies for the conducting of such. All such conditions must be taken into consideration. And these must be extended over those periods in which all such expectancies are taken into consideration. Unless this IS done, such group might become easily top-heavy. But not if there is the consideration taken, that this—whatever it may be—is protection, never as investments.

16. In the formulating of plans for barns, homes and the like, and the rural or farm, these may be an entirely different nature. These may be banded into groups that pledge themselves, by a stipulated contribution—which may be very nominal,—with each loss by ANY given factor, as may be indicated in the contract itself,—to contribute to the needs of their fellow member, their fellow associates. This may be made into such as to present a very moderate, yet a very safe plan,—as safe as the sincerity of each individual is, as combined in such a group organization.

17. These, to be sure, may be analyzed by the entity and brought into activity in such a way as to make an appeal to EVERY individual who seeks protection, not investment.

2533-002

Thus, eighth-house decisions need to have the right kind of purposes as for all of the other houses. Planets and signs color the requirements and the needs. These decisions affect all external possessions as described, but there is one more possession people may not have considered. That possession is the soul in the body, and the decision is the time to die. Doing so may or may not be under total control of the will. But the soul, a thing possessed for a while by the body, exits through the eighth house to another realm and thence to another sojourn and eventually to another body until these journeys can be ended.

NINTH HOUSE

We have now arrived at the house that provides experiences and knowledge to or with other people. It is a house of expression for that which is learned from the past. As part of the learning experience, professors and other students are met at college. It is where other people make contact during travels. It is where others are found who read or listen to what one has written, sung, played, or said. Occupations falling into the ninth house include writers, publishers, playwrights, teachers, lawyers, lecturers, opera singers, actors, actresses, musicians, commentators, reporters, and the like. All are communicators. They impart information, knowledge, culture, feelings, or perceptions.

The average astrologer may know this side of the ninth house reasonably well. There is another side, however, that they most likely have missed altogether. That side is subconscious remembrance of planetary sojourns and the applications of lessons learned for the benefit of other people. In a long reading for a mathematician,* another ninth-house occupation, Edgar Cayce discussed some of the concepts incorporated.

3. In giving that as may be helpful in the experience of this entity, the approach would necessarily for the entity be from the mathematical standpoint.

4. For the entity in its every relation is not merely method-

ical (for it does not partake so much of this) but mathematical.

5. Anything in its activity that would pertain to puzzles of a mathematical nature, or charades or word building would be of interest to the entity.

6. Hence such an approach is that which would arouse the more interest, and unless it may be made a practical experience would not become of much use or of much experience for this entity.

7. In the understanding then, gain this; that:

8. As in numbers one builds upon the other (as units) and all are formations or divisions or multiples of units of one, so the universe and the expressions of all natures within same are the manifestations of that one force, one power, one spirit, one energy known as or called a Universal Force, Creative Energy, or God.

9. Hence there is a purposefulness in every experience; and this may be worked out, just as mathematically as any problem of such a nature.

10. That there are those relative relationships through Influences through which an entity or soul as a unit passes becomes then natural; or a natural consequence just as Conscience IS, Life IS, God IS.

11. Thus these ofttimes become misunderstood by those who give too great an importance to an individual activity or experience.

12. For just as an experience of a soul or entity into the material plane is purposeful as a lesson, as a schooling, so the Influences through which the entity passes become as those influences in an individual experience in the material plane affecting the entity as Environment or Heredity. And these are just as motivative in the activities of an entity in any experience as the influences from material activities that are as hereditary or environmental.

13. For as a soul enters it is spirit, as God is Spirit. And as

there is the building through the material associations of that through which there may become Life or activative force (which is as an entity's activity), these become then as Influences for judgements or parallels of such influences in the experience of an entity, a soul, a mind. For remember, Mind (as is called) is the Builder.

14. The Influences from sojourns in Environs from without the material plane are as the innate or MENTAL urges that may come as dreams or visions or the like; while the Influences from the material sojourns or individual appearances in the earth are as the earth—earthly HEREDITY that may come in what we know as the emotions—or those influences that may be sensed by the emotions.

15. Yet all of these work or build as it were one upon another, making for that Body-Politique as it were that is known as an individual entity or soul in the material plane.

16. In this entity's experience then from the astrological aspects (MENTAL urges from sojourns from without the material plane, as indicated above), we find these become as the heady; or Aries—and Jupiter, Mercury, Saturn and the activities that become natures that are INNATELY builded; as: the desire for travel is an innate force from its influences in Saturn (which are the changing forces).

17. But the influences from the indwelling in Mercury make for the high mental efficiency and mental abilities; while those from Jupiter become as a protective force—and as the entity will build within self.

18. No matter WHAT may be the circumstance as it were of the entity, it is one that will build or CREATE or make for those influences that become as staying forces with the entity.

19. Hence we will find in some experience in this present life much of this world's goods will be a part of the entity's expression; also much travel in many of the varied lands and environs will be a portion. These are shown INNATELY as expressions that will become a part of the entity.

20. As to how these will come about depends upon the ma-

terial application, or the application of those Influences that arise from the earthly or material sojourns that become as emotions in the experience.

1462-001

Whenever Edgar Cayce says mind is the builder, the reader should recognize that in all relationships whatever is expressed from that building emerges through the ninth house and its planets. Expressed, communicated, or taught are key ninth-house words. However, distinctions between experiences and accomplishments need to be understood because such activities are sometimes confused. Accomplishments fall into the domain of the twelfth house, while experiences and the transfer of ideas are in the ninth. Planets and the sign on the ninth-house cusp provide tone and flavor. For example, a person with Mercury in the ninth house with further influences from Venus and Jupiter was told:

9. The abilities should be expressed in writing short stories and eventually a full length book, whether fiction or only part fiction and historical, or that as counsel to others. The exact type of this writing may be indicated as the entity would apply itself and progress. Thus in its studies, in the completion of its schooling, the entity should study journalism or short story writing. These should be the preparations.

10. Apply the urges latent in Mercury, as well as in Venus and Jupiter, or measure to others—under whatever circumstance may arise—that ye would like for others to do to thee.

11. If these tenets are held as truths and practiced in the entity's relationship to others, it will bring harmony and peace within self and then with others.

12. Ye may not give to others that ye do not possess thyself. The ability to accomplish, the ability to attain to whatever is chosen as thine ideal, in spirit, in mind, in fact, lives, within self. The entity itself must apply these.

3807-001

We prepare to write or speak or sing by studying (third house). Today we might include computer training and networking. Then we publish, present, lecture, or get on the information highway (ninth house). Expressions to the outer world pour through this latter domain.

Most adults have the confidence of their skills, but some people are timid unless invisible to others. They may be frightened of getting up in front of a crowd. Training can help. Joining an organization such as Toastmasters has aided innumerable people as they were transformed into better public speakers. Others may gradually meet the public with greater assurance as they mature. Edgar Cayce shed the right light on this phenomena:

Q-67. What causes my inferiority complex?

A-67. It is NOT an inferiority complex; rather the lack of giving or allowing full expression of that INNATELY known to the entity from its deep experiences in matter and the activities of the many. Because of the FEAR of convention and what others will say. Hence one of the greater forces as may be had, allowing self to be loosed by the influences of the vibrations of the body—in the Appliance—and the abilities to unify the concentrated efforts, ye may indeed learn the lesson as that Teacher of Teachers gave; that abiding in the truth, it SHALL make you free, and will bring to thy remembrance ALL that is helpful since the foundations of that ye know as the earth!

1473-001

Saturn is the planet that typically shows where fear lies. But Saturn can also be a steadying and calming influence, or a place to hold back. Every planet has more than one side, just as the complementary houses show alternate sides. That personal fear to receive everyone's attention (ninth house) is an input by self back over in the third house. Thus, every opposite house has a continual interplay back and forth across the horoscope (through the color white, if you remember). In the following reading, what is felt by self skips to the third house, but all of the rest of the comments apply to the ninth.

21. In the Mercurian sojourn we find that again, as in the Venus forces, of the appreciation of learning; high-minded, but depreciating as it were those who rely upon their own abilities in learning for their activities in associations with others. For the entity knows there are deeper forces and influences that are felt and experienced by self in such relationships.

22. Hence the entity sees the beauty of the influence of

learning, yet realizes its subtle force that may be the undoing of others—if they rely upon same rather than upon that which PROMPTS the activity of such.

23. Where it may be used for the benefit of the many, rather than the confusion of the many or the few—these are appreciated in the experience of the entity.

1648-001

When called for, distinctions were made between the pure astrological influences and those coming from prior sojourns. How the individual spoken to could tell them apart is a question that Edgar Cayce answered in the next reading that involves the ninth house. He spoke of natal planets, progressed planets, and the emotional or sensory forces that caused a love for travel.

18. Jupiter, making for the benevolent forces in all of these, will bring in the latter portion of the experience—and it should begin within at least the present year—more satisfactory conclusions as to travel, as to unusual scenes,—indicated both in Venus and in Uranus, as well as in Saturn. These should in the latter portion of this present sojourn find material manifestation. For the love of travel is indicated, not only by the astrological but from the material sojourns, as will be seen by the very varied experiences in the material sojourns.

19. The astrological influences arise as latent forces, or as the dreams or the thoughts of the entity, while the influences from the material sojourns find expression through the emotional or sensory forces of the material body—which ofttimes are confused, especially by those who attempt to study or to materially apply mystical forces. For, the emotions of the body do not wholly correspond to spiritual awakenings.

2144-001

The emotions and sensory forces are not the same. They come from different sources. Whether there is importance in distinguishing between them is up to the individual, but an astrological adviser might have trouble in doing so. Everyone is psychic to a degree. Astrologers use their psychic abilities more than most people because they have to. But, it would be well for astrologers to know more about the distinctions between purely astrological aspects and subconscious memories of planetary sojourns. In this next reading Edgar Cayce goes into far more detail for the person he was trying to help. The ninth house is where all of this information could be found.

5. While it will require some self-analysis,—study that as may be given here, in the light of thine own experience, as to inclinations and urges that have been latent, partially or wholly manifested in thy present experience; applying that indicated for instruction and edification to make this experience the more helpful.

6. When the material sojourns and the astrological aspects are correlated, these are indicated—as warnings, as well as helpful influences:

7. One very capable in most any line of endeavor.

8. One who may use a great deal of intuition in its experience or associations with others, yet warnings in these are indicated from uses made of same in other experiences.

9. Beware of an individual, or individuals with casts in the eye. Such as led, such may lead thee astray.

10. With the psychic abilities, or intuition, latent and manifested, the entity easily makes decisions—in its judgments on others. This may oft lead the entity astray in its judgments.

11. Judge with that fairness, that open-mindedness as ye would be judged by others.

12. That there are weaknesses and inclinations in the experience with some of thy associates, thy relations, thy companions, is evidenced. Judge not too harshly.

13. DO apply thyself in activities, in any form of activity requiring inspiration for its better performance; as in music, as in writing, as in speaking.

14. Any of these phases of thy abilities may be magnified in the present, as to allow an outlet for many urges. And these, with the purposes as indicated, should give the entity oppor-

tunity for expression in such measures as to be a helpful influence in the experience of many.

15. In latent urges, two great influences are apparent. They may be compared to hereditary and environmental influences in the material plane. But these, of the real self, are the spiritual environments, the spiritual heredity.

16. Spiritual heredity, then, is a combination of what the entity or soul has done with its opportunities for creative influence in this and all other experiences. That inherited is what the entity has made of such.

17. The spiritual environment is the sphere of activity in which such influences have found expression, whether in this or in the other environs of this same solar system; much as the manners of activities in the earth have been in the various classes, the various ages, the various periods through which each soul passes.

18. Body, mind and soul are one, just as the Godhead in dimensions is presented in the material plane through Father, Son and Holy Spirit.

19. From sojourns, these we find in the experience of the entity:

20. Venus gives the appreciations, as well as the abilities in all forms considered or called the arts in the material plane. This includes abilities and activities as a speaker, writer or musician, as well as conversing with, reasoning with, and meeting individuals on their own plane and speaking—proverbially—their own language.

21. There are the abilities for attracting individuals to self, as it may choose in seeking companionships.

22. Consider the warnings indicated,—judge not too harshly, that ye be not also judged. For, with the measure ye mete it is measured to thee again.

23. In Uranus we find interests in the mystical, the occult, the psychic; as well as the moods, as may be termed, when

they give expression in materiality, from the activity of the mind upon mental, spiritual and material aspects of associations, of thought, of spiritual interpretation of conditions in the experience of the entity.

24. We find in Jupiter the benevolent influences, the abilities to see many groups, many phases of human experience; also the ability to analyze things, conditions and circumstance.

25. In this phase, too, comes the ability for the entity to become a universal helpful influence in its activities, as well as the opposite,—miscomprehension, misapplication of spiritual law, that may lead many—as well as self—to disturbing, distorting conditions mentally and materially in the experience.

26. We find in Saturn the change that has been, may be wrought. For this is the environ in which there is purification; not putrefaction, but purification; though judgments of the entity may vivify or putrefy the activities of others, when judged by the standards as set by the entity.

27. Do not attempt to have double standards for others or for self, or for certain groups. For, the Lord thy God is One, and is not a respecter of persons; but He would—wills—that all should be equal one with another.

28. As to the appearances of the entity in the earth plane,— these find expression in the emotional nature. And, as indicated from sojourns in Uranus and in Saturn, the entity has the spiritual emotions, the material emotions. Their purposes should be one. The judgments in same may oft be misconstrued.

29. Not all of the appearances in the earth may be given at this time. These are chosen to indicate that phase of experience that, as we have indicated, is evidenced in the composite phases of the entity's urge latent and manifested in this particular period.

2581-002

Furthermore, this reading was chosen to indicate some of the effects attributed to the planets mentioned. Their effects are distinctive. They should form a part of everybody's education, and higher education is under the auspices of the ninth house. Note that higher education is shared.

For another person Edgar Cayce said:

5. In giving those experiences of the entity in the earth, and the other dimensions through which the entity may pass that give innate and manifested experiences:

6. We find influences in Mars, in Mercury, in Jupiter, in Venus. Thus the entity has a very active mind, ever setting up standards for groups or individuals or for those activities of those with whom the entity may be associated; not in a dictatorial manner but rather as one that would be helpful in such.

7. Then the entity is the natural teacher, the natural director of certain characters of activities, and especially—even in the present—of that which has to do with the outdoors. And as we find, even in the present, if the entity would apply itself to physical education for the teenage, especially girls we would find not only harmony within self but a channel through which the entity may shine out as an example, in which many in all walks of life may be aided.

8. Remember, in such a program to include first spiritual education, next physical—that of exercise, that of proper dress, proper tone of hair, proper care of hair, proper care of body, proper activities that will bring out the better attributes of each individual. For all may have heads and eyes, feet and arms, and a body, yet all may put them to different usages—but all to the glory of God. For God, the Lord thy God is ONE!

9. Physical, mental, spiritual education, social activities all should be to one purpose. Not too much of the satisfying of the emotions but that the body as the temple of the living God may be a more beautiful place for thine own worship as well as those that may be directed by the activities of the entity.

10. In Mercury we find the mental ability, in Jupiter the universal consciousness, in Venus art, music, reading. All of these should become a part of the entity's activity. Just as in the physical, train those of various temperaments as to what they should read, as to what they would do about their abilities as home makers, as clerks, as secretaries or stenographers or whatever

the choice, that there should be decorum in their activity as befits one using such activities—to the glory of one purpose, and that purpose not self but using such abilities to the glory of God—and then they will ever be to the honor and to the helpfulness of self.

11. Those are the tenets, the truths that the entity should apply in its activities.

3350-001

Thus, every house has greatness, even those that astrologers call cadent. The ninth house is cadent. An archaic meaning of cadent is falling. Cadent houses fall behind the strong cardinal houses, but they also have cadence or rhythm. And, they are essential. Man could not do without education and imparting of knowledge if forward progress is to be made. Man could not realize cadence with other souls if it were not for the ninth house.

TENTH HOUSE

The tenth house sits at the top of the chart and is one of the four cardinal houses. It is king of the mountain and dominates. It is the house of power and reputation in society. This is where an individual exerts authority from whatever the position is in life, and it is where authority is exerted upon the individual. Hence, it has to do with hirings and firings, with controls, orders, or commands applied in any relationship with others, and with honors or awards. Everyone who receives acclaim typically finds it to be indicated astrologically by a tenth-house aspect, including aspects to the Midheaven. The type of acclaim is shown by the signs, planets, and aspects involved. The aspect is either with a planet in the tenth or with its ruler.

In youth, with the father typically away at work, the mother becomes the fourth-house authority figure in the home. But either can be present in the tenth-house world at large. Here, Edgar Cayce goes far back among a mother's reincarnations to explain:

Q-36. What were the past associations with the present mother, what are the urges and how may they be best used in the present?

A-36. In the Egyptian experiences, when the positions were much reversed. Thus often the questioning as to who shall be boss.

2969-002

Bosses are tenth-house people. When the fourth and tenth houses are emphasized in a horoscope, such as with intercepted houses or when filled with planets, that person is born to lead. If Martian forces are indicated, it could be an officer's role in the military. If Jupiterian forces are present, the aspirations for being an executive or CEO are present; growth will be a major objective. Each of the planets has its own connotations, and it matters not what the sex.

7. Also from Jupiter and Venus do we find the abilities of the entity in the COMMERCIAL or active field of activity as being well manifested in the abilities as an executive; not often found in one of the sex, with the ability to control or to counsel or to aid in the relationships where such great numbers of individuals may be influenced by the activity. Yet these are manifest in the experience through sojourns in these relations. Hence are the necessities in the entity's experience for entering into these activities in the commercial or material world; in such lines as in large corporations, large associations that deal with the activity of many individuals, may the entity find that which will not only be well in the experience for material activity but for the developing of abilities in the mental and material ways.

513-001

9. From those influences builded in Jupiter and Mars, we find the executive abilities in the direction of organization that requires detail, or that as respecting CLASSIFICATIONS—and that deals with individuals, as well as with things. While to the entity, INNATELY, those of individuals RATHER than things are the INTERESTING things in life, the EFFECT that is had upon individuals by reactions in the experience of individuals, through various lines or endeavors, is of interest. Hence the entity should be, or could be, a politician—and in those fields where executive forces, as well as some active force of self is required, in data or records, or the like, would be—or would have been well; or in any field where there is the reaction of individuals upon those of facts AND figures, these are the fields of endeavor; OR where public policy, public reaction, GROUP

and CLASS reaction, these are the fields that are of the greater interest; as also those of ferreting out UNSEEN, or those of ferreting out problems that are hard to understand—this is the characterization that influences the entity, or is LIKED by the entity, especially, in the READING matter.

10. Those influences that will come in Mars and in Uranus:

11. Mars' influences have made for those little differences that have arisen in the experience of the entity, when LITTLE differences between individuals have grown in sudden heat or activity as to CHANGE the whole experience in the affairs of the entity in the present. This has occurred some once or twice; more in the younger days than in the present, though as we find—if the entity allows same, this will occur again in April or May. Keep even tempered, then, and even minded. Do not be overwrought. But, should changes come about—then rather seek in those fields of the political, than in those of the commercial.

12. Those influences from Uranus will be most active or in the life. These, as we find, will be in or through the next two or three years. WERE the entity to associate self, or to consider SERIOUSLY the research into such fields (as it has in others) that influence individuals, groups, or peoples' lives, the entity could become a real executive in such an undertaking also; for THIS has, as we see, also much to do with policies, or feelings, or reactions of individuals or groups, or the like—see?

5463-001

Both readings are interpretations of the astrological positions of the planets with their distinctive influences upon careers. The signs were not mentioned, but there is always a blending of planet and sign characteristics. The executive good at details or classifications had to have a strong Virgo influence in his tenth house. The information from the signs was simply given without mentioning them.

But, in keeping with Edgar Cayce's general approaches, he also gave admonitions. Raw power can be used in many ways. For the soul's development, power must be used in the right ways, else destiny will be delayed or set back.

2. In entering the earth's plane in the present experience we find the entity coming under the influence of Mercury, Jupiter, Venus and of Uranus.

3. In the astrological aspects, then, we find these above the ordinary; for in the various phases as have been and are presented in the astrological chart, or astrological conditions, this entity should be in places of power, position, wealth, and of one guiding the lives of many. Hence we find there are other influences entering the outcome or the life, other than those of purely astrological conditions.

4. Then the urge as is seen through the experiences of the entity in the earth plane, in respect to urges as seen from an astrological condition and the various spheres of indwelling that the entity has attained through the experiences, brings conditions that NEARLY approach many of these, that fail through the application of will in various planes or experiences as related to earth's experiences—see? Well that these conditions were properly understood, that the various individuals who may have proper access to what the varied experiences of an entity mean, as to how one may then apply self in earth's experience to the BETTERMENT of the individual towards its development.

5. Let it be understood, however, that one that would be greatest among men, or man, will be the servant of most men. Not in that idea as is ordinarily meant, as of servitude, but of SERVICE to most individuals, and not in place of high position, either as of one considered social, or financial, or of material worldly goods as the criterion for the judgement of success of an individual. Rather let it be understood that these places, these positions, are as the outgrowth either of that merited, or of that plane chosen through which one tempts or tempers self as to one's ability to become the servant, or to render service to fellow man, thus fulfilling the whole law of what, and for man's, indwelling in earth consists.

270-015

To have the power to lead other men and women is a tenth-house issue. To render actual services is a twelfth-house matter. From an astrological standpoint, these differences need to be kept in mind. However, Edgar Cayce's message was clear. Whatever power we have over fellow human beings must be applied in a constructive way or else the user of that power loses. As the next reading indicates again, the best of the leaders are servants of all.

Q-81. Would you consider my present work and position a work suitable?

A-81. A work suitable for the stepping-stones. As ye apply thyself in the work in which thou art engaged, ye will find this will bring about greater opportunities in broader fields of service. And "He that is the greatest among you is the servant of all."

1650-001

Both the astrological aspects and the sensing of planetary sojourns influence one's vocation. Moreover, planets in a number of houses other than the tenth exert their influences. The ruler of the Ascendant often points to a particular involvement of the whole body. The ruler of the sixth house shows the nature of one's work personally. The ruler of the second house indicates the ways in which money can be made. The ruler of the tenth house located in a different house is often suggestive of what a person might do in life. With these signatures acknowledged, a horoscope can help in pointing out the directions that might be taken in finding a suitable occupation. Those are in cases of doubt or for those who desire more clarification. But then one's work is somewhat like love. A soul mate is usually known when met, without the aid of astrology or outsiders or anything else. A desire to enter a field is usually known automatically—especially to those with organized minds.

5. In the astrological, or from those sojourns that are termed astrological, we find one of high mental abilities through the Mercurian, the Martian, the Venus, the Jupiterian and Saturn. All have their influence in the experiences of the entity; each according to the will—and this in the application of that as lies in the abilities of the entity through its sojourns in the earth has used these for woe. These may be used in the present for that as may make amends, as may make for an atonement in the present or an at-onement with Creative Forces. And that should be, that must be that which the entity leaves with each

individual for whom, to whom he may give that as is their astrological or astronomical aspects, that have a bearing upon the latent or the material urges of an entity. These are as tests, the urges that arise—and the test is ever that they must be measured by that as is the standard, the ideal of an entity.

6. For while the mental abilities are high, so is the self importance, so are those influences that make for the entity desiring those urges for position, for fame, for power.

7. Power in the hands of those that consider not from whom this power arises, this power is given, becomes as a millstone to each and every soul.

8. So in the application of those abilities, those influences wherein there are the urges for the application of self in these directions, hold fast to an ideal founded not in earthly things, founded not in ONLY mental things but spiritual application of the mental forces, mental abilities, not only of self but in others. And he that is wise considereth the way of the spirit. What be the fruits then of the spirit? What be the motivative forces?

9. Gentleness, kindness, long suffering, brotherly love, patience—these be the measuring sticks, these be those influences that must govern each and every activity in the relationships to not only individuals but to opportunities in giving, in aiding, in assisting others that seek for thy understanding.

1221-001

Power is a gift from the Creator, but power misapplied becomes a millstone. Authority is a trust, and treating others with respect is an essential ingredient in the way it is exercised. Moreover, honor and the adulation of others come from the way each entity handles this trust. Awards in life may be for other reasons than managing people, but the same rules apply.

The cry of the judge, the seeing of the medals, the awards, shows to the entity that necessity of being prepared. As has been given and as has been instilled into the mind forces the necessity of preparation for any force whatever that may be presented into the life of the individual, that necessity of being prepared to meet the conditions, mentally, morally, and in that oneness of spirit with Him who is the giver of all good and perfect gifts. For when that oneness is made, the entity sees, though same may be a blank in the eyes of others, through His strength, through His assistance, all becomes in that way and manner the success. Then heed it.

341-012

Be prepared.

ELEVENTH HOUSE

This is the house of entertainment, sales, friendships, envisioned projects, and mass planning. It is where the spontaneity of ideas is expressed. It is where the imagination is let loose on other people. It is where spirit soars. Trusts, corporations, syndicates, and campaigns evolve from such projections into the future.

With regard to theater, perhaps it would be well first to make certain distinctions. An opera role that is learned and sung, a movie or stage role that is studied and presented, these belong to the ninth house. But a comedian is another matter. Their methods are far more impulsive, and they ride on the collective spirit of the audience. Hence, comedians, the people who make us laugh and enjoy humor, are shown by their eleventh-house planets. The friendships we enjoy are there too. Great salespeople are found in this house; they can cause clients to pleasantly imagine new capabilities if they will just buy the products being offered. This is where imagination takes external form and where all strategies, schemes, and titillating notions affecting other people are expressed.

And the purpose of each soul's entry into an experience is not only to apply the material and mental self for the enjoyment of what may be called the material pleasures but these if they are of and making for constructive influences to individuals as to the manifestations of Creative Energies, or of God, then does a soul, an entity, manifest and experience the greater blessings of a manifestation in the material world.

For unless the Creative Forces or the divine within each self find an answer in the lives of others that gives expressions for a channel of manifestation of those influences, little does life become to such individuals. For sooner or later it must pall upon them. Thus interesting self in the lives, the experiences of others in a constructive way and manner that is tempered or directed ever through the impulse as arises from the spiritual self and import, brings peace and harmony that those who have not been active in such CANNOT, DO NOT know.

1238-003

This reading so exactly expresses the eleventh house. This is where "Creative Forces or the divine within find an answer in the lives of others." Ideas conceived by an individual meet the public. Moreover, having fun with friends is just as important a manifestation of spiritual expression as many others.

9. Know that with what measure you mete it is measured to you.

10. If you would have friends, be friendly. If you would even have fun, make fun for someone else.

3440-002

21. We find in Jupiter the universality of the entity's abilities, as well as the application of same. Hence those activities in which the entity should engage, and in which it will find the greater abilities for expression, should have to do with the general public, as masses; yet the expressions individual. Hence in the radio first would the abilities find the outlet for the better activity of the entity,—in story, in the expressions in same— but always, the more oft, the lighter, the comic or the laughter producing vein.

2655-001

Perhaps the key to the eleventh house is the expression "Mind is the Builder." Liking other people is a manifestation of the mind, and it leads to cooperative works. Enjoying one another is one of the best ways to gain in mutual endeavors. Creative plans for shared benefits are far better than benefits for oneself alone. This includes the ideas of limited partnerships, corporations, land use planning, and mutual benefits organizations.

8. But first we would give these: Know that all that comes into materialization or into physical being is first patterned in mind and in spirit. Mind is the builder, and your purpose is dependent upon what spirit—or what mortar, what water—

those things that go to make materiality active in the earth—
you use, as to what is the character of the body mind or structure that ye, as an entity, create.

9. Just as in the activities in directing those associates
about you, if ye become interested in others, others are interested in you! Are ye selfish in all your planning, no matter how
you may cover it up with pretty words, if it is for yourself you
are using the selfish spirit; then it becomes as the Frankenstein
in thyself before it is through. You have experienced some
such. You know what is meant. If you attempt to become active
in selling to others, unless there is the same sincerity in that
approach to selling—as if you were in the other individual's
place and you present what you are selling in the spirit of cooperation—again it may turn upon thee and devour thy very
self.

10. For the law of the Lord is perfect and ye as a child of
the divine may apply it to the works of thy Lord and Savior, or
to His wayward son, Satan.

11. Astrologically we find the urges latent and manifested
in Mars, Mercury, Jupiter and Venus.

12. A very active individual; you are going to be doing
something, even if it is doing wrong. That is to your credit, not
to your discredit. But keep on doing something, and if ye seek
with sincerity you will be given the way. It is he who is satisfied,
who sits down, who fails. Who lost his talent? The man that
was afraid, or the man who was vigorous and active? In thy
experiences, then, seek first to know thyself and apply thyself
in making thy own paths straight. Or, better illustrated first be-
hold the beam that is in thine own eye and you'll see more
clearly to remove the mote from thy brother's eye. So it is in
thy dealings and in thy activities.

3541-001

Edgar Cayce was a pretty decent astrologer when in trance.
His interpretation of the planets was better than most, and always he came up with those nuggets of guidance that are so
important to everyone on earth. Observe how he identified the
individual's second-house talents that could be used to benefit
self in the fifth house and to benefit others in the eleventh. The

latter benefit is much to be preferred. And 'tis better to have loved and lost than never to have loved at all.

The next two readings show more of this prowess. A number of house relationships are given, as in reading the entire horoscope, but the eleventh stands out.

5. In Jupiter—we find as one dealing with things, with conditions, and—as we find—this will be the greater RULING factor in the latter portion of the entity's present experience and sojourn, especially when there is a conjunction or square of the Jupiterian influence with that of the strange influence, or Uranian influence, and this should bring a material and a physical change in the experience of the entity in the coming spring, in April or May. As we find, the same will have to do with peoples and their relationships in life, as well as places and things. Hence will make a decided change. All these—all these relationships, to be sure—are altered or changed, dependent upon the application of self's will as respecting same; for as an entity's relationship is governed by the surroundings or environs, as well as hereditary influences, these are the makings OF the will as RESPECTING that an ENTITY holds as its criterion, or as its ideal. This, in this PARTICULAR entity, dealing then with things, with peoples, with people's relationships, will call ESPECIALLY for the ACTIVITY of the mental being and ITS relationship with its own ideal. Insofar as this change, as we find, would come, has to do with self and with self's own material interests. Then, these would be better that such a change, or such altered relationships, be considered rather seriously. Do not jump at conclusions; neither be too hasty in making connections or associations that might eventually bring some entanglements that would have to do with relationships with others in financial matters.

6. In those conditions as are made in the entity's experience as personalities, these—as seen, with respect to the will's influence:

7. One that would ever make a good salesman in dealing with other peoples, provided that to be sold has a tangible value in MATERIAL things. This would not imply that there are not spiritual valuations, or mental planes in the entity's experience. This depends a great deal, though, upon the entity's application of its ideal as relationships to such conditions.

348-014

10. One that sees the comic or humorous side of most every situation, and through the abilities of such we find the companionship and associations of the entity are often sought. These abilities may be used for weal or woe.

11. The activities should include ANY phase of an association or organization that requires a good personnel man; whether this is an organization such as a circus, a school, or as a representative for a group or organization or individual. But in whatever activities the entity may engage, it should be as the personnel man.

12. From the astrological sojourns we find influences in Mercury, Venus, Jupiter, Saturn and Mars. But Mars, for this entity, is rather the urge than the affliction; rather the benevolent urge towards the many interests the entity finds in its associations with groups and with individuals.

13. And indeed may this entity be called friend by other individuals who have abilities but who do not have the ability to push forward. Use, but do not abuse, these abilities. Abuse of same may work to the disadvantage of thy experience in the spiritual, in the mental and in the material things.

2986-001

Every house, every astrological aspect is a two-way street. Each house has an opposite. The effects of aspects can be positive or negative. Benefits may accrue, or they can be taken away. The eleventh house is no different in this respect than the others. Neptune can show deceitful friends or mystical friends. Uranus can cause one to gravitate toward either professional friends or those who would shock. Mercury friends can make promises and not keep them, or they can be television commentators. Every planet has these multifaceted sides.

15. In the Venus influences we find the friendliness, the ability to attract others to self, the ability to make friends easily and to hold those who are necessary to the entity not only in the way of friends but in mental or material ways. Yet the very same influence often allows the entity to become (according to those who are so material-minded) one subject to being preyed upon by others because of the goodness or the kind feelings of the entity.

16. Thus disappointments have often arisen in the entity's experience with friends whom the entity has befriended, and because of promises made and left undone.

17. Yet as there have been the experiences of turning within, we find that again no inharmonious reactions have been in the entity's experience.

1010-012

To continue with some of the untoward possibilities, no planetary position should ever be regarded as goody-goody.

10. Astrologically we find that Mercury, Mars, Jupiter, Venus are all parts of the consciousness of the soul-entity. Thus no one will ever call this entity lazy. Sure it gets tired, sure it needs recreation, but not the character of recreation that it sometimes is thought or felt, but rather know change of activity as may be indicated in Mars and not getting angry about anything but keeping in the Jupiterian influence of activities, of things, knowing that these work together for good to those who love the Lord. This doesn't mean just being "goody-goody", but good for something—something definite. Be the best husband there is on the road, be the best salesman in the whole group and you will find that in a very short while there will be much difference, if those set periods are adhered to—not just something to take up a little time, but set a definite period morning or evening, or both even, though it be five or ten minutes—let nothing interfere, pray. Then live like you pray. Then listen, and ye may be very sure the answer will come back to you and ye will soon find everyone much gladder to see you coming. Ye will find all will be ready to assist you in being the best of whatever ye choose as the active service, and soon ye will be given a new place in the general organization where ye can carry on to greater expansion in preparation, in expanding the fields of service with those with whom ye are associated.

5368-001

Whatever the eleventh-house planets express, the possibilities are endless. They always show relationships with others and can be most often turned into benefits unless the individual retreats into becoming a recluse. Ideas do not travel far when kept entirely private.

9. From the influences in Uranus we find the extremes; and indeed the entity has in the present experience known extremes—the good, the bad; the enjoyment of luxury in a manner and the husks of life itself as it were.

10. Yet the entity has "come through" with a shining hopefulness that should be as a light for many. And it may be only said to the entity:

11. Hold fast to the faith that has prompted and does prompt thee in thy dealings and thy relationships and thy activities with others; and ye will find—yet—greater contentment and peace coming in this experience.

1556-002

Optimism and doing one's best will be rewarded in the end. Pessimism will be met by what was envisioned as well. Choose which one you want.

TWELFTH HOUSE

Finally, we come to the most misunderstood, yet possibly the greatest house in all of astrology. Mutterings of astrologers can be recalled about hidden enemies, jails, hospitals, dangers from big animals, and the like. One would be expected to believe that this house only involves dangers and confinements. While those things can come to pass, the more exciting effects are extremely constructive. This is the opposite house to the sixth of personal service. Hence, it is the house of service to mankind. That automatically makes it important for all destinies. No person in any field of endeavor is likely to leave something worthwhile to posterity without a strong twelfth house. No public servant could become one without a strong twelfth house.

Q-54. I have been told, by what I have believed to be an inspired source, that my destiny is to be of outstanding import.

A-54. It should be, in those fields as has been indicated—as in the diplomatic service of thy country.

1497-001

The twelfth is the natural house of Pisces. In a manner similar to that sign, the interests may be multifarious and follow almost any direction, including the circular. Occupations may be of virtually every type that results in service to others. Heads of service companies are strong in this house. Farming is an important twelfth-house occupation, because other people are fed by their efforts. Diplomats and government employees who serve their country are obviously included. Restaurant owners, waiters, and waitresses perform twelfth-house services. Then, there are the doctors and nurses whose occupations are for the purposes of nurturing health and overcoming illnesses in other people. In no way is this house limited to hospitals and jails. Playwrights, actors, writers, great teachers, justices of higher courts, makers of laws, breakers of laws, historians, those who gave the world great art, great sculpture, great symphonies, great new inventions, and many, many others have this influence. All are yang-type accomplishments. Yet there are those well-qualified people who feel themselves unworthy in twelfth-house activities.

4. In giving the interpretations of the records here, many phases of this entity's record would be worth MUCH to those who oft find themselves troubled as to circumstances and conditions, and especially those who so oft are feeling sorry for themselves.

5. But to give the interpretations as we find them here,—these are chosen with the desire that this be a helpful experience for this entity; yet those about the entity in the moment may learn a lesson from this entity.

6. In choosing that as will be indicated, we find that what the entity has done about its ideals, its purposes in the present, speaks much more than the mere inclinations that are indicated from astrological aspects or from earthly sojourns; though one may easily find indicated that thread of truth, as the entity has applied in its present experience and present sojourn, of a continuity of intent and purpose,—also that which has ever brought and ever will bring helpful, hopeful influences into the experiences of all; the desire to be in an at-onement with the Creative Force in its relationships to man.

7. And its dealings have been in that way and manner as to demonstrate those tenets, those truths,—yea, those laws per-

taining to such, "As ye would that others should do to you, do ye even so to them."

8. Irrespective of what the environs or circumstances have brought into the experience, the entity has looked upon such, and hoped, wished, acted in that manner—in its dealings with its fellow man—as it would that there be shown unto self. Not as one attempting to impel or control without a purpose, but in a manner in which it has attempted—through its voice, its abilities, its purposefulness—to bring into expression, into the experiences of others, that as would give a more hopeful outlook,—as in its music; in its abilities to create, manifest, or express the GLADNESS in the heart; that others might take hope, might put away FEAR and know that God is in His holy temple, let the earth and the earthly things indeed keep silent!

9. Not that disappointments have not come to the entity; not that individuals have not broken their word with the entity; yet in its experience, in its dealings with others, the entity has so lived, so acted, as to indeed merit that which is the promise of the GREAT COMMANDMENT, that carries with it the first promise from the Maker!

10. Then, who is thy mother, thy brother, thy sister? He that doeth the will of the Father!

11. Hence the entity has manifested and brought hopeful, helpful experiences to others; through its abilities manifested in its art, its temperament, its artistic activities, its musical temperaments; its abilities towards interpretation of verse, of song, of music, of nature and its relationships.

12. Hence, the entity has thus enjoyed, and does enjoy in its experience among its fellow men, not only respect, not only worshipfulness and respect, but LOVE,—love that maketh the world of men's affairs more harmonious, that puts away hate from the heart and mind.

13. Thus, the entity attempts to give that activity into the experiences of others in such a way and manner that they too may know the freedom that such brings in its experience.

14. That astrological sojourns have had their URGE is in-

dicated, but little of such becomes of great meaning in the experience of the entity. For, as indicated, much MORE is brought by that which the entity HAS used and applied of its abilities through its sojourns in the material plane.

15. Thus, the entity has experienced in this sojourn a great EMOTIONAL life,—through those periods of associations where sorrows from every phase of man's experiences have touched the entity; yet the entity has raised its voice (though at times appearing to self as weak) in hope that is found in those promises of the truth expressed in, "Be ye faithful unto the end, that the joy of the Lord may indeed be thine."

16. FEW have so expressed this in and through their periods of temptation, their periods of sorrow and disappointment, their periods of GLADNESS and the enjoyment of the good things of life; yet the entity has held these as the principles, the purposes, the aims,—from which ALL, every one, may take and learn a lesson,—that INDEED the good things are those that may not be bought with the specie or gold or silver. While these are judgments or measures in the material associations that are necessary in dealing with one's fellow man, that which brings happiness for which the world cries; that which brings harmony for which people are calling; that which brings peace among brethren of a household, a city, a nation; lies not in the seeking of such.

17. For, as has been indicated, it is the love of that power and might which such gives that brings sin to the more individuals, to states,—yea, to nations, and to those in political power.

18. Though the entity has seen and experienced in its associations the feeling of same, it has tempered all in such relationships, in its dealings with others, with mercy and judgment.

19. Thus the entity finds itself now in those periods of activity in which it may look back upon its sojourn in this material plane and say, "Lord, thy humble servant hath kept thy promise. Keep thou, show thou the way."

20. This is indeed one in whom many, many may take

thought, and learn to pattern their lives, their ways, by that counsel which the entity has given, does give, as it meets those in its relationships day by day.

21. Thus may the entity in these periods of activity in this sojourn give help and hope, and YET bring to fruition—by the counsel to others—the helpfulness that lives on!

22. For, know,—only the growth in grace and mercy lives forever. ONLY such is eternal,—love that passeth understanding!

23. And to create hope and harmony in the minds and hearts of those ye meet day by day is that purpose for which each soul enters a material experience.

24. Thus does it grow to fruition by or through the seed of the spirit of truth.

25. As to the appearances in the earth,—we find these have been quite varied, and quite far apart in some, yet quite close together in others, as may be indicated by the periods of activity.

26. Before this the entity was in the French land, during those periods when there were rebellions in the land, when there were those activities that had been known or heard of that brought those influences and forces into the land of the entity's present nativity.

27. Hence the entity, with some of its kin in those experiences, journeyed to the land of the present nativity; in the name then Jean Paulusa de Lafayette.

28. In the experience the entity gained; for as it sought for itself, for its fellow men, the spirit of freedom of speech, the freedom for the worship of God according to the dictates of its own consciousness, so did the entity encourage those of that period and of that land.

29. So did the entity bring into fruition a land that bears the stamp of those who may bring greater and greater knowledge to a sin-sick world.

30. Blessed indeed are they who harbor and manifest, in their dealings and relationships with their fellow men, God's own purposes with mankind.

31. Thus may the entity find, in these experiences and these stirring times when there are men MAD for power, that might which comes in the still small voice within of "Keep thine own skirts clean! Condemn not thy fellow men that ye be not condemned!"

32. Thus may the entity find that those turmoils and strifes, too, will pass away, and only love and hope and harmony remain. For out of turmoil and strife, as the entity saw and experienced, has grown a hopefulness that has provided and does provide shelter under the wings of Him who has given, "Be ye perfect, even as thy Father in heaven is perfect!"

33. Thus may the entity take hope, and bring into the experiences of others—with its abilities as were gained in that sojourn—the right of each individual to give the expressions of itself in a HELPFUL, HOPEFUL way and manner.

2166-001

What one has just read is the attitude and accomplishments of a great man—probably one who has progressed further toward his destiny than some of the rest of us. Edgar Cayce gave advice to him, but at the same time he was giving advice to others as well. He disclosed principles and guidelines that apply to all people. In many ways these revelations show what life is all about and the beneficial lessons that can be learned. These are ministrations. All ministers, priests, rabbis, and spiritual leaders fulfill some of the principles identified. They have twelfth-house occupations. But then, every occupation can become twelfth house if the entity so wills.

This next long reading is about such a minister, about theology and spirit. It contains even more of the things we should know as laypeople, with warnings as well.

3. What an unusual shape! as if this in itself had much to do with that the entity has had to do with the unifying of thought of those who have sought to interpret the records left by the sages, as ye would call, of old.

4. This in itself would appear to signify that the entity's application of self in the present will find a greater outlet for itself in seeking the correlation of those tenets and truths left by those in the eons and ages, that have attempted to leave for posterity—or man—a vision of that which prompted the activities of human endeavor throughout the ages.

5. And as to how they are, as through the solar as well as the years as by the fixed stars, come into the experience of man to bring a new order in the dealings with the elements, and the activities of same as related to the associations of man's endeavor.

6. Is there little wonder then that television, radio, flying have a DEEP influence? Not so much the act as the influence such has upon the relationships of man as his brother, under the varied climes or varied aspects of the experience.

7. But to give the interpretations from the records of time and space, or the Akashic records, of this entity called [1473] in the present:

8. Those influences—as the entity experiences—that arise in the relationships to mind as the controlling factor in the experience of a human entity, are correlative and have their relative relationships to the astrological aspects, the numerological influences, as well as those from sojourns of an entity or soul in materiality or in matter.

9. Hence we find, while these are influences—relative— none of these surpass the will of the individual entity.

10. For the will is a portion of the soul-entity, a part of—or creation itself. And as every atomic structure of the bodily force is in relationships as one to another, so each soul in its relationships to a universality of activity, of evolution, as of the very movement of itself through time and space, becomes a part of an influence.

11. Yet will is dominant even of that.

12. Hence choice and will become the predominant forces; and the urges that arise in the human experience as from this

that makes for that which is ruled by the mind, ruled by the influences from the astrological aspects, may allow itself to be influenced, or may influence those in other aspects to a greater or lesser degree, according to their relative relationship from a numerological aspect.

13. As One is the factor, and every division of same becomes a portion of that unit, so do we find from the astrological aspect the influences from Jupiter, Uranus, Venus, Mars, Saturn, with the effects—for this entity—of the Moon and the Sun.

14. For Two becomes a factor in the experience of the entity; not as a divided influence but rather the abilities to weigh or compare in the experience of the entity two degrees beyond that of many with whom the entity may find even much in common.

15. In Jupiter we find influences accredited by astrology as not only protectorate but as disseminating among the masses.

16. Hence the influences in which the entity may find itself engaged, or the influences that arise from its material activity will affect many—the masses rather than the individuals; though to be sure reaching same through individual application.

17. From Uranus we find the EXTREME influences. Hence the entity's experiences are those as of just ready to grasp the meaning of much being sought, in the interest of the occult and the spiritual influences and forces; and again to the very depths of "No use—it escapes me!" These then become factors in the experience of the mental forces of the entity, in which there is manifested from the spiritual aspect the Mind—AND Choice, AND Will.

18. Venus as the friendship or love influence has very unusual aspects, with the aspects of Jupiter, Uranus AND Saturn with Mars. There are very few whom the entity trusts ENTIRELY; yet holding friendship, love, and those influences ordinarily accredited in Venus as of the beautiful, as of the music, as of those factors in same, as that which may bridge often that which is lacking in this full trust.

19. The influences of Saturn make for the changes that have been at definite periods in the experience of the entity in the present sojourn, and into the way of its mental thinking—not only that but as to the environmental forces or influences, and the manner of application as related to same.

20. Mars has made for those forces where anger, wrath and the like have become such at times that the necessity of choice became paramount to be weighed with those innate feelings that all of such experiences are worthy of being considered, and not thrown aside lightly; neither are they to be dwelt upon in such measures of manners as to become paramount.

21. For the creating of anger breeds contempt. Contempt gone to fruition breeds strife, and makes for disturbing forces that become—in the experiences of the entity—those things that bring inharmony.

22. As to the influences that arise from sojourns in the earth, we find these are unusual as compared to most.

23. For, as from the very shape (a harp) of the record itself, we find the entity's creating or making—through many of the sojourns—those activities that make for ONE becoming so much more outstanding than the others that it becomes as a thread through the whole efforts of the entity.

24. To be sure, its horizon of vision becomes lost in the confusion of time, in the confusion of circumstances oft; yet there may be seen the thread throughout those sojourns that we find influencing the entity in the present.

25. Not that all are given here, for as the very cycle of numerological aspects turns about, or as the wheel of fortune or fate (as may be termed by some) goes about its activities, irrespective of that which is done, then opportunities come.

26. Each awareness of an association brings its influence that arises from the emotions created from the portions of the experiences in the varied spheres of activity in the earth.

27. These then are given that from same there may be gathered hopeful, helpful aspects for practical application in the

activities of the entity in its relationships as one to another.

28. That ordinarily termed or called theological in its nature has become almost nil in the experience; while that termed SPIRITUAL has grown and does grow more and more paramount in the activities of the entity.

29. That these (the theological and the spiritual) have grown and are growing farther and farther apart in the affairs of man as a whole, as is viewed by the entity, is a fault—a failure of man to grasp the ONE thought, the ONE ideal, that would be held in such a way as to know that these must be ONE, in that "I AM my brother's keeper!"

1473-001

Edgar Cayce gave numerology some credence, along with astrology. But the purposes were often the same. They were aids in understanding principles to live by. From his words, from the world's religions, from parental teachings, and many other sources we know that doing good is a preferred mode of living. Certainly, doing good is to be preferred over doing bad. Boy Scouts and Girl Scouts learn to do good deeds. But simply doing good deeds is not enough if the attitude is wrong. The worst offense is to put oneself on a pedestal and say, "See here what a good person am I. See what I have done." Self-glory and self-praise are especially to be avoided. This is why making contributions to worthy causes in order to see one's name in print should be questioned as a desirable practice. Anonymous giving is to be much preferred if the soul would develop farther.

2. In entering the present experience we find the entity coming under the influences from the astrological aspects of those things that have made for very peculiar and unusual experiences in this sojourn of the entity. And while the interests of the entity for those things that would or do make for the soul development have been paramount, there have been at least two very definite periods and changes in the activities of the entity. For during a portion of the present experience and sojourn, those conditions that surrounded the body that were more of the material nature made for and have produced those experiences where the thoughts, the purposes, the activities were more in not self-indulgence but rather in self-glory, self-praise, self rather than that aid to others. Yet when there have

been the extremities, or the physical needs of the body, these extremities have brought in the experience those associations and those seekings for that innate, that longing which has been a portion of the dream of the entity from its earlier periods and early associations; and during these there has been that which has come very close to those expressions where the entity has seen deep into the unseen forces and influences in the material affairs of others. This has not always been pleasant. To make these more constructive, more effective in the lives of those whom the entity may contact will be for the greater activity, and for those things that may bring to the experience of the entity in the present that which will be the more satisfying. And bringing contentment and happiness in these periods when there must come again, and will come those visions and those dreams, those longings not for the pleasures of an earthly experience but rather as a joy in a service for the fellow man— during these latter portions of the entity's sojourn in this experience.

3. As to the astrological aspects, we find these varying quite from that ordinarily termed the astrological chart or astrological map for one under these environs. For the signs more of those things that are as omens, as periods in the experience of the entity's application in the present sojourn from its activities in individual sojourns in the earth, have brought and do bring much more than all the astrological aspects. For being, as it were, in a temperament—through the driving at times of its own mental self—these that are as from the emotions, rather than from those innate that have been awakened or may be awakened—have become the impelling influences in the experience of this entity, [3823] as called. For while the sojourns in the earth make for those periods that have seen the various activities in the affairs of people, the interest of the entity is in people, places, and conditions of people in places, rather than in the minutia or detail that has become at times the driving forces—and the necessity of the body to supply same for the individual needs. Hence the life has become something of a drudge, rather than being purposeful in every act, in every day, in every contact, that such may be more helpful, more hopeful to others; thus keeping for self the well-rounded life that there may be the better, the greater service rendered in an individual experience. For the soul, as it seeks expression in a material world, is not for naught—but rather that it, the soul, in its en-

virons, may be prepared for the greater appreciation, the greater understanding, the greater application of the spiritual realms in which it has its inception.

3823-001

Thus, if life becomes a drudge in spite of good deeds, it is highly likely that the purposes are wrong. In no case is it a good idea to withdraw from society for long. Being a temporary recluse may have merit as a time for reconstructing one's actions, gathering forces to start a plan of action, or establishing new goals. But withdrawing altogether from this world, no matter how excused, is sinful and is wrong.

8. Then, first study to show thyself approved unto God. Let thy yeas be yea, thy nays be nay. Look more to a spiritual awakening, a spiritual understanding.

9. This does not make one a recluse, but rather—if same is applied in a conscientious and consistent manner in the experience and the dealings with the fellow man, it will bring of itself—as has been the promise ever—contentment and greater blessings materially, mentally, socially, financially.

10. But if these are forgotten, then the inclinations to be self-indulgent and to glory in accomplishments are the result. Because of the natural high ideals, let not those influences of a social nor of an economic nature turn thee aside.

11. As to the urges from the astrological sojourns,—we find Venus, Jupiter, Uranus being the greater influences or forces; and these are independent one of another oft in their influence.

12. Hence there are periods when there is the desire to withdraw from a general social surrounding. There are other periods when the activities or urges from Venus, as a combination with Uranus, increase the desire for greater social accomplishments, greater economic accomplishments.

13. All of these are well, provided—as has been indicated— these are not allowed to become that sought, rather than the same being a result OF a conscientious life lived for the good works of every nature.

1950-001

Living "for the good works of every nature" should be the goal of every soul. This is so in spite of a constant barrage of negative news items. In the news media, blaring reports of criminal activities occupy minds. Murder has become soap opera. The degradation of entertainment to levels that would not have been accepted only a few decades ago is a decidedly backward movement. Acts of vilification are being championed as new forms of pleasure. Yet the mores of a society move slowly like a pendulum, and the time should be near when movement peaks and starts back in the other direction. Throughout this period many good people can be found who act with benevolence. Much in this world does not result in distasteful news or screaming headlines. Much of life is wonderful, to those who seek it, and good citizens should strive to make this side of life stronger.

12. Thus we find from the astrological aspect, in Venus there is the influence as to beautiful things, the depicting of these in one manner or another. And if there would be the application, the entity might make a great contribution to the human relationships through either the pen or the brush as to whether the choice is in this direction or not depends upon the entity; for there may be the same character of expression found in depicting characterizations, or activities in which there is the laudation as to abilities of individuals or products that might be advertised or distributed.

13. Thus creative forces as arise form associations of ideas or ideals are a part of the consciousness, both from the material sojourns and the astrological aspects.

14. Hence in any field of service in which the entity might find this means for expression would be the outlet in which there might be not only the material gains, and mental satisfaction in attaining to ideals and idealistic principles, but the helpful forces brought to individuals as well as to groups and masses.

15. However, never attempt that on which the entity is not itself sold!

2310-002

Know thou art well—pleasing in those things, those services thou hast rendered to thy fellow man, and that thy name is written in the Book of Life, that thou wilt be called into a greater service through those accomplishments. Though to self they may appear to be small, know that man looketh on the outward appearance but God looketh on the heart.

702-001

And so we have made the full circle around the wheel of a horoscope. It started with a recognition of self in the first house and has ended with a culmination of all the other lessons in the twelfth. The next question is, "What happens to the soul at the end of this series of journeys?" Edgar Cayce was not without an answer.

3. At the correct time accurate imaginary lines can be drawn from the opening of the great Pyramid to the second star in the Great Dipper, called Polaris or the North Star. This indicates it is the system toward which the soul takes its flight after having completed its sojourn through this solar system. In October there will be seen the first variation in the position of the polar star in relation to the lines from the Great Pyramid. The dipper is gradually changing, and when this change becomes noticeable—as might be calculated from the Pyramid—there will be the beginning of the change in the races. There will come a greater influx of souls from the Atlantean, Lemurian, La, Ur or Da civilizations. These conditions are indicated in this turn in the journey through the pyramid.

5748-006

The soul completing its mission in this solar system by reaching the end of the twelfth house goes to Polaris. For those of us here now, souls from the Atlantean, Lemurian, La, Ur, or Da civilizations are coming in. Many more sojourns would appear to be in the offing, and the objectives of all should be to complete progressive stays in our solar system.

With this thought in mind, nothing could be more appropriate than the prayer Edgar Cayce gave when asked:

THEN, LET THY PRAYER BE:

LORD, USE ME IN THE SERVICE OF MY COUNTRY, IN THE SERVICE OF MY FELLOW MAN, IN SUCH A WAY AND MAN-

NER THAT I MAY DO SO TO THY NAME AND GLORY. AND MAY IT BRING THAT AWARENESS, THAT CONSCIOUSNESS OF THE CLOSER WALK WITH THE CHRIST.

361-015

14
SELF-HELP

WHETHER THE READER has astrological knowledge or not, these revelations have clearly shown that the greatest benefits and the most powerful self-help come from helping others.

We are all in this world together. Edgar Cayce has clearly pointed out how astrology can be used to improve relations among all people. He also made another significant point:

> And as ye find in self the manner in which ye would treat others, ye will find in self help physically and mentally.
>
> 3359-001

From this short reading and the last two chapters, perhaps the thought that might enter a person's mind is, "What are the specific ways that greater knowledge of astrology and these special revelations from Edgar Cayce can help me personally?" That question might be asked by both those individuals who already have familiarity with astrology as well as those who do not. For astrologers with quite a bit of knowledge about astrology, the probability is high that they have learned a great deal more from the readings. The main question is whether they will change their ways because of them. For those who only know a little about astrology, the reasons may appear to be more important because there are so many revolutionary ideas to absorb. They have the advantage, however, of not having to unlearn false ideas. The real answer for everyone is to figure out how to use true knowledge gained in your own life for the benefit of mankind. Edgar Cayce dwelled upon this thought over and over again, in many different ways. That guiding principle in life is how you will advance the furthest toward your own destiny. Providing assistance in the right way, without being intrusive, so the recipients can better fulfill the purpose of their own lives is far more important than selfish personal triumphs. By example, Edgar Cayce showed that astrology is a wonderful ally for fulfilling this objective, and its study can be extremely enlightening.

Q-36. In what way should astrology be used to help man live better in the present physical plane?

A-36. In that which the position of the planets give the tendencies in a given life, without reference to the will. Then let man, the individual, understand how WILL may overcome, for we all must overcome, if we would, in any wise, enter in. Not that the position gives man the transport, but that that force as manifested in the creation of man wherein choice between the good and evil, exercising highest will force, may be manifested the greater in man. DO THAT.

3744-001

A belief is now held that it would be desirable to share additional findings gathered from perfect natal horoscopes, even if met by skepticism and suspicion. Perfect natal horoscopes are defined as those that are totally functional. Every one of them has been verified by comparing all of the planetary indicators with the nature of the individual and by testing progressed aspects against known, dated major events. All astrological fundamentals are in accord with no exceptions. All progressed aspects match the selected timetable of urges exactly. By now, it should go without saying that perfect horoscopes are believed to be the ones chosen by souls using their willpower. Collectively, they have the power to reinforce what is known about astrological fundamentals. Individually and collectively, every one of these perfect natal horoscopes has been in complete agreement with Edgar Cayce's revelations. Test results and observations from verified horoscopes are simply too important to remain hidden.

Taking a broad viewpoint first, there are two main technical differences between these verified horoscopes and the usual horoscopes currently being published and used in behalf of clients: 1. They are cast for a spiritual birth time, rather than a reported physical birth time, often being several hours apart. 2. Both natal and progressed parallels of declination are included. The importance of parallels and contraparallels of declination come to the forefront during verifications. About 20 percent of all horoscopes could not be verified without them, because they are the only appropriate aspects matching the forces present at the time of the event.

Inspection for serviceability shows another major difference between these two types of horoscopes. The verified horoscopes are strikingly practical. Horoscopes for physical births are only partially practical, often being conspicuous for omitted indicators. A good astrologer should be able to recognize the soundness and integrity of a soul-selected horoscope without hesitation.

When reviewing parallels of declination together with aspects in celestial longitude, additional information becomes evident. In particular, contraparallel aspects provide great opportunities for spiritual advancement, because they always involve interfaces between people. Contraparallels supplement the oppositions, sesqui-squares, squares, and semi-squares that demand attention and signal encounters. These aspects in celestial longitude occur at 180°, 135°, 90°, and 45°. Some might call them the dark aspects.

Q-33. What is the meaning of the dark aspects in my horoscope?

A-33. These are tendencies for the warnings that have been indicated, that there are those virtues and vices. Hence the need for the ideals to be set in creative forces. Whose is the earth? Then keep the ideals in the correct way and manner, and shadowy expectations should be eliminated by the truth and of life itself.

3656-001

All aspects are as signposts. The most disturbing aspects are the ones that vibrate the strongest with the greatest amount of harmonic reinforcement. Considering 360° as being a full wavelength, these reinforcing aspects angles occur at half-wave, quarter-wave, and eighth-wave angles: namely, 180°, 90°, and 45°. They are sometimes called the even harmonics because they occur at intervals of the full circle divisible by the even integers,

2, 4, and 8. The one-and-a-half times sesqui-square at 135° is often included in this list of hard aspects, although weaker. Sustained vibrations, or sequential reinforcements, are produced by even harmonics during earth's daily rotation. They are the most difficult to overcome, requiring "ideals to be set in creative forces." This angular category establishes the greatest amount of resistance and instigates the greatest tests in life.

Third-wave and fifth-wave aspects angles occur at 120° and 72° respectively. The third-wave is usually divided twice again to form angles of 60° and 30°. This group of angles is sometimes referred to as the odd harmonics. None of these aspect angles are as disturbing as the even harmonics described in the preceding paragraph, because they appear to incorporate periods of rest during earth's daily rotation. Therefore, they provide the greatest amount of harmony in relation to important happenings.

Conjunctions and parallels involve planets in the same angles. They provide direct contacts on a tête-à-tête basis. Moreover, conjunctions and all parallels of declination are fully sustained during earth's daily rotation. Therefore, they fall into the hard camp.

Help comes through astrology from optimizing opportunities by knowing when any of these aspects will occur, the category they are in, the stage they will be set upon, and the characteristics of potential events. Then preparations can be more complete, and willpower can be more fully exercised than without such information. Verified horoscopes can show exact milestones to the day. Supporting aspects fill in numerous details.

Q-11. Anything that might warn of approaching attacks?
A-11. Has it not been illustrated for thee? If the good man of the house knew when the thief was coming, he would be prepared. To be prepared would be to have the sword of the spirit, the purpose of the mind; and the conditions will not be broken up.

2828-005

If an attack is coming, it is better to have defenses on line and prepared—much better than being caught off guard. Nervous breakdowns might be avoided if the victim is not overwhelmed by surprise. If a new pleasant encounter is coming, it is better to have consideration beforehand of the opportunities that will present themselves. Advancements or worthwhile ventures might be optimized by making the most of one's chances.

Success most often comes about through helping hands. More hands than two usually result in expansion of benefits. Those people who achieve much in life often sense this fact and moments of good fortune, but prior notification would be even better for them and their allies.

Thus, the tendencies in ourselves and others are what we should be looking for in accurate horoscopes. Integrating and exercising these leanings for good, as opposed to evil, should be among our most positive and productive goals. There is no other tool with greater power to reveal tendencies than astrology. All of us have psychic abilities to a limited degree. If one has developed psychic abilities to the point that the Akashic records can be tapped, as Edgar Cayce did, that would be better. But, short of such abilities, astrology is probably the next best approach. Astrology has been available to virtually everyone for aeons, even when some intellectuals have cast it aside. The systems in different regions of the world may have differed, but some way of looking toward the stars for guidance could be sought.

Q-20. What is the correct system to use in astrology—the Heliocentric or the geocentric system?

A-20. As we have indicated, the Persian—or the geocentric—is the nearer correct. But, as we have also indicated, these—the astrological urges—are ONLY tendencies! Choices must be made, and the application of self to the universal laws is effective—in EACH life!

Do these things as we have indicated.

Analyze all that has been given. See how it fits into thy longings, thy hopes; and ye will find that it may be made practical in the daily life.

933-003

All known civilizations have practiced some form of astrology—from ancient Sumerians, Egyptians, Persians, Greeks, and Celts to aborigines of every land, to Indians (of India as well as tribes in the Americas), to the huge populations of China and Japan, to Europeans, Russians, South Americans, Central Americans, Australians, Madagascans, and modern man throughout the world. The forms of astrology have differed, but an enormous proportion of the human race has held some form of belief that warranted study and utilization. While archaeologists might debate the issues, real monuments in stone were devoted to astrological purposes—partially or wholly. Many are visible today.

The pyramids of Egypt, Stonehenge of England's Salisbury Plain, similar structures in France, observatories of the Maya in the Yucatan of Mexico and Guatemala are prime examples. Among most of these earlier civilizations, astrology was an elevated study performed by the most advanced of their people. No other science was more important. In rejecting astrology today, modern scientists do not know what they are missing.

> The entity then among those that were raised to the position as the TEACHER of the young, and ESPECIALLY gifted in the interpretation of those things as were presented by what was termed the genealogist, archaeologist, and the scientist of the period, especially as related to chronological orders and of astrological influences.
>
> 5424-001

But all fields of knowledge rise and fall, or rather they move cyclically. Over the past three to four hundred years, astrology has moved through a nadir. In most of Western civilization, astrology is still below the waterline where it took a dive for malpractices. Malpractice continues, but there are signs that give hope. Some irregularities are being corrected.

The fact that irresponsible astrologers were denigrated at various phases of history is perfectly understandable. It is all the more understandable when the knowledge contained in this book has been understood. Astrologers of all ages have made the kinds of mistakes that Edgar Cayce discussed. It is their attitudes that makes a difference. When unwilling to change from their own egocentric viewpoints, they will certainly continue in darkness. When willing to listen and heed Edgar Cayce's advice, there is hope.

That anyone should look down upon astrology today—well, that is understandable too. But the attitude of the critic is again what makes the difference. Edgar Cayce was a benign critic and very polite. Others would deride, taunt, or attempt to humiliate. Siding with science versus supposed superstitions is one matter. Looking down one's nose at all of astrology suggests another sojourn on earth is needed for such a person to work off a karma of conceit. The rest of us might accompany these types of critics by working off karma for other reasons, but it is not likely that Edgar Cayce and his source, or sources, of information were wrong. A more valid concern would be to oppose those astrologers who would continue to mangle its functions.

As to the application of self respecting the astrological forces,—these as we find are only urges. As to what one does WITH and about same depends upon choices made.

Hence the needs for each soul, each entity to have a standard, an ideal by which the patterns of the life, of its associations with its fellow man, may be drawn.

1710-003

Astrologers badly need standards. However, in their defense, many have been unaware of all of the ramifications disclosed in Edgar Cayce's readings. Their ideals may not have been well chosen for lack of insight. They have only been able to operate from knowledge previously received and what they have found inwardly that seems to work. How this information was obtained and translated into personal action has been an important activity. How they might react to these revelations is also very important. All astrologers reading this book now have an opportunity to set matters straight—or straighter.

First and foremost, every astrologer should recognize that three births take place for every newborn baby—the spiritual, physical, and soul. They can be hours apart. Let's be realistic and more precise, they can be four-and-a-half hours apart, or possibly more. Such differences in spiritual and physical births have been verified through functional horoscopes. No physical birth time observed to date has given a horoscope that was completely applicable to the person! Professional astrologers will do their clients and themselves a disservice if they do not recognize this fact. They will not be exercising their willpower for greatest benefits unless they strive to ascertain the spiritual birth times for horoscopes.

In addition, while it takes a bit more effort, they should try to verify the horoscopes they have cast for total and complete functionality, because a perfect horoscope was chosen by each soul to match the earthly sojourn. A perfect horoscope is 100 percent functional. A horoscope chosen by the soul is not based on just any sliding analog function of time. It is based on a finite time, like a pulse. The accuracy in casting such a horoscope must be increased if the faster-moving signposts are to be recognized. Hour-minute times are inadequate, because they do not correctly identify the Midheaven and Ascendant. Adding seconds as a vernier to an hour-minute spiritual birth time can result in improvements if the proper corrections for the nonspherical shape of the earth are taken into account. Extra attention needs to be paid to the Midheaven and Ascendant, because they define some of the most important signposts in every life. No horoscope can be considered completely verified unless at least one progressed Midheaven or Ascendant aspect has been related to one of those major events.

Furthermore, to increase the accuracy of horoscopes, know that degree-minute coordinates for the place of birth are inadequate. Latitudes and longitudes should be improved to degrees, minutes, and seconds. No horoscope should be cast for a city center unless the village is tiny. Babies are rarely born in the city hall or state capital. Geodetic surveys can pinpoint birthplaces to within one square meter. The soul pinpointed its birth to an equivalent precision.

Day-for-a-year progressions are absolutely essential for the greatest benefits to be realized. An inability to obtain day-for-a-year progressions means that preparations and training in astrology are still inadequate to do justice to this greatest of ancient sciences. Those astrologers who cannot find correspondences between real-life experiences and day-for-a-year progressions have a long way to go before they have truly mastered the art.

Remember that a horoscope wheel thrown together with name, date, birthplace, and alleged physical birth time without bothering to show the declinations does not do the individual for whom the horoscope was cast, the astrologer who accomplished the deed, or any other knowledgeable person much good. Such horoscopes are often published without explanations, because they cannot be properly explained. Records show that approximately 58 percent of all progressed aspects for major events are the parallels of declination. The physical birth time horoscope wheel does provide a starting point for good work to be accomplished, but this flawed picture is always inadequate. Exercising willpower to benefit others is a good use of time for casting and verifying more accurate and definitive horoscopes. Information that is precise can be of great value. Crude horoscopes are of much less value. Falling back to transit-based astrology or solar charts when inaccuracies or unknown times are present still provides benefits, but understand how much greater the benefits could be if verified horoscopes were used. The objective should be to maximize constructive purposes.

The experience of data or information as concerning the application of an individual entity during sojourns in the earth, and its activities at such periods as well as the application through what may be called the astrological aspects, is for constructive purposes.

And as each entity has individual or definite experiences or activities to be regulated or guided, or prompted in activities, it lends assurance—if there comes the answer to the self WITHIN to prompt self in seeking.

For as the will of each soul is that it may make itself as one with the Creator yet knowing itself to be itself, then that which would aid or help, or give hope, or give that which would be as a helpful experience would be well. This is the purpose of such information.

That which would prompt or direct, or force, or call for that which would bind, becomes destructive.

Hence there must be the answer WITHIN!

1151-009

All astrologers should find constructive answers within by trying to cast the most accurate horoscopes possible and by using parallels of declination, as well as celestial longitudes. Answers will be more constructive if the horoscope matches the soul's choice of time. The easiest way to find that match is by pinning down the exact longitudes and declinations of the rapidly moving Midheavens and Ascendants—both natal and progressed. This very recommendation is feared and avoided by many contemporary astrologers because of the difficulty in recognizing those important correlations. However, astrologers must get around this fear and address the important declinations as well. They need to delineate horoscopes with the relative strength of all soul-chosen aspects in mind. Remember that relative strength is a function of the apparent slow deviation in position of the planet each day as observed from the surface of the earth. If a computer program is being used, it would be wise to find out whether or not it calculates and displays natal and progressed declinations of the Ascendant and Midheaven in addition to natal and progressed declinations of planets. Some do not even show the progressed longitudes of the Ascendant and Midheavens, except indirectly. That is bad news, and it strongly shows a lack of understanding on the part of the originators.

If the software program you have access to does not incorporate these features, then an obvious deficiency has been encountered. The next course of action is a matter of choice as to how will should be exercised. At a minimum, the author of the program should be informed so that corrections can be made. If enough users voice their concern over these omissions, then revisions might be in the offing. Most sellers of software will listen when a sufficient number of their customers request a change.

Since traditionally minutes were the lowest level of numerical entries in manual calculations, they have simply been repeated for machine consumption. Hopefully one's astrological program has some form of adjustment that can modify hour-minute entries in time and degree-minute entries in longitude and latitude. Some have adjustment capabilities for time. Otherwise, manual interpolations might have to be performed—a silly thought when a powerful computer is sitting there. Between these two entries, time is the more important. Moreover, sidereal times must be used in the calculation of horoscopes, not clock times. Else errors of three or four degrees can ensue. Programmers and program reviewers who do not know much about astrology have little conception of these needs, and their remarks or viewpoints can be misleading. However, in this modern world of high technology, more exact answers are befitting.

An intelligent astrologer will be persuaded by Edgar Cayce's words to modify what they have been doing in accordance with what has been given from the Universal Mind. Modifications of procedures ought to include information gained through the exercise of willpower after stepping up to the higher levels of accuracy recommended. Experience from use of perfect horoscopes runs deep and makes a straightforward, sharp impression. Much less can be learned about an astrology based upon approximate or extremely inaccurate horoscopes. Receiving knowledge through Edgar Cayce's revelations that conflicts with earlier practices does little good unless willpower is thereafter combined with wisdom to remedy the situation.

As for the person who started with little knowledge of astrology but who wishes to receive astrological advice, it would be best to determine whether or not the astrologer being consulted has the requisite knowledge and experience. That might prove to be a trifle awkward, like trying to decide on a doctor by asking questions about credentials. However, in case anyone did not know already, there are vast differences in the capabilities of doctors, irrespective of qualified schooling. And the same goes for other professions. It has been said that only the top five or ten percent in any profession are the true thinkers and leaders. Astrologers do not differ in that regard. Many levels of service may be provided. If one is looking for capabilities beyond a few basics, it would be desirable to know whether or not the recommendations to astrologers given by Edgar Cayce are actually known and followed. If one is so inclined, a few well-chosen questions can quickly determine status.

Or the reasons and desires for personal information might be so compelling that it will be decided to plunge into astrology personally. Under these circumstances one might come to expect that certain gnawing omissions or differences between what astrological books say and what is known about your own life will appear. Almost always in the past a horoscope delineation will contain much that is true, but those anomalies or uncertainties may be present as well. They can only be exterminated if the horoscope is altered to the time of spiritual birth—usually, but not always, earlier than the physical. The average difference between spiritual birth and physical birth is about one-and-a-half hours! To repeat, because it is so important, the progressed Midheaven and Ascendant are keys to verifying accurate horoscopes, because they are the fastest moving elements. When progressed Midheavens and Ascendants correspond with the most important milestones in life, one can be assured that the horoscope is reasonably accurate. Not before!

In entering the present experience for this entity, and in giving that which may be helpful in the present experience, well that the astrological as well as the innate influences in the experiences of the mental and soul development of the entity be considered in their proper relationships.

First, in entering, we find the entity coming under the influences from the astrological sojourns; not because the planets were in a given position but the indwellings of the associations of the entity-soul in these environs having an influence, as: . . .

670-001

Proper relationships with respect to "innate influences in the experiences of the mental and soul development of the entity" can only occur when the horoscope is correctly cast. However, you should understand by now that forces other than the purely astrological can produce urges that come forward to help in times of need. In addition to astrological aspects in the traditional sense, there are the latent, submerged memories of past-life experiences and the awareness created from prior planetary sojourns. These promptings probably show one's leanings toward astrology in the first place, otherwise the quest for self-help would not have turned to astrology. An astrologer is fairly limited to just interpreting the astrological map and not the special urges from sojourns. On the other hand, sojourns may produce the greatest reactions. A sojourn on a particular planet always carries with it the astrological characteristics of that planet. You may be in a much better position than anyone else to recognize these added moods, impulses, inspirational thoughts, or other forms of urges in yourself. Such forces are integrated with the horoscope. Knowing and feeling cosmic influences from positions of the planets and from sojourns can cause far greater awareness of the signposts established by your own soul.

In giving that which may be helpful to this entity in the present experiences, respecting the sojourns in the earth, it is well that the planetary or astrological aspects also be given. It should be understood, then, that the sojourning of the soul in that environ, rather than the position, makes for the greater influence in the experience of an entity or body in any given plane. This is not belittling that which has been the study of the ancients, but rather it is giving the UNDERSTANDING of same. And, as we have indicated, it is not so much that an entity is influenced because the Moon is in Aquarius or the Sun in Capricorn or Venus or Mercury in that or the other house, sign, or the Moon and Sun sign, in that one of the planets is in this or that position in the heavens; but rather because those positions in the heavens are from the ENTITY having been in that sojourn as a soul! This is how the planets have the greater influence in the earth upon the entity, see? For the application of an experience is that which makes for the development of a body, a mind, OR a soul. For how has it been written? "He that knows to do good and doesn't, to him it is sin." Then, the altering or changing fact or in an influence is the application of the WILL, that which makes a soul, an entity that dwells in that called man or woman (means the same)—capable, through this gift of the Creator, of being one with the Giver.

Then, in this entity, the experiences or sojourns in the environs in the earth's solar system are those things that make for

MENTAL urges innate and manifested, according to the WILL OF the entity or body now known as [630].

630-002

And so seeking self-help can be a complex mission beset by large gaps in knowledge and confused by the status quo. This book may have uncovered just a little bit of knowledge that will be helpful. One can gain much, much more through experience. Virtually every astrologer has learned from experience and can relate those cases where benefits were truly obtained, but one must realize that the positions of the planets are only a piece of the puzzle. Always something will be missing if the purely astrological interpretation is the sole source of information. Rather then, when facing such a dilemma, to turn urges for help into urges for helping others with the guidance of good astrology. By that means greater good will be done.

Begin with the spiritual attitude, First know in self what ye believe about spiritual things. As was given by the lawgiver, don't look somewhere else. Neither call on heaven, until you have set your own heart and mind aright. For lo, thy redeemer liveth in thy own activity. And as ye find in self the manner in which ye would treat others, ye will find in self help physically and mentally. This will change thy whole outlook on the purpose of life. Do not question as to what others will say or do but find in thy self how and why God, in His wisdom and mercy, has given thee the opportunity—for thyself, [3359]—to be a witness for Him, thy God in the earth.

Find that, and ye will begin then with the correct attitude. For, that we find in spirit taketh form in mind. Mind becomes the builder. The physical body is the result.

3359-001

APPENDIX

A. AN OLD SOUL'S CHOICE OF HOROSCOPE

EDGAR CAYCE'S HOROSCOPE has been incorrectly cast and published just like the horoscopes of most other important people. One of the two shown herein has been verified.

Old souls have had many sojourns and accomplished many important things for other people. Edgar Cayce's soul most certainly should be classified as old, and it would be well to study his latest reincarnation.

In Thomas Sugrue's *This is a River*, Edgar Cayce's grandmother is quoted as having said he was born at three o'clock sharp. That was most likely Sun time. Another source quoted the physical birth of Edgar Cayce to have occurred at 3:03 PM in what is now the central standard time zone. That source was Edgar Cayce himself, and he was referring to his physical birth time. He was born on March 18, 1877, in a farmhouse south of Hopkinsville, Kentucky, beside what is now State Highway 107. A horoscope blindly cast for either one of the stated times, date, and location would show late Leo or possibly early Virgo on his Ascendant (see Figure 6). Those Ascendant signs are out of the question. He did not have a large, big-boned frame, a rectangular face, broad shoulders with narrow waist, or a regal per-

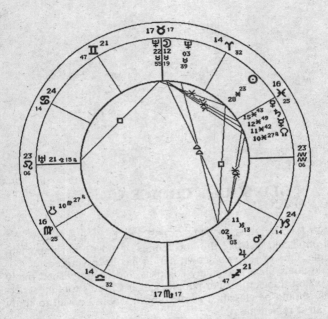

EDGAR CAYCE
MAR 18 1877   3:03 PM CST
HOPKINSVILLE   KY
36N52   087W27
MAR 18 1877   21:03:00 GMT
Tropical   Placidus   True Node

Figure 6. **Physical horoscope of Edgar Cayce. The Ascendant does not match his appearance or personality, and on this basis alone it must be thrown out.**

sonality of Leo rising. Neither did he have triangular features, a thin-bridged, down-pointing nose, or the meticulousness of an individual with Virgo rising. His preoccupation was not with numbers or precise details in his waking life. These false horoscopes, based upon physical birth times, would have placed Pluto near his Midheaven, which might cause pause for thought. Pluto shows tremendous resourcefulness. However, his Sun would then be in the eighth house, an entirely wrong place for this predominant source of energy. He had no inclination to be hired as an accountant or financial adviser. It is true that he tried to sell insurance once, but that eighth-house vocation did not last long.

The reading below gave interesting information about locations of planets in his horoscope and about personal traits of Edgar Cayce himself:

> The inclination of man is ruled by the planets under which he is born. In this far the destiny of man lies within the sphere or scope of the planets. With the given position of the Solar system at the time of the birth of an individual, it can be worked out,—that is, the inclinations and actions without the will power taken into consideration.
>
> As in this body here [Edgar Cayce] born March 18, 1877, three minutes past three o'clock, with the Sun descending, on the wane, the Moon in the opposite side of the earth (old moon), Uranus at its zenith, hence the body is ultra in its actions. Neptune closest in conjunction or Neptune as it is termed in Astrological survey, in the ninth house; Jupiter, the higher force of all the planets, save the Sun, in descendency, Venus just coming to horizon, Mars just set, Saturn—to whom all insufficient matter is cast at its decay—opposite the face of the Moon. Hence the inclination as the body is controlled by the Astrological survey at the time of the birth of this body, either (no middle ground for this body) very good or very bad, very religious or very wicked, very rich or always losing, very much in love or hate, very much given to good works or always doing wrong, governed entirely by the will of the body. Will is the educational factor of the body; thence the patience, the persistence, the ever faithful attention that should be given to the child when it is young. [GD's note: I believe above birth data was volunteered because Mr. Thrash did not accept birth data from EC and parents.]

254-002

The comment about Mr. Thrash not accepting Edgar Cayce's birth data is an astute remark. It questions the time as given for unknown reasons, but that was a correct assessment. Even Edgar Cayce's discussion of his astrological survey is a mixed bag, and it deviates in a manner that will be reviewed shortly.

But first, the equations to determine this soul's choices were applied. They produced four potential horoscope times with indicated Ascendants in a window established by the 3:03 PM CST input time. This six-hour window was open between 10:03 AM and 4:03 PM CST (or between 10:13 AM and 4:13 PM True Local Time). Note that all four horoscopes are computed for True Local Times (about ten minutes from standard times):

True Local Time	Ascendant
10:31:57 AM	23° Gemini 34.6'
11:26:46 AM	6° Cancer 10.1'
12:33:14 PM	20° Cancer 23.2'
1:28:03 PM	1° Leo 38.9'

No output was obtained within one-and-a-half hours of 3:00 PM. No horoscope was produced having a Virgo Ascendant. The nearest time to the physical birth time gave the Leo-rising horoscope. Leo on his Ascendant can be quickly eliminated, because he was not a big, heavy man with a constant desire to be the center of attention. Although he was tall, the Gemini horoscope planets simply do not fit. This leaves two Cancer-rising horoscopes. The choice between these two is rather easy for this mild-mannered individual. It must be the horoscope with 20° Cancer 22.7' on the Eastern horizon. Incidentally, this horoscope is for a time that is two hours, thirty-nine minutes, forty-one seconds before the mark at 3:03 CST. That is a typical difference between a spiritual and physical birth time.

Before proceeding further with proofs of this choice, the paragraph in reading 254-002 describing Edgar Cayce's horoscope will be analyzed. Some difficulties are present, because there is an apparent midway jump from the spiritual horoscope (Figure 7) with Cancer rising to the physical birth chart (Figure 6) with Leo rising and then back again. Perhaps with his extremely broad insights that maneuver is not so strange after all. The Sun is past noon and on the wane in both horoscopes. The Moon is on the opposite side of the earth in both horoscopes. The earth is always opposite the Sun in astronomical calculations. With Sun in Pisces, earth is in Virgo. Thus, the Moon is an "old Moon" in the third quarter from the earth. "Uranus at its zenith" does not apply to the Midheaven of either horoscope. It does apply to Uranus being in Leo at the opposite extremity from its own sign, Aquarius. Leo is a zenith for Aquarius. "Neptune closest in conjunction" is the first conjunction appearing above the horizon in the Cancer-rising horoscope. The Neptune conjunction in the physical horoscope is not the first from any benchmark. Yet a conjunction closest to either the Ascendant or the Midheaven is a natural observation.

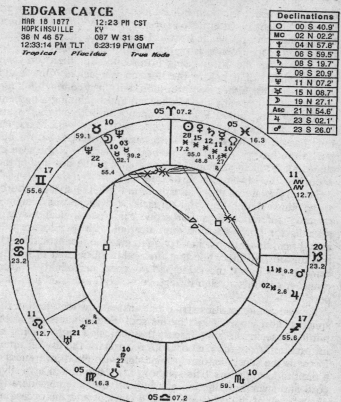

Figure 7. Spiritual horoscope of Edgar Cayce. This horoscope has been thoroughly tested, and much can be learned from it.

"Neptune as it is termed in Astrological survey, in the ninth house" fits the 3:03 PM horoscope. This is where "in Astrological survey" apparently alludes to a change of views back to the physical horoscope that the average astrologer would have produced. Edgar Cayce may have been mindful that no astrologer of their acquaintance would have been reviewing the horoscope not "in Astrological survey." But then he continues and eventually returns to the spiritual horoscope. "Jupiter in descendency" is correct for both horoscopes. "Venus just coming to horizon" might be interpreted several ways. Venus is just past the Midheaven and headed toward the horizon in the Cancer-rising horoscope. Venus is in the seventh house and closer to the horizon in the Virgo-rising horoscope. But there are two planets ahead of it before the horizon is reached. One could make a case for either interpretation, but "just coming" fits the concept of just passing the Midheaven and beginning a descent to the horizon. Jupiter is in descendency in both charts. "Mars just set" fits the spiritual horoscope extremely well. Mars has long passed the horizon in the physical horoscope. Saturn opposite the face of the Moon fits both horoscopes if the face of the Moon is taken as being at right angles to the position of the Moon, or the Moon seen at its quarter.

The aggregate of these interpretations fits the spiritual horoscope much better than the physical. Yet there was that momentary reference to a horoscope "in Astrological survey," perhaps for purposes of communicating with astrologers who would read this information, trying to give them consolation. He had to know all the while that the real displacement of his Ascendant was into Cancer. He had a Cancer personality, and no other. A one or two sign difference was often quoted for other people.

Several configurations strike one instantly when viewing this spiritual horoscope picked by his soul. Four planets are in the ninth house in the sign Pisces; they coincide with passing on information from the past or from records for the use of others. Pisces is the sensitive, omnipotent sign with great awareness of a multitude of factors. The symbol of two fish linked by a silver cord and swimming in circles is indicative of the consideration given to all of the components of a concept and the occasional delay in making an optimum choice. This placement by house and sign has extraordinary power to reveal information unknown to other people. Moon and Neptune are sextile to the ninth-house group. They are conjunct in the practical sign Taurus and tenth house. These two planets relate to his dreams and ability to provide useful cures when in trance. Such activities were the basis of his reputation, in addition to showing his work in photography. His Sun is the most elevated planet. That is a noble position. Pluto in the eleventh house indicates the competence and professionalism of many friends. Uranus in the second house indicates sudden and frequent changes in personal fortunes.

We know that Edgar Cayce had many indirect relationships with other people. The seventh house is blank, and that discloses such indirectness. We also know that he was a happily married man, and his wife was his helpmate. These are facts. Saturn, the ruler of Capricorn on the seventh-house cusp, is located in the ninth house surrounded by Mercury, Venus, and the Sun. This reveals the cooperation of his partner and the separations in distance from her at times. It also portrays the usual separations in distance from his clients.

This initial view of Edgar Cayce's horoscope is only for planets in longitude. A review of the declinations is in order. Jupiter and Mars are parallel to each other. Both are Southern declinations. This causes their influences to be like conjunctions in longitude, but with the added connotation that associated events will be personal and inwardly directed. The Ascendant is within 01° 07.6' of a contraparallel with Jupiter. His Ascendant has a Northern declination, but his Descendant would be Southern and in harmonious aspect. The result is that his Descendant is widely parallel to Jupiter and Mars. The Descendant relates to partners, including a spouse. Jupiter always represents expansion. His relationships with others were constantly undergoing pressures for more readings, often with a relative or friend interceding. His wife conducted many of the readings. Both Jupiter and Mars are in his sixth house that give suggestions as to his accomplishments. Mars shows the insistence of those wanting readings and the impositions upon his time and health. Mars also signifies the people who tried to use him and did for a while.

Most of the aspects with other planets are harmonious, especially the Moon-Neptune pair that connote trances. They facilitated his efforts that were conducted in a relaxed mode of self-hypnotism. Neptune is the planet of hypnotism. However, a square to his Midheaven is present, and that describes the professors, doctors, and other skeptics. The adverse Jupiter aspects to both his Midheaven and Sun show they came in numbers. Some tried to besmirch his reputation. Legal confrontations are indicated, even though his accusers did not win. Without the specific parallels of declination (including the Ascendant contraparallel) and the special knowledge we have gained about them, something would have been amiss in this horoscope, although every other indicator appears to be correct. The declinations have supplied the missing links.

The careful steps used in validating this horoscope will be reviewed briefly, but without going into a lot of additional detail.

First is the Ascendant sign. Cancer fits his appearance very well. He has the ovate head shape and the strong family attachments of Cancer. His features were rounded. He was a man with strong feelings, and Cancer is a water sign. Whatever dominance he had in personal or business matters was mostly kept in the background. He avoided conflicts and backed away from confrontations. These are Cancer traits. Some astrologers might argue that he was tall for a Cancer-rising native, because Cancer-rising people are usually average in height. But tallness does occur now and then, just like shortness applies infrequently to Sagittarius-rising people.

Next are the locations of the planets. All have actually been accounted for already. Uranus in Edgar Cayce's second house square Pluto indicates the financial adventures with friends that did not result in personal gain. Pluto in the eleventh house portends resourceful, down-to-earth types of friends. David Kahn is a good example of one who aided his ninth-house activities but could not manage to produce money from a joint enterprise. The eleventh house is the place of such plans and enterprises. Pluto relates to below-ground raw materials, but not necessarily oil or gas. A favorable Neptune aspect to these planets would have been required for realization of gains in an oil exploration venture. That aspect was not found, and the venture came to naught. The square aspect between Uranus and Pluto introduced obstacles that were present and were not overcome.

Yet Neptune is a co-ruler of the sixth house. Its favorable contacts with the Moon and trines to the other sixth-house planets favor photography as an occupation, although for its satisfaction, not necessarily for its remuneration. Neptune can be associated with the chemicals used in developing pictures and with the illusions created by photographs. Although Neptune had a tenth-house placement, neither oil nor photography made Edgar Cayce famous. His fame originated from his clairvoyance, another side of Neptune.

Mercury, Saturn, Venus, and the Sun in the ninth house and in harmonious aspects with every other planet in the horoscope, except Uranus, represent the readings. He gave over sixteen thousand of them (14,249 being recorded). Sun inconjunct Uranus matches the difficulties encountered when readings attempted to enrich his personal fortunes. The vast majority of those for other people had positive outcomes.

Sun in Pisces and Moon in Taurus made for his deep insights and kindly disposition. He was popular among the people who knew him. The Moon's location fulfills one of the verification tests. Is it properly in the tenth or eleventh house? Only a few minutes' difference in time could have caused an exchange of houses. With a reasonably accurate latitude and longitude used in the calculations, no error was anticipated. Moon in the eleventh house would have indicated many emotionally charged popular appeals supporting his work. There would have been more public enterprises planned than there were. His list of friends would probably have included more celebrities. The number of enterprises would have come and gone frequently. By contrast, with Taurus Moon in the tenth house, his popularity was stable. It was not based upon flippant schemes. It was down-to-earth and based upon solid achievements. People could count on him to come through whenever they faced trials or tribulations. Those accusations of fakery from the Neptune placement were mitigated by association with this earthy Moon. The array of harmonious aspects with so many other planets did not allow the accusations to stand. The Moon passes this test by a whisker of time. A whisker of time is all that is needed to verify that this horoscope is correct and not one with the Moon in the wrong house.

Next come the day-for-a-year progressed aspects. Day-for-a-year progressed aspects are the most powerful verifications of all when they include aspects to or from the Ascendant and Midheaven. So many events are documented that this task was comparatively easy. Every event checked was accompanied by appropriate progressed aspects, as anticipated. Showing a large number of these aspects and events would not be more convincing at this point, because the fit of the man to the horoscope is so strong. Thus, only a few will be mentioned. He proposed marriage on March 7, 1897, when his progressed Moon was sextile Venus within 0° 3.3'. This was an emotional experience, and Venus represents the female contact and nature of the milestone. Edgar began traveling on February 1, 1900, as a salesman and insurance agent when progressed Mars was contraparallel his Ascendant within 0° 2.8' (that is not the same as a progressed contraparallel from the Ascendant). The outcome was not especially propitious. He married with several aspects present on June 17, 1903. The most significant indicator was progressed Descendant semi-sextile Mercury within 0° 1.7'. Progressed Uranus was parallel his Jupiter with 0° 1.0'. Progressed Jupiter was trine Neptune within 0° 4.6'. Progressed Sun was also contraparallel Mercury within 0° 1.7', and that may have had something to do with the ceremony. Formation of the Association for Research and Enlightenment was agreed upon June 6, 1931, when Edgar Cayce's progressed Moon was conjunct progressed Neptune within 0° 2.1'. He died on January 3, 1945, when progressed Ascendant was contraparallel progressed Saturn within 0° 0.3' (or eighteen seconds) and progressed Moon was sextile progressed Ascendant within 0° 3.8'. The first, fourth, and eighth houses were involved, and those energized houses always accompany a moment of death. The world lost a wonderful human being on that well-timed occasion, scheduled by his old soul.

When astrologers claim a progressed aspect, and it is 1° to 10° from the theoretical angle they err in that assertion. Subjective orbs within four minutes might be reasonably acceptable. Orbs of degrees are not. Note that every progressed aspect mentioned for events in the life of Edgar Cayce was closer than four minutes to its theoretical aspect angle, except one. That 4.6' deviation was for a secondary, or supporting, aspect, and it could have been omitted from the discussion.

There were no intercepted houses, so this test could not be applied. Intercepted houses increase the power of the house pair involved. When present, they usually have sufficient strength to indicate occupations or major avocations.

The last test normally used is to confirm the integration of all these detailed elements. The overall picture of this horoscope fits Edgar Cayce without question, unless his own reading that seemed to combine the spiritual and physical horoscopes might have caused a bit of confusion. The confirmed horoscope was a perfect fit, as always. The progressed aspects were extremely accurate. Many nuggets of information can be discerned from this map of his life when it is examined closely. What he always wanted to leave for posterity was a hospital and university. Mercury, ruler of the twelfth house, is in the ninth. His principal legacy is in the form of words and spoken remedies, now recorded. Yet both the hospital and university did come to pass. A Cancer Ascendant almost invariably produces a family man. He was always close to his wife, children, and relatives. Leo on the second-house cusp shows that he was most imperial about private money matters. Often he did not have money, but when he did, spending could be liberal. All of us have an imperial house with Leo on the cusp, but it can apply to any of the twelve houses. This time it applied to Edgar Cayce's second house most appropriately.

By the way, Leo is not to be looked down upon. This sign, as all of the others, has many positive virtues. One of them, when on the second-house cusp, is to spend freely on gifts for others, an admirable trait.

Virgo on the third-house cusp is represented by Mercury in Pisces, sextile Moon. No wonder his mind wandered in school, but when he slept on his textbooks his recall was precise. That is fitting of Virgo, who knows all of the details. Libra at the fourth station is ruled by Venus. Venus is well placed in Pisces, and Edgar was always close to his mother. Scorpio, with dominion over the fifth house, indicated fruitfulness, but some problems would be encountered because its ruler Pluto is square Uranus. Let those who knew him best be the judge of that. Jupiter, the primary ruler of Sagittarius, is in the sixth house of employment. Jupiter is not in an agreeable sign, much preferring Cancer. This caused some irritation and need for change. Photography did not bring in enough money. There is the trine to Neptune that provides an outlet with photography, but the squares and presence of Mars also in the sixth house created disruptions. Other ways to gain income had to be pursued. Capricorn's ruler Saturn is located in the ninth house. His marriage was extremely favorable. Yet he left his family to travel away from them on certain occasions when he was trying to get a new job or support them. Aquarius on the cusp of the eighth house is ruled by Uranus and Saturn. The eighth house pertains to the possessions of partners and other associates. The Uranian influences were the ones that did not pan out when working on joint ventures. Those activities confined to the ninth house were more favorable. Jupiter and Neptune have impacts upon the ninth house in addition to the four other planets located there. Action to record his readings, to start an organization that would communicate the intelligence from those readings, to build a hospital, and to start a university match the patterns shown, even though difficulties were encountered.

Most of the aspects in celestial longitude are harmonious, with the exception of the square and inconjunct to the Sun. However, it is the Mars parallel Jupiter aspect that in this case caused most of his problems. Mars always connotes strife, even when the aspect is favorable. This same Mars parallel Jupiter aspect impacts the tenth house as well. This is where the orthodox doctors, insiders, expert debunkers, and other investigators blunted their swords trying to prove fraud or deceit. With Taurus on the cusp of the eleventh house, friends always came to his aid. Venus, the ruler of Taurus, is so well placed, high in the horoscope and next to the Sun. However, Venus is also conjunct Saturn, and there were always restraints. Gemini on the cusp of the twelfth house has its ruler Mercury well placed on the other side of Saturn. Again, caution and constraints were always present, but he did succeed in leaving a great deal of knowledge to the rest of the world.

That was a swift journey around his zodiacal circle, but it leaves no doubts with respect to the timing. Every placement rings true. With the importance and variety of past lives Edgar Cayce revealed about himself in the readings, we can conclude that his was an old soul indeed. Its choice of a horoscope for this past earthly sojourn was masterful.

B. APPLICABILITY TO AN ENTITY

The Association for Research and Enlightenment is an entity. Its perfect horoscope derived using the same methods as for a human being should be an interesting closing subject for study.

The first attempt at computing the horoscope of an entity using the equations normally applied to human beings was for the Declaration of Independence chart of the United States. This was done at a convention on the casual suggestion of a passerby. In only a fraction of one hour, several potential national birth times were computed for the day of July 4, 1776. Verification steps that could be readily applied at that moment confirmed one of the horoscope times.[9] The results were startling. Characteristics were in agreement throughout the wheel just as they would have been for a person. All progressed aspects timed events to the day. This new revelation was just as inspiring as those for people. Edgar Cayce had said that astrology was applicable to every corpuscle.

Since that discovery of apparent soul-picked horoscopes of entities, those for a number of cities and corporations have been computed and confirmed in much the same way. What would be more fitting now than to calculate and interpret the horoscope of the Association for Research and Enlightenment?

According to Thomas Sugrue's *There is a River*, a meeting was held on June 6, 1931, at Virginia Beach after a series of

[9] The True Local Time was 5:51:29 PM, and 21 Sagittarius 3.8' was on the Ascendant. The coordinates for the signing in Philadelphia were 039 N 57:13 and 075 W 11:05.

discouraging events had occurred. Atlantic University was in desperate shape due to lack of funds. It was eventually closed in 1932. For similar reasons the hospital had to be closed and returned to Morton Blumenthal, a benefactor before the depression ate into his profits. Edgar Cayce signed his house back over to Mr. Blumenthal. An earlier association of people who had benefited from the readings, calling themselves the Association of National Investigators, folded. This latest meeting was composed of members who had joined that organization, mainly those who had benefited from the readings. There were 67 loyal survivors. To paraphrase the words of Edgar Cayce:

"Last winter, when the hospital closed and the association was dissolved," he said, "I sent a letter to everyone on my mailing list. Each of you received one. In it I asked a question: whether in your opinion another organization should be formed. If this work of mine is worthwhile, I asked you, tell me so. Tell me what, in your opinion, is its value. I don't want to fool myself, or anyone else. If it has all been a mistake, I want to quit now, before any more damage is done.. . . ."

That meeting provided the inspiration to form a new corporation. Once again Edgar Cayce went into trance, and among many other things he said about the new organization was the following:

In coming into existence as an organization in a material world, it is necessary that there be that which represents MATERIAL values, the EXCHANGE in material affairs, yet ALL should—WOULD this be made a HELPFUL organization, institution, active—have THIS realization: that it MUST be founded upon that that is LIVING, that is truth, that grows, that expands, that brings hope, cheer, LIFE itself into the minds, the hearts, the souls of individuals.

254-057

The Association for Research and Enlightenment was incorporated in Richmond, Virginia, on July 7, 1931. The articles of incorporation were signed by thirteen people: David W. Kahn, Ernest W. Zentgraf, David Levy, Hugh Lyne Cayce, L. B. Cayce, H. H. Jones, Paul Kaufman, C. A. Barrett, Florence R. Edmonds, F. D. Lawrence, F. H. Scattergood, Wallace Hardin McChesney, and Esther Wynne. Sixteen people were named as trustees, including all of the signers. H. H. Jones was named as president. Mildred G. Davis was named the secretary-treasurer. As usual for a new corporation, articles of the certificate had been signed earlier. All signatures had been notarized by Gladys Davis back in June. All papers were typed, signed, and placed in the proper order. Approval had been granted by B. D. White, Judge of the Circuit Court for the County of Princess Anne, Virginia. Submittal of the charter to the Commonwealth of Virginia, Office of the State Corporation Commission, in Richmond occurred on July 7, time unknown. If like most corporations, this submittal was before noon. Most corporations are born in the two-hour period between 10:00 AM and 12:00 noon, or occasionally a little after. This was an excellent period for calculating potential horoscope times.

Before starting the calculations, a single astrological viewpoint was held to be necessary. The A.R.E. had to have a strong ninth house, just as the horoscope for Edgar Cayce. The principal purpose of the A.R.E. was and is the dissemination of information. A mismatch would exist without a strong ninth house.

As luck would have it, 32 candidate times were derived—a rather large number. At first, differentiation might appear to have been an overwhelming task. The majority of these times had Virgo rising. Two had Leo rising, and two had Libra rising. The Libra-rising horoscopes were the ones closest to noon, but a rapid overview of these horoscopes was extraordinarily revealing. Almost all of the candidate horoscopes had very weak ninth houses until the two Libra-rising horoscopes were inspected. One and only one had the third and ninth houses intercepted. This means that a sign of the zodiac was wholly within each of those two signs. That means both the intercepted signs and the signs on the cusps of those two houses contributed energy, making them stronger. From this knowledge about interceptions, the anticipated and necessary strengths in the information houses were found. All subsequent verification steps responded to that single horoscope shown in Figure 8.

In the final analysis, selection from the 32 candidates became a relatively swift and easy task. Besides, the personality of the A.R.E. is much more Libra-like than Virgo-like. Appearance of things is all-important. Harmony and balance are far more significant to the A.R.E. than being meticulous with paperwork, billings, or analyses. Libra tends toward cultured approaches to life. All of the A.R.E.'s good works, the way the organization is viewed by outsiders, and its position in the world of esoteric

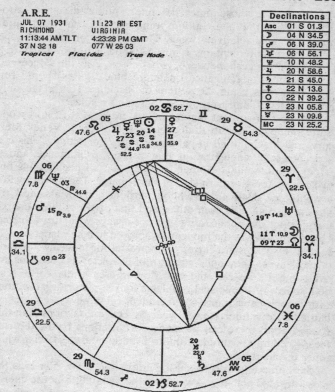

Figure 8. Horoscope chosen by soul of the Association for Research and Enlightenment. The third-ninth-house interceptions and parallels of declination are very meaningful.

information dispensation are far more sophisticated than average. These are Libra traits.

A horoscope time only a few seconds earlier would have lost the third-ninth-house interception and caused the second and eighth to be intercepted. It is true that the A.R.E. loans books, but the main thrust is certainly not to loan money, sell investments, or insure customers. Those would be likely occupations of a corporation born with second-eighth-house interceptions.

A little before those times the interceptions disappear altogether. With the interceptions omitted, the third and ninth houses became relatively weak. This recognition of horoscope times versus interceptions is just as good a test as one for a planet near a cusp between two houses. Anyone concerned about such strong reliance on intercepted houses should run their own tests using the system of Placidus. This is the only house system found to produce consistent results.

The most prominent feature of the entire A.R.E. horoscope is the lineup and quality of declinations. Pluto, Sun, Venus, Mercury, and M. C. are all in parallel within 71.6 seconds. This is a very powerful configuration that assures prominence and a strong reputation. The other factor is that all declinations but two are on the Northern side of the equator. Ten out of twelve are outgoing, dealing with a public responsibility. Mars and Uranus are also parallel each other, and that provides more energy for meeting the public, although not always without problems. Uranus in Aries is the pioneering-spirited handle planet of a T-square. T-squares are extremely powerful for inducing a parade of challenges. They build strength of character as problems are overcome. In this case the esoteric purposes of the A.R.E. can be a source of ideological problems for people or organizations with whom associations are intended. Mars always equates to battles or forcefulness, even when aspects are favorable. In this configuration there can be many perturbations below the surface. Keeping appearances on an even keel are essential while other incidents erupt.

The horoscope in celestial longitude is striking. Venus is the most elevated planet and would be the main ninth-house energy source if it were not for the interceptions. Venus is the ruler of the ninth-house cusp and the Ascendant. It is in the literary sign Gemini. The complexities of these arrangements fit the association perfectly.

Jupiter, Mercury, Pluto, and the Sun are prominent in the tenth house of reputation. They are in the sign Cancer, and that causes its people to be members of the A.R.E. family. However, all four planets are opposite Saturn and square to Uranus. These configurations show formation of the corporation out of adversity and the constant struggle to survive and grow. Fortunately, Saturn is in its own sign, which is favorable in the long run. Saturn may take a while, but it endures. The orientation for a corporate home is toward the traditional. The Arctic Crescent home became the first headquarters. This move was in full accord with the sign Capricorn.

One other positive confirmation of the Midheaven is its Cancer sign. The man for whom this organization was all about had Cancer rising.

Neptune in Virgo and the eleventh house is closest to being semi-square Pluto. This Neptune placement indicates a dramatization of chronicled information. The semi-square indicates a problem in keeping the organization socially acceptable and respected by learned men and women. The Libran influence from the Ascendant and the Leo influence from the cusp of the eleventh house strive for high levels of acceptance, as opposed to being companions with what has been called the lunatic fringe. Some would-be friends are adherents of more radical esoteric practices. They might opt for lower levels of mystical involvements. However, by concentrating upon professional and accepted methods of disclosure, quality and high standards of appearance for all publications and presentations, and words carefully recorded by Gladys Davis and others, the illusory side of Neptunian friendships are kept in bounds. The solar types of friends, represented by the Sun's rulership of the eleventh-house cusp, are prominent. Many are altruistic in nature.

Mars represents masculine energy. In the twelfth house Mars strives to do things aggressively for the world's people. In Virgo, the actions tend to be more studied than athletic, more detailed and word-oriented than combative. The trine to Saturn is helpful in pursuing practical, carefully planned, and time-consuming courses of action. The sextile to Sun and the other tenth-house planets is useful in gaining recognition. The inconjunctions with Uranus and the Moon represent opportunities, but they can be accompanied by people problems at times.

Uranus and Moon are in the pioneering sign Aries. Uranus causes creative methods to be utilized in recruiting new members. The Moon's presence signifies popularity. Thus, some new members are new world in character; some aspire to the acceptance of important figures; and some join because the clairvoyance of Edgar Cayce simply appeals to their emotions. The circulating files and library are benefits tied to the Moon. Uranus is the dominant T-square handle planet, but the Moon shares this role. This makes the Moon a coconspirator in recruiting drives. An Aries Moon has a cooler, less emotional nature than average and almost always is in forward gear. Much energy is consumed.

This horoscope of the A.R.E. maps an informative picture of what the organization is really like. Those who work there understand and would probably agree with the assessment given thus far. But for further validations we need to check the progressions. Day-for-a-year progressions provide increased energy levels to corporations in much the same way that they do for people. The nature of the energy surges and the dates need to coincide if this is to be identified as the perfect horoscope. Fortunately, the history of the A.R.E. is known to many people. Unfortunately, the exact dates of many events were not always printed for public consumption. Often the month and year were recorded, but not the day. However, there are a sufficient number of dated events to proceed with some degree of confidence.

For example, the first study group was formed on September 14, 1931. This was only a little over two months after the A.R.E. was incorporated. A number of planets and angles in high Northern declinations reached their maxima and returned to natal positions within that period. The Midheaven was parallel its own place; the Ascendant was parallel its own place; and Sun was parallel its natal position. In addition, progressed Venus was parallel progressed Mercury within a half minute of arc. Venus was semi-sextile Jupiter within 0° 2.7 minutes of arc. With this parade of aspects the event had to be significant. The lessons created at that time developed into *A Search for God.* One might conclude that this was no ordinary study group. It took some very important, long-lasting, and effective actions.

By the following year the A.R.E. published its first bulletin. This was September 1932. Often, when the exact day is not specified, reasonably accurate confirmations can be obtained by using the middle of the month. This is especially true when the movements of planets forming aspects are relatively slow. A progressed horoscope for that date shows Venus parallel Mercury within six seconds. Venus's declination was relatively slow-moving, and it gave quite a confirmation. The ninth house of publications became extraordinarily active, as would be anticipated. Saturn was exactly opposite Pluto in longitude. Launching this publication was probably a major effort that did not necessarily come off smoothly. But the progressed Midheaven was still parallel to its own place within 0° 1.7'. The effort had to be well-respected, and it had to be successful.

Edgar Cayce, the inspiration for the A.R.E., died on January 3, 1945. Progressed Saturn was square progressed Uranus in this horoscope within 0° 1.4'. That in itself was an adequate mark in the timetable of events and most appropriate. However, progressed Midheaven was also parallel Sun within 0° 3.7'. By translation the progressed IC, being the cusp of the fourth house, was contraparallel the Sun. That supplementary aspect carried a lot of meaning. The event was newsworthy, and it impacted the heart and soul of the organization. The publicity was widespread. The key parent of the A.R.E. had passed on.

In early March 1945 Thomas Sugrue's *There is a River* was republished by Holt, Rinehart and Winston, Inc. An early 1,000-copy numbered edition had been issued first in 1942. It was later published in many editions by Dell Publishing Company, Inc. By that time, sales had grown considerably. This book in its many releases had a major impact on membership. The main significance of the second printing astrologically was that a date to the nearest month was available. In early March 1945 progressed Venus returned to a parallel with its own natal position within 0° 1.3'. Progressed Moon also came to a swift parallel with Mars. The Venus aspect in particular was pertinent, because it occurred in the ninth house of publications.

Jess Stearn wrote *The Sleeping Prophet* in 1965. Doubleday agreed to publish this book, and their first edition came out in January 1966. What makes this event so important to the A.R.E. is that it was another publication that had a major impact on membership. Doubleday has a comparatively large sales volume. The publicity caused thousands of readers to make their initial contacts. Midmonth January was used for a progressed horoscope. Progressed Midheaven was semi-sextile progressed Neptune within 0° 1.2'. Neptune, coruler of the third house, reflects the publication by an associate of the A.R.E. (third-house Sagittarius). Jess Stearn might be regarded as an associate, whereas Thomas Sugrue could be thought of as a member of the family. He had lived with the Cayces. At any rate, Jess Stearn's book reflected favorably upon the reputation of the A.R.E. Progressed Saturn and progressed Pluto were within 54 seconds of an opposition. Doubtless, the sudden influx of new members caused some good problems and necessary changes at headquarters.

As a rule, a minimum of three dated events are considered necessary to confirm a horoscope by means of accurate day-for-a-year progressions. Therefore, at least three are required for all serious efforts. Five have been given above for the A.R.E.'s horoscope, although several were only dated to the nearest month. The main problem has been the omission of specific days and months for important events in the A.R.E.'s history. A large number of activities were simply recorded for the year of occurrence, and that thwarts the precision being sought. However, there should be little doubt at this point about whether or not the horoscope is correct. All of the available tests have been positive. A horoscope selected by the soul of the A.R.E. has no room for negatives or exceptions. This horoscope will stand on its own merits, just as Edgar Cayce's horoscope and his astrological revelations do.

LIST OF ILLUSTRATIONS